RESTRUCTURING GENDER RELATIONS
AND EMPLOYMENT

Restructuring Gender Relations and Employment

The Decline of the Male Breadwinner

Edited by

ROSEMARY CROMPTON

OXFORD
UNIVERSITY PRESS

OXFORD

UNIVERSITY PRESS

Great Clarendon Street, Oxford OX2 6DP

Oxford University Press is a department of the University of Oxford
It furthers the University's objective of excellence in research, scholarship,
and education by publishing worldwide in

Oxford New York

Athens Auckland Bangkok Bogotá Buenos Aires Calcutta
Cape Town Chennai Dar es Salaam Delhi Florence Hong Kong Istanbul
Karachi Kuala Lumpur Madrid Melbourne Mexico City Mumbai
Nairobi Paris São Paulo Singapore Taipei Tokyo Toronto Warsaw

with associated companies in Berlin Ibadan

Oxford is a registered trade mark of Oxford University Press
in the UK and in certain other countries

Published in the United States
by Oxford University Press Inc., New York

British Library Cataloguing in Publication Data

Data available

Library of Congress Cataloging in Publication Data

Restructuring gender relations and employment: the decline of the male
breadwinner / edited by Rosemary Crompton.
Includes bibliographical references and index.
1. Women—Employment—Europe. 2. Men—Employment—Europe.
3. Work and family—Europe. 4. Sex role in the work environment—
Europe. I. Crompton, Rosemary.
HD6134.R47   1999   331.25—dc21   99–19786
ISBN 0–19–829469–7
ISBN 0–19–829608–8 (pbk.)

1 3 5 7 9 10 8 6 4 2

Typeset in Times
by Hope Services (Abingdon) Ltd.
on acid-free paper by
Bookcraft Ltd
Midsomer Norton, Somerset

ACKNOWLEDGEMENTS

Many people have contributed to this book, which has been constructed around an ESRC funded project (R000235617), 'Gender Relations and Employment'. The first project seminar was held at the University of Kent in 1994. This was attended by, amongst others, some of the future interviewers for the project (Marie Cermakova, Irena Hradecka, Irina Aristakheva, and Elena Mezentseva), as well as Gunn Birkelund and Nicky Le Feuvre, who directed the project research in Norway and France (and were also involved in interviewing). My debt to both of these colleagues is considerable. Fiona Harris joined the project as a Research Associate in 1995. The second project seminar was held at the University of Leicester in 1996, and further interviewers on the project were among the participants at this seminar, including Merete Helle and Jaroslava Stastna. The third project seminar was held at the University of Bergen in 1997. At this seminar, there were presentations from Birgit Pfau-Effinger, Jane Millar, Anne-Lise Ellingsæter, Randi Kjeldstad, Kari Skrede, and Sue Yeandle, as well as papers deriving directly from the project, several of which are published in this volume. Many other people have attended all or some of the seminars, including Anna Pollert, Annie Phizacklea, Mary Crow, Sabine Gensior, and Ann Nilsen. I would like in particular to thank Jacquie O'Reilly, who both attended the first two seminars and also read and made very useful comments on the first draft of Chapter 1 of this book. All of the other contributors to this volume have read and commented on the first chapter before publication. Papers from the project have also been presented at the ESF Network on Gender Inequality in the European Regions, and I would like to thank Simon Duncan, Diane Perrons, and Birgit Pfau-Effinger, the organizers of the network. During a visit to Australia in 1997, as a visiting Fellow at the Australian National University, I gave a number of papers deriving from this research. Janeen Boxter read and gave useful advice on an earlier version of Chapter 6. Papers have also been presented at the University of Nottingham, the University of Leicester, the University of Warwick, GED-DIST/CNRS (Paris), the European Sociological Association Conference in Essex in 1997 and the Gender, Work, and Organization Conference in 1998. A first version of the final chapter was presented to the Work, Employment, and Society Conference in 1998. Throughout a series of meetings and seminars, therefore, many people have contributed to the arguments and ideas contained in this book. I have not been able to name them all, and I hope that this acknowledgement will suffice. Finally, much of this book could not have been written were it not for the willingness of 154 women to be interviewed about their families and employment careers. As the chapters in this book demonstrate, these were extremely busy people in demanding jobs. My thanks to all concerned.

Rosemary Crompton
Canterbury
December 1998

CONTENTS

LIST OF FIGURES

LIST OF TABLES

ABBREVIATIONS

CES   *Certificat d'Études Specialisées*
DDL   domestic division of labour
DES   *Diplome d'Études Specialisées*
ELFS   European Labour Force Survey
ESRC   Economic and Social Research Council
GP   general practitioner
GRA   gender-role attitudes
ISSP   International Social Survey Programme
SCPR   Social and Community Planning Research

LIST OF CONTRIBUTORS

Gunn Elisabeth Birkelund   *ISAF, Universityof Oslo, Norway*
Rosemary Crompton   *City University, London*
Anne Lise Ellingsæter   *ISAF, University of Oslo, Norway*
Jane Millar   *University of Bath, England*
Fiona Harris   *University of Leicester, England*
Birgit Pfau-Effinger   *University of Bremen, Germany*
Nicky Le Feuvre   *University of Toulouse le-Mirail, France*
Sue Yeandle   *Sheffield Hallam University, England*

1

The Decline of the Male Breadwinner: Explanations and Interpretations

ROSEMARY CROMPTON

INTRODUCTION

The social sciences—and sociology in particular—underwent a period of rapid expansion from the 1960s onwards. However, during this period in which the social sciences were putting down their roots in academe, they were virtually gender free. Major social actors were, implicitly or explicitly, assumed to be men. Sociological theory was grounded in the classic trilogy of Marx, Durkheim, and Weber. Each of these theorists treated gender relations as being of little or no relevance in developing their explanations of the social. Marx saw women's oppression as a by-product of the development of capitalism. The bourgeois requirement for heirs explained the restrictions on middle-class women, whilst working-class women were available for super-exploitation in the labour force. Women's liberation, it was suggested, would be achieved with their full representation in economic life—which meant employment (Engels 1940). This policy was duly followed in the state-socialist societies of Eastern Europe. Durkheim's attitude to women and gender reflected the prevailing discourses of his age. He argued that physical and emotional differences between men and women—including the smaller cranial capacity of the female sex—rendered them unsuitable for full participation in the public sphere (Durkheim 1964). Unlike Durkheim, Weber was a supporter of social and civil rights for women (Thomas 1985), but, nevertheless, his theoretical work uncritically reflected gendered assumptions relating to the division of labour. In particular, both the worker and the bureaucrat were described as free of social ties and domestic responsibilities—that is, as (implicitly) male.

During the 1960s, most empirical sociology also operated with similar assumptions relating to the gender division of labour. It was assumed that men were the major breadwinners, and that women's responsibilities rested largely with the domestic sphere. Thus major studies of class and stratification, for example, drew upon samples of men only (Blau and Duncan 1967; Goldthorpe 1980). It was taken for granted that men were the major actors in the public realm and that their experiences, therefore, could be used as representative of those of the family—including any women. Similarly, in the sociology of work and industry, the standard worker was built upon a masculine model of full-time, lifetime, uninterrupted labour-force participation (Feldberg and Glenn 1979). The model of the male breadwinner, therefore, in which men assumed the dominant role in the public sphere of employment and civil society, whilst women assumed responsibility for the domestic sphere of home and family, was incorporated into sociological theory and research in a taken-for-granted fashion. This model, of course, was always gendered, in that it rested upon a particular division of responsibilities between men and women. However, the manner of its incorporation into the social sciences meant that it was assumed to be natural, rather than as reflecting a particular set of *social* arrangements.

By the end of the millennium, however, there have been major transformations both in the gender division of labour and in social-science theories and explanations. In western Europe, Scandinavia, Australasia, and North America, social and economic change, as well as continuing pressures from second-wave feminism, has meant that the remaining formal barriers to women's participation in civil society have been removed. Levels of educational attainment amongst women have risen, and women's labour-force participation rates have continued to rise.[1] Thus the male-breadwinner model of the gender division of labour is undergoing a process of transformation, and in this book we will be exploring some of the consequences of these developments.

However, the manner in which we understand and explain changes in the gender division of labour will reflect our theoretical understandings of these phenomena. It is difficult to exaggerate the impact of feminist theories and criticisms on theoretical thinking within the social sciences during the last quarter of the twentieth century. Debates in social-science theory, therefore, as well as in feminism, have interacted in important ways in developing explanations of the social and material changes in the situation of women, and it is to these that we now turn.

FEMINIST THEORY AND RECENT SOCIAL THEORY

Second-wave feminist theory insisted that social structures are actively gendered, rather than simply reflecting natural differences relating to sex, as classical theorists such as Durkheim had assumed. Thus it was argued that the male-breadwinner model of the division of labour was, in fact, a reflection of patriarchal, rather than natural, processes. For example, dual-systems theory (Hartmann 1982; Walby 1986) argued that occupational segregation (as manifest in the concentration of women in low-paying jobs together with their exclusion from better-paying jobs and the professions) ensured that capitalists were able to benefit from women's cheap labour, whilst men (breadwinners) remained dominant in the home.

However, although these arguments should not be dismissed out of hand, there are problems in using the concept of patriarchy as a general term to understand the situation of women in relation to men. Criticisms of patriarchy have been extensive, and may be briefly summarized.[2] First, the concept is essentialist inasmuch as it is premised on the inherent capacity of men to exploit women. If patriarchy is defined as 'a system of social structures in which men dominate, oppress, and exploit women' (Walby 1990: 20), then it is not possible to avoid the assumption that relationships between men and women are *inherently* unequal and hierarchical. Secondly, it has been argued that the concept is ahistorical, and lacks sensitivity to the experiences of different groups of women. It was argued that the category 'woman', as developed in early theories of patriarchy, was in fact a reflection of a white, Western, middle-class stereotype, obscuring the experiences of women of different ethnicities and classes, at different times and in different places (Eisenstein 1983).

Thirdly, there are difficulties in conceptualizing patriarchy as a single system. Male violence against women, for example, arguably derives from rather different sources than the historical exclusion of women from particular areas of economic activity. Duncan (1994: 1177) has argued that the concept of patriarchy gives a 'necessary causal basis' to the study of gender divisions. However, if different manifestations of gender relations have different causes, is it helpful to label this agglomeration as a 'patriarchal system'? Against these kinds of criticisms, the concept of patriarchy may be defended by pointing to the fact that most of the evidence over millennia of world history demonstrates that men have, indeed, dominated women. However, the very complexity of gender relations means that domination is not universal within all areas of social and personal life. There are, for example, non-patriarchal relationships in the workplace, and, as we shall see, by no means all state policies in respect of women may be described as 'patriarchal' (Crompton 1998*b*).

If the difference between men and women is characterized in terms of oppression/exploitation, then, by definition, an absence of patriarchy is indicated by an androgynous gender equity (see Walby 1994: 1353). As already noted, occupational segregation, as an indicator of women's inferior labour-market position, has occupied a central role in the theoretical frameworks developed by Hartmann and Walby. An absence of patriarchy, therefore, would be indicated by an absence of segregation. However, measures of occupational segregation are so constructed that an absence of occupational segregation would mean that women's distribution in the labour force was *exactly* proportional to their representation. Empirically, this situation is highly unlikely (Hakim 1992).

This point raises another long-standing issue within feminism—that is, 'equality vs. difference' (Barrett 1987). Feminists have always had to confront a difficult paradox, deriving from the fact that women's social roles have been long regarded as an expression of natural difference. Should women, therefore, seek absolute equality with men (that is, to achieve some kind of androgyny), or should male/female differences (particularly in relation to childbearing) be taken into account in shaping institutions and policies relating to women. 'Welfare' feminists have focused upon these differences in seeking to improve the situation of women (as carers) and their families. However, to identify the need for special treatment for women runs the risk that difference will be seen as inferior (Banks 1981). Nevertheless, one does not have to be a biological determinist in order to recognize that biological differences, together with the kinds of feelings and emotions that are associated with interpersonal relationships (of all kinds), are likely to result in persisting differences between men and women, and these are likely to be reflected in the occupational structure. As Cockburn (1991) has argued, men and women are the same *and* different. Therefore, any account we give of gender relations and their structuring (as well as their transformation) has to confront and grasp this contradiction, which patriarchy is unable to do.

In this book, therefore, we will use the neutral term 'gender relations' to refer to the relationships between men and women, and 'gender system' (or 'gender regime') to describe the totality of these relationships (see e.g. Connell 1987).[3] Gender relationships may be patriarchal, but they are not *necessarily* so, and, indeed, have demonstrated considerable variation over both time and space. The gender system is instantiated through the development of institutions such as educational systems, welfare states, employment regimes, family law, religious differences, and national cultures. A gender system, however, does not necessarily represent a coherent totality, not least because its elements reflect differences in power between the sexes, as well as their cooperation in economic and social reproduction. Indeed, a major theme that informs many of the chapters in this book is that women (and men) may consciously seek to transform elements of the system. Thus gender systems reflect both the specificities of national historical pasts and presents, as well as the universalities of cross-national (or global) developments—such as, for example, the contradictions and tensions generated by women's pursuit of their individual rights through the discourse opened up by the bourgeois ideals of modernity.

However, although we have criticized the use of patriarchy as a universally applicable explanatory tool, the concept does retain an emphasis on the necessity to explore and explain gendered *structures* in order to comprehend the situation of women—and men. Over the 1990s, however, the postmodernist and post-structuralist 'turn' in social theory has had a very significant impact on feminist thinking (Barrett and Phillips 1992). The post-structuralist critique of the humanist assumption that there are essential features in common in terms of which human beings (and thus men and women) can be defined and understood has been carried forward into a view of the constructed subject as constantly in process, never unitary, never complete. Thus gender is seen as performative, as having 'no ontological status apart from the various acts which constitute its reality' (Butler, cited in Marshall 1994: 110). In consequence, there has been a tendency systematically to downplay the significance of structures—and this would include patriarchal structures—in explorations of gender.

More generally, the postmodernist trend in social theory has been associated with a turning-away from the grand theories and meta-narratives of modernity, whether of Marxism or liberalism. There has been an increasing focus upon the individual, as well as upon the transformations in social and interpersonal relationships that are held to be integral to the development of 'reflexive modernity' (Beck 1992; Giddens 1992; Beck and Beck-Gernsheim 1995). Indeed, the growth of feminist theory may be seen as having contributed to these developments in bringing to the fore the requirement that social science incorporate the investigation of emotions, embodiment, and those aspects of the private sphere that had previously been marginalized as women's issues. Those who have taken up the arguments of Foucault (such as Butler, cited above) assert that questions of sexuality are central to the construction of the individual's identity—and, indeed, that this fact is one of the key features of modernity. Thus the investigation of masculinity and femininity has become a major topic in its own right (Connell 1995). Much of this work has emphasized the social and cultural variability of masculinity and femininity—a position that, in the case of Connell, has also been linked to the possibility of a positive transformation of masculinity.

However, during the 1970s and 1980s, there emerged a school of new essentialists (Gilligan 1982; see discussion in Segal 1987), who argued that women were not only different from, but superior to men. Women's caring, nurturing, and flexible qualities were positively contrasted to masculine qualities of aggression, emotional distance, and rigidity. The new-essentialist feminism stands in sharp contrast to post-structuralist feminism, with its emphasis upon femininity and masculinity (indeed, sexuality in general) as a constantly-to-be-achieved project, rather than a constant presence.

Nevertheless, the reasoning behind the new essentialism (as with post-structuralism) has tended to be psychological and/or cultural, rather than structural, reflecting the 'turn to the individual' in social theory.[4] This strand of feminist theorizing, however, appears to have reached something of an *impasse* as far as its relevance to empirical research is concerned. The postmodernist rejection of grand theory and meta-narrative, together with the substitution of the notion of discourse, runs the danger of leaving us without a subject to investigate. Within feminist theory, the emphasis upon diversity and rejection of general categories (such as 'woman') as essentialist has led to a stalemate. As a consequence, Maynard (1995: 273) has argued that feminist theory is 'in danger of focusing only on epistemological and philosophical issues, rather than on how gender operates to construct life chances differently for women and for men, and the subordinations which result from this'.

We would argue, therefore, that, rather than stretching explanatory concepts in an attempt to develop an overarching theory that accommodates all eventualities (as, for example, Walby 1994 has attempted to do in developing the concept of patriarchy), or being forced to choose between apparently incompatible alternatives (such as structuralism versus post-structuralism), we should attempt to work within apparently contradictory perspectives. More may be gained from a pluralistic approach that works with different explanatory frameworks rather than from an attempt to achieve either a synthesis, or an alternative theoretical approach.

A recent example of this kind of argument is to be found in Marshall (1994), who suggests that we must explicitly recognize the tension between the use of 'woman' as a universal category and the reality experienced by actually existing women, who may or may not share a unified gender identity. Marshall (1994: 112) argues that: 'Recognizing this tension, it seems more appropriate to speak of "gendered identities", implying a recognition of plurality and difference without abandoning the notion that gender *does* play a part in constituting the subject' (emphasis added). A parallel tension exists between gendered structures and gendered subjects. Gendered structures both describe and impose an order on individuals, but are nevertheless developed and interpreted by these individuals—the order they impose is not universal. Thus as Marshall (1994: 115) argues:

It is the recognition . . . of the *tension* between individual and society, between subject and structure, that allows us to proceed in a dialectical fashion in reconceptualizing gendered . . . identities as relationally and historically *interpreted* . . . according to certain historically available modes of interpretation . . . To express in another way the two poles of the debate which need to be grasped simultaneously, the content of gender is infinitely variable and continually in flux, yet the salience of gender categories is persistent.

It may be suggested that here we are returning to a perennial topic within sociology; that is, the agency versus structure debate. What Marshall's discussion illustrates is the need, not to seek a synthesis of different perspectives on this issue, but to work creatively within the tensions it generates. Gender relations are structured in contexts— employment, families, and state institutions—that play a major part in reproducing the gender order (or gender system). However, these structures are negotiated and interpreted by changing and flexible gendered subjects. Both the structures, and the manner in which individuals and groups work on them and interpret them, may be investigated empirically. Thus a key element of *feminist* socio- logical explanation is also a key demand of sociological explanation more generally. This means taking a position of analytical dualism— that is, distinguishing the 'parts' from the 'people' in order to exam- ine their interplay, but recognizing that neither of them can exist without the other (Archer 1996a, b; see also Layder 1994).[5] The constitution of gendered structures presents to the subject a binary conception of gender, the foundations of which may appear to be natural. Relations between men and women may have generated these structures, but nevertheless they pre-date the actor. The dis- tinction between structure and agency characteristic of analytical dualism also enables us to explore the processes and possibilities of change in gender relations. These are opened up by the 'tension between public and private, political and personal, mind and body, masculine and feminine' (Marshall 1994: 114) that individuals attempt to resolve in the construction of their biographies and iden- tities.

In summary, our discussion of feminist and recent social theory has developed five main points:

1. We should abandon the attempt to build a single overarching system or theoretical explanation of gender relations—such as patriarchy—and adopt a position of theoretical pluralism.
2. However, theoretical pluralism should not be associated with a collapse into the relativism implied by some post-structuralist authors. Structures still count, and gender is not simply perfor- mative. To theorize gender exclusively at the level of the subject runs the risk of letting social relations disappear, and seeing gender as primarily located at the individual level.
3. Accepting theoretical pluralism means that different dimen- sions of the complex whole of gender relations may require dif- ferent explanatory frameworks.
4. One dimension of difference (which has nothing to do with postmodernism or post-structuralism) is, however, central to any account of gender relations. This is the biological differ- ence between men and women emphasized by (so-called) wel- fare feminists. The significance of this difference is changing and socially constructed but, nevertheless, persistent.

5. Thus gender relations are historically specific and need to be understood as such.

In this process of theoretical clarification, we have also emphasized the importance of taking a position of analytical dualism—that is, of the necessity of exploring the impact of gendered structures, whilst at the same time also recognizing that men and women have the capacity to change these structures.

In the next section we will investigate the extent and nature of the changes in women's employment, and their related circumstances, particularly in Europe. We will also explore some of the concepts and theoretical frameworks that have been developed in order to analyse and understand these changes. Our discussions will also serve to illustrate the theoretical points we have developed in this section.

RESEARCHING GENDER TRANSFORMATIONS CROSS-NATIONALLY

Although we have emphasized (see point 5 above) that gender relations are historically specific, and thus the importance of particular national and historical factors in their structuring, there are nevertheless important cross-national continuities in the changes taking place in the situation of women.[6] Rates of female employment have been rising in all OECD countries (OECD 1994), and women are expected to continue to play a major role in the labour market (Eurostat 1996). In 1992 an average of around 68 per cent of men and 44 per cent of women in the EU were economically active; and, on some EU estimates, women are anticipated to be 48 per cent of the labour force by 2020. As many commentators have noted, this shift has come about because of deindustrialization and the shift to all kinds of service employment—that is, in financial services, retail, and so on, as well as welfare and other areas of state provision such as education and health. Educational levels have been rising amongst women (nearly half of the student population in Europe is now female), and more women are moving into managerial and professional jobs.

Changes in women's employment have been accompanied by significant demographic shifts. In all European countries[7] there has been a rise in the age at marriage, an increase in rates of divorce, and a decline in fertility. These trends appeared earlier in northern European countries than in the south, where traditional marriage, establishing male dominance, was enshrined in law until relatively recently. Nevertheless: 'Everywhere in the Community, despite substantial differences that exist among countries in the socio-cultural sphere and with respect to legislation—especially that relating to divorce—third births have been declining, marriages are taking place later, births outside marriage and cohabitation are increasing and the divorce rate is increasing' (Hall 1993: 106). European fertility is now below replacement level. It is the lowest in the world and has been described as a 'second demographic transition' (Sporton 1993). By 1995 total fertility rates (TFRs) in Europe averaged 1.43 (a TFR of less than 2.1 is generally regarded as being below replacement level). Amongst the countries discussed in this book, in 1995 TFRs ranged from 1.87 for Norway to 1.17 for Italy.[8]

At the same time, household size has been declining, as have the number of marriages, and there has been an increase in cohabitation outside marriage, particularly in northern Europe and Scandinavia. The declining popularity of marriage is indicative of a new European marriage pattern, which does not mean that people are not forming relationships, but, rather, that the position of marriage as a regulator of sexual relationships is weakening. As the number of divorces indicates, marriage is not only less frequent but also increasingly fragile. The crude divorce rate for the European countries has risen from 0.5 in 1960 to 1.8 by 1995. Although divorce is everywhere on an upward trend, national variations in legislation mean that there is considerable cross-national variability—for example, the UK had a rate of 2.9 in 1995, as compared to only 0.5 for Italy.[9]

The causes of fertility decline are complex, but demographers have argued that both the increase in women's employment as well as changes in social mores are of major importance:

Within the West, the parental function is no longer deemed to be as socially gratifying as in the past. Attitudes have changed from the child-centred, altruistic values that characterized the first fertility transition in the nineteenth century to the more individualistic, post-materialist values of today. Low fertility levels prevailing at the end of the demographic transition were engendered by the parental desire to have fewer 'quality' children. Today, very low fertility may be associated with greater individualism as couples no longer plan their lives around the birth of a child and his or her future. (Sporton 1993: 58).

Not surprisingly, these very visible changes in employment and family structures have attracted an increasing amount of attention from social scientists. The increase in women's employment worldwide has been investigated in comparative studies that have grappled with attempts to explain the persistence of gender difference (and inequality) in employment (see e.g. Jensen *et al.* 1988). Gender equality in employment has become an important objective on the European social agenda, and the EU has sponsored extensive research into women's employment, as well as associated policy matters such as childcare. The European Commission has recently committed itself to mainstreaming gender into all its policies and practices (Rubery *et al.* 1998). Economists and labour-market analysts influenced by feminist arguments have explored, comparatively, the articulation of family and labour-market systems (Rubery 1988). Recent comparative work has had a major focus on part-time work, which is both female-dominated and an expanding form of employment (Bloßfeld and Hakim 1997; O'Reilly and Fagan 1998).

Comparative research, therefore, has monitored change and development in women's paid work in different countries. This work has revealed that, although women's paid work may everywhere be on the increase, nevertheless there are also important national differences in both the level and the structuring of this employment, reflecting historical variations in the development of national institutions and cultures. This societal-systems approach to comparative analysis (see e.g. Maurice *et al.* 1986; Rubery *et al.* 1998) seeks to explain women's employment outcomes through an understanding of the processes of its structuring. There is an explicit recognition of the complexity of this institutional structuring, and of the difference in outcomes at the national level. The societal-systems approach, therefore, has many parallels with the gender-systems approach that we develop in this book, in that it is pluralistic and would avoid universal or single-theory explanations (as argued in points 1 and 3 of the previous section).[10]

A very important source of the institutional structuring of, and variation in, women's employment has been the welfare state. Debates relating to the welfare state have been a major arena within which the continuing significance of the difference between men and women (see point 4 in the previous section) have been discussed. During the 1970s and 1980s feminists were highly critical of the part played by state welfare in the reproduction of masculine dominance.

Gender differences were built into the structuring of the welfare state from the very beginning. Pateman (1989) has argued that, whereas men were incorporated into the welfare state as individual citizens— that is, as workers who could contribute to social insurance—women were incorporated as members of families—that is, as wives and mothers. Men were employees or potential employees, heads of households or potential heads of households; women were dependants who made claims on the welfare state through their relationship as a member of an employee's household. Women were not, therefore, full citizens, as they did not have direct access to the provisions of social citizenship. In many countries, the welfare state was explicitly constructed on the male-breadwinner model of the family (Land 1994). For example, the author of the major report that shaped the British welfare state (Beveridge 1942) wrote that 'the great majority of married women must be regarded as occupied on work which is vital though unpaid, without which their husbands could not do their paid work and without which the nation could not continue'. In the National Insurance Act of 1946 wives were treated differently from their husbands for insurance purposes. Married women (if they were working) paid lesser contributions for reduced benefits, and could even opt out of benefit payments on the assumption that they would be supported by their husbands (Pateman 1989: 194). Women's unpaid domestic work was, therefore, not regarded as making an independent (or productive) contribution worthy of social insurance.

Welfare states, however, are not homogeneous. Male dominance is not necessarily reproduced through their actions, (for example, in situations where benefits are paid directly to women), and feminists have been active in the development of maternalist state policies (Orloff 1996b). Indeed, it has been argued that states may work against established masculine domination through the development of woman-friendly policies (Hernes 1988), and, as we shall see in Chapter 3, Scandinavian welfare states have been particularly active in this regard. Throughout the 1990s Esping-Andersen's (1990) characterization of different welfare-state regimes has been very influential in exploring welfare-state variations. He identifies three clusters of welfare-state regimes. The social-democratic regime cluster is typified by the Scandinavian welfare states, which are universalistic, so that all citizens are entitled to a high level of state-provided social supports. The corporatist (or conservative) regime cluster is based upon insurance rights; thus there are strong ties to the labour market, and welfare benefits reflect existing wage and salary inequalities (for example, in France, Germany, and Italy). In contrast, in liberal (or residual) welfare states, welfare benefits are means-tested and are provided only for those in greatest need. Because the state provides only a minimum, a market develops—and may even be encouraged—for the private provision of welfare needs. The USA is a major example of such a welfare state, although, since 1979, Britain has moved much closer to this model and may now be considered to be a liberal welfare state.

Esping-Andersen has linked his analysis of different welfare-state developments to a broader account of the emergence of post-industrial society, which he sees as generating important gender-related changes in the labour market (Esping-Andersen 1993*b*). In social-democratic welfare states, post-industrialism has been associated with the expansion of highly professionalized welfare-state employment in which women predominate. In corporatist welfare stares, service employment has not expanded to the same extent, and the family is regarded as the major service provider. This has restricted the growth of women's employment. In liberal welfare states, government is more of a passive force and the market has been relied upon to create jobs. Low wages have been the major source of service job growth. Women have moved into both the 'good' as well as the 'bad' jobs that have been created. There has been not only an expansion of business-related professional services, but also an explosion of unqualified service jobs. Despite these cross-national variations, however, Esping-Andersen (1993*a*: 236) argues that 'the service economy is everywhere associated with the evolution of two gendered labour markets. Except for routine administrative and sales jobs, the traditional fordist economy remains predominantly male. The evolving services are becoming a women's labour market.'

Esping-Andersen's work, therefore, emphasizes the importance of social institutions and structures in the shaping of particular configurations of the gender division of labour and thus gender relations (see point 2 in the previous section). However, his work has been subject to extensive debate and criticism, by feminists and non-feminists alike (see Sainsbury 1994). One major feminist criticism has been that his analysis takes no account of the unpaid (or caring) work of women (which has been largely linked to childcare or biological difference), and thus women disappear from Esping-Andersen's analysis once they disappear from the labour market (Lewis 1992). In Chapter 2 of this book, Millar develops these arguments. She emphasizes that an explicit recognition of the work of caring, as well as of paid employment, helps us to understand the significance of the fact that women receive benefits from welfare states as mothers and as workers, as well as as dependent wives. Comparative analysis, moreover, suggests that welfare states have not necessarily been universally modelled on breadwinner principles, even in the recent past (see Pfau-Effinger, Chapter 4 in this volume).[11] Nevertheless, in all countries states are attempting to redefine family obligations and to restructure welfare states, and Millar's discussion suggests the direction(s) that might be followed.

It is in the Scandinavian welfare states, however, that there have been the most deliberate attempts to develop welfare policies that match the *de facto* reshaping of the gender division of labour and the erosion of the breadwinner model. In Chapter 3 Ellingsaeter focuses in particular upon the case of Norway, a country that has actively developed work–family policies with the aim of promoting gender equality. Ellingsæter describes the way in which 'political fatherhood' has been placed on the agenda in Norway. Related strategies include policies such as the 'father quota' in childcare leave, designed to increase the amount of caring work that is undertaken by men.

Although it is the case that Esping-Andersen's framework is problematic in many respects, his work has nevertheless been of considerable value in understanding important aspects of both the growth of women's employment, and its variable nature. One general methodological principle that the contributors to this book would have in common with Esping-Andersen would be his emphasis on the need to be cautious of universalistic explanations, and to be sensitive to the fact that different historical starting points can produce very different contemporary mixes as far as women's employment is concerned.

This point is also emphasized within a further dimension of comparative institutional analysis developed in this book. In Chapter, 4 Pfau-Effinger develops a primary focus upon gendered systems as such, rather than welfare states alone. In this Introduction, 'gender system' has been used as a neutral term to describe the totality of the relationships between men and women at both the individual and the institutional levels. Others have been more specific. For example, Hirdman describes gender systems as operating on three levels: the cultural sphere, social institutions, and socialization through gender roles. Hirdman employs the notion of a 'gender contract' to describe historical developments in Sweden, from the 'housewife contract' of the post-war period to the 'equality contract' from the 1960s onwards (Hirdman's work is discussed in English in Duncan 1994, and O'Reilly and Fagan 1998: 16). Gender-systems approaches have many parallels with societal-systems approaches in that they embody an explicit recognition of both the complexity and societal specificity of the structuring of gender relations and employment. Pfau-Effinger's comparative analysis argues that culture, institutions, structures, and social actors are interrelated within gender systems. Different societies are characterized by different cultures of motherhood, of which the male-breadwinner model is only one. Thus in Finland, for example, the model of the family economy prevailed into this century, in which women managed farms whilst men worked in the wage economy. As a consequence, women's entry into waged work, she argues, has been followed by the development of 'public motherhood', in which the state assumes the major responsibility for childcare.

In Chapter 5, Yeandle develops these arguments further in her comparative discussion of non-standard employment, and the division of breadwinning/caregiving in Germany, Italy, and the UK. She shows how differences in sectoral mix, welfare provision, and family arrangements have contributed to cross-national variations along both of these dimensions. Institutional analyses, therefore, have emphasized the continuing significance of cross-national differences in the structuring and nature of both gender relations and their associated patterns of women's employment. However, it is important to remember that these national differences are cross-cut by important similarities, even global continuities. The universal shift to service employment has included financial, retail, leisure, and personal services, as well as welfare—understood broadly to include education and health as well as direct welfare services. In all of these sectors, what have been conventionally assumed to be women's jobs have predominated. At the same time, deindustrialization has removed many jobs that were conventionally regarded as male—in mining, steel, and heavy industry. Employment in industry has become more capital intensive, as technological change has replaced human labour with computerized control systems (Crompton *et al.* 1996).

Although it is, in practice, difficult to disentangle the different elements contributing to changes in paid work, technological shifts have also been accompanied by changes in the political climate, which have also had an impact on the nature of employment. Although these trends have by no means been universal, since the beginning of the 1980s there has been an increase in attempts to marketize or commodify all kinds of social relationships, from relationships within organizations, to those between different parts of the same enterprise, and between different functions and fractions of the state. Within organizations, these trends have been accompanied by an increasing managerial emphasis upon individual *performance*, rather than on ascriptive factors such as seniority—or gender. As women's levels of formal educational and vocational qualifications have also been rising, many women have been well placed to take advantage of these changes, and have found themselves able to move into higher-level professions and occupations. (For example, in finance, one of the fastest-growing sectors of employment, between the 1980s and 1990s women increased their representation in management by 12 per cent in the USA, 11 per cent in the UK, and 9 per cent in France (see Crompton 1998*a*).) However, at the level of the household, marriage and cohabitation patterns mean that, whilst many women, as individuals, may have benefited from these developments, marketization has also been accompanied by increasing social polarization and exclusion for both women and men.

In this section, we have made brief reference to other recent comparative work (particularly O'Reilly and Fagan 1998 and Rubery *et al.* 1998) that has many parallels with the theoretical and empirical approaches developed in Chapters 2–5 of this book. This kind of work has focused, in the main, on the significance of different institutions and/or *structures* in the shaping of gender relations and employment. The chapters by Millar, Ellingsæter, Pfau-Effinger, and Yeandle may be seen as a development of these analyses in that they both extend the range of comparisons and suggest how institutions might respond and adapt to changing circumstances. However, in our theoretical discussions in the previous section, we have emphasized the importance of maintaining a simultaneous focus on human *agency*, as well as structure. Indeed, recent social theory has emphasized the significance of increasing individuation, together with changes in interpersonal relationships, which have emerged as a consequence of change and development in the gender division of labour (Beck 1992; Giddens 1992; Beck and Beck-Gernsheim 1995).

Beck argues that the position of women in industrial society was in fact ascribed or feudal. Whereas men had to be released from traditional constraints in order to be able to participate in the industrial labour force, women's position was assigned to that of home and family, and a lifetime of domestic labour. Thus, according to Beck, in industrial society modernization was only partial—particularly as far as women were concerned. Women, however, have gradually established and secured their rights as individuals. As a consequence, however, 'the nuclear family, built around gender status, is falling apart on the issues of emancipation and equal rights' (Beck and Beck-Gernsheim 1995: 1–2). Thus Beck and Beck-Gernsheim (1995: 14) predict that 'we are in for a *long and bitter battle*; in the coming years there will be a war between men and women, (emphasis in original). The male-breadwinner model, they argue, was one of the cornerstones of industrial society, and it will not be transcended without conflict—over jobs, over the domestic division of labour, over child-bearing and child-rearing (indeed, as we have seen, this conflict is already evident in both declining fertility and rising divorce rates).

Beck's arguments concerning the contemporary transformations of gender relations are but one element of his wider thesis concerning the development of risk societies, in which risks, particularly ecological risks, become general, extending beyond the control of particular classes or status groups. He suggests that the regulatory frameworks of classes, religious authority, and other traditional groups will be replaced by the 'reflexively modern' *individual*. In a similar vein, Giddens (1991, 1992) has argued that in 'late' or 'reflexive' modernity the individual has increasingly become the source of, and responsible for, his or her own biography. The erosion of traditional ties and conventional social arrangements has resulted in the emergence of the 'pure relationship'—that is, a relationship independent of formal ties that is entered into out of choice and then 'reflexively organized, in an open fashion, and on a continuous basis' (1991: 91). We would agree that there have indeed been considerable changes in personal relationships and family life, that the range of ways of living or lifestyles have become much less dependent on convention and tradition, and that individual choice and preferences have become of more importance in determining them. Thus we would not seek to ignore or reject the significance of human action in the shaping of both individual lives and social institutions. However, as critics of Beck have pointed out, his analysis gives considerable causal weight to the power of norms and ideas, and their innate logic of development, in transforming human society (Rustin 1994). Thus his analysis of other forms of economic, political (and gendered) powers, which still limit human agency, is somewhat partial.[12]

We should also note that, as we have argued, the feudal or male-breadwinner model of the gender division of labour, on which Beck's analysis rests, has by no means been a universal phenomenon historically. We have emphasized that the manner in which gender regimes have been constructed has varied, not only over time but also as between different nation states. Beck's analysis has at its core an individual who has been remarkably successful in acquiring the capacity to choose.[13] A similar emphasis on the significance of choice in explaining women's employment patterns in particular is to be found in Hakim's recent work (1995, 1996*a*). Hakim argues that occupational segregation, resulting in the concentration of women in particular jobs, and particular types of work such as part-time work, may be seen as the outcome of the choices made by different types of women. She has described women in part-time work, for example, as 'uncommitted' workers who have 'chosen' this kind of employment. We have been careful to argue that women's family and employment patterns will, indeed, reflect diversity amongst women as a whole. However, we would also emphasize the importance of the analysis of the *structuring* of these choices, as well as of their variety. As we shall see, this variation can result in considerable differentiation of biographical outcomes, even in reflexive modernity.

We have already outlined how Chapters 2–5, through the comparative analysis of gender systems, institutions, family practices, labour markets, and so on, describe and explain the structural changes, tensions, and developments brought about by the erosion of the male-breadwinner model. In the chapters in the second half of this book, there is incorporated more of a focus on agency, and on the way in which individuals negotiate these structures and live out their lives. In this process, they also contribute to their transformation. All of these chapters draw on empirical research carried out as part of a cross-national project funded by the Economic and Social Research Council (R000235617), the British Council, and the University of Bergen. The project (Gender Relations and Employment: A Cross-National Analysis) was directed by Rosemary Crompton, and Gunn

Birkelund and Nicky Le Feuvre have been closely associated with it. The next section of this Introduction describes the project and its methodology, as well as discussing some of the research findings that have already been published.

GENDER RELATIONS AND EMPLOYMENT: A CROSS-NATIONAL ANALYSIS

Cross-national comparative research has been conventionally categorized as representing either a broadly positivist approach, which seeks to establish continuities that may then be used to support universal or lawlike assertions, or, alternatively, as being largely concerned to understand the particular nature of events and circumstances that have generated a particular (that is, unique) outcome (Kohn 1987). However, the Gender Relations project was designed to explore both similarity *and* difference. Thus the research has established the significance of *different* national institutions in structuring patterns of women's employment and gender-role attitudes (Crompton and Harris 1997*a*), but, as will become apparent in Chapters 6–9, these differences are cross-cut by cross-national *continuities* at the occupational, interpersonal, and individual levels (Crompton and Harris 1998*a*, *b*).

As we have argued in this chapter, gender relations are produced and reproduced via already existing institutions, norms, and practices, as well as through the ongoing relationships between individual women and men. The project, therefore, was designed to investigate gender relations at three societal levels: macro, meso, and micro. As noted in our previous discussions, the institutional structures reproducing the gender order include educational systems, welfare states, systems of occupational regulation, labour markets, and so on, as well as legislation, etc., pertaining directly to women. Systems of regulation and legislation are often linked to an 'equality agenda', which has been widely adopted, at a national and transnational level, since the Second World War. The countries chosen for comparative analysis in the Gender Relations project reflected the variations in welfare-state regimes identified in Esping-Andersen's typology: the UK (liberal); France (corporatist); Norway (social democratic), and Russia and the Czech Republic (state-socialist self-welfare).[14]

In relation to the equality agenda, human-capital theories have explained women's relatively disadvantaged labour-market position with reference to their lack of qualifications and employment experience. The research design did not, therefore, focus on such 'disadvantaged workers', but on women in professional and managerial occupations. This strategy also facilitated a systematic contrast between these two occupational types, which enabled us to focus on the impact of meso-level structures—in this case, occupations—on the structuring of gender relations at the occupational and individual levels. Biographical work-life interviews were carried out with women doctors, and retail bank managers, in all five countries. Standardization was achieved via a number of simple rules to be followed by all interviewers. All doctors had to have completed their post-registration qualification, and all bankers had to hold managerial positions. All had to be currently employed. The women had to be aged between 30 and 55.

To summarize: the research framework, and associated research methods, were as follows:

- *Macro-level*: focused on the nation state. It included:
    - (i) Nationally available descriptive statistics including census data, government, and other reports, for all five countries. These national case studies included (amongst other topics) information relating to education systems, family policies, welfare states, occupational and labour-market structures, as well as the equality agenda.
    - (ii) Data collected by the International Social Survey Programme (ISSP) (Family and Gender Roles Module) for Britain, Norway, and the Czech Republic.[15]
- *Meso-level*: focused on the occupational structure. It included case studies, for each country, of the development of medicine and retail banking.
- *Micro-level*: focused on individuals and their relationships. It included biographical work-life interviews with fifteen women, in each occupation, in each country (154 interviews in all).[16]

Chapters 6–9 all draw on different aspects of this comparative empirical work. In the development of the project our approach has been, first, systematically to examine the impact of the structures, institutional and normative, shaping gender relations and employment. Subsequently, through the analysis of the biographical interviews, we have examined the way in which individuals have acted out their interpersonal and employment careers. We have demonstrated the importance of different national cultures and institutions in shaping gender relations, arguments that are reinforced and developed in Chapters 2–5 of this book. In previous publications deriving from the project (Crompton and Harris 1997*a*, *b*), we have shown that a three-country (Britain, Norway, and the Czech Republic) comparison of national level survey (ISSP) data indicates that gender-role attitudes are the most liberal in Norway, and the most conservative in the Czech Republic, with Britain somewhere in between. These differences are, we argue, systematically related to differences in national cultures and institutions.

The case of Norway has already been briefly discussed. It is a Scandinavian social-democratic country at the forefront of both gender-equality and family-friendly policies, which are reflected in liberal gender-role attitudes. In contrast, the British government has not attempted to develop 'active' gender equalization or transformation policies. Thus legislation has given women formal equality of opportunity, but (until recently) the government has not actively promoted women's employment through (for example), the provision of childcare—and indeed, Britain has had the second lowest levels of childcare provision in Europe (Phillips and Moss 1988). As an ex-state-socialist country, the Czech Republic has actively promoted women's employment. Pro-natalist policies in support of motherhood have also been accompanied by extensive maternity leave and allowances (Scott 1974; Heitlinger 1979). It might have been thought, therefore, that national attitudes to mother's employment would be relatively positive. However, we found that Czech attitudes to women's employment and gender roles were in fact rather conservative, reflecting the lack of emphasis given to domestic labour in the ex-state-socialist countries (Buckley 1989). Indeed, attitudes to Western feminism throughout the ex-Soviet Union are somewhat negative. The employment of women has been linked with their forced employment during the era of state socialism (Crompton 1997), and gender-role attitudes tend to be stereotyped in consequence (our interviews in both the Czech Republic and Russia confirmed this at the micro- or individual level.

In Chapter 6, Crompton and Harris carry forward their three-country comparison of gender-role attitudes in order to examine the way in which these attitudes are reflected in the division of labour in the household. Using the ISSP data, it is demonstrated that more liberal gender-role attitudes are linked with less conventional patterns of the domestic division of labour. In this chapter, evidence from the work-life interviews in Britain, Norway, and the Czech Republic is used to demonstrate that the domestic division of labour between doctors and their partners has a marked tendency to be rather more conventional that that between the bankers and their partners. This finding was one of the first indications of a systematic pattern of difference in the work–family biographies of the doctors and bankers, in all countries, that cuts across the cross-national differences we have identified.

We link these occupational differences in work–family biographies to the characteristic differences in the manner in which 'professional' (doctors') and 'managerial' (bank managers') occupations are organized, and the possibilities they offer to those in these occupations (Crompton and Harris 1998*b*). Medical careers require long-term forward planning, and we found that many doctors had developed similar strategies in respect of their family lives as well. This had often resulted in a somewhat gender stereotypical domestic division of labour. In contrast, bankers had made their careers by responding to organizational demands, in which domestic life had often had to take second place, and, if it was to be managed at all, more often than not required more than average assistance from a partner. The meso- or occupational level, therefore, provides further evidence of the importance of occupational *structures* in shaping personal lives.

Nevertheless, we do not see women, or their employment decisions, as being in any sense entirely determined by particular national or specific occupation-related structures and institutions. In Chapter 7, therefore, Crompton and Harris explore the diversity of the work–family decisions (and their origins) that had been made by women in similar jobs (see also Crompton and Harris 1998*a*). In so doing, we found that there could be identified amongst the women we interviewed (and it should be remembered that *all* of them had been successful in employment terms) a minority who were superwomen, and that this minority were equally distributed amongst the doctors and bankers. Thus macro- and meso-level structural patternings are criss-crossed by personal characteristics not necessarily linked to occupation or nation. In Chapter 8, Le Feuvre develops a 'sociology of experience' in order to suggest how both personal *and* occupational experiences contribute to the transformation of logics of action that are linked to particular personal and occupational outcomes. This analysis returns to some of the central concerns of social and feminist theory discussed in our previous section, in that it illustrates the range of ways in which the women interviewed 'do gender'—and in some cases, offer active resistance to it through the development of gender reflexivity.

This return to some of the concerns of contemporary feminist theory is also a central theme Chapter 9 by Crompton, Le Feuvre, and Birkelund which examines the feminization of the medical profession in Britain, France, and Norway. As women move into previously male-dominated occupations and fields of employment, it has been suggested that these occupations might themselves be transformed as a consequence. However, it would seem that an internal (re)segregation of the medical profession is under way, in that many female doctors consciously seek out specialties that are at least compatible with family life. Although we would not be in favour of essentialist arguments concerning the feminization of previously masculine occupations, we suggest that gradual occupational change might nevertheless be under way, in that the medical profession will have to adapt to the fact that increasing numbers of its members (men, as well as women) might be workers *and* carers.

All of the chapters in this book may be read as individual contributions to the range of debates relating to gender relations and employment. However, our aim is to have gathered together here rather more than a set of disparate essays (albeit in a similar academic field). We have, therefore, placed the Conclusions to this Introduction at the end of the book, as Chapter 10. The reader may choose whether to examine Chapter 10 now or after having read the intervening chapters.

NOTES

1. These countries cover a large part of the globe, but, nevertheless, we recognize that the trends we identify and discuss in this book are by no means universal. The expansion of Islamic fundamentalism has been accompanied by both a loss of civil rights, and/or the imposition of social and physical restrictions on women, in many countries. In Eastern Europe, the collapse of state socialism, whilst improving the situation of some women, has also meant the closing-down of state nurseries and the removal of other protections such as statutory representation in legislative bodies. It has long been a criticism of feminism that socialist theory and practice paid little attention to the private or domestic sphere, being dominated by materialist and

productionist analyses (Buckley 1989). In practice, gender relations and ideologies in Eastern Europe seem to have been, and continue to be, very traditional amongst both men and women (see e.g. Heitlinger 1979; Crompton and Harris 1997*a*). Some of the chapters in this book incorporate material from Eastern Europe, but our major focus remains on 'Western' societies.

2. See Walby 1986, 1990, 1994, 1997; Acker 1989; Bradley 1989; Duncan 1994; Pollert 1996.

3. More extensive discussions of gender-systems approaches may be found in Duncan 1994 and O'Reilly and Fagan 1998.

4. Giddens's account of 'intimacy' draws heavily on psychological object-relations theory (Chodorow 1989) and has similar problems in avoiding essentialism in its characterization of masculine and feminine.

5. In a previous publication (Crompton and Sanderson 1990) Giddens's notion of 'structuration' was utilized in an analysis of occupational segregation. However, following from the arguments we have developed above, the notion of 'analytical dualism' is preferable to that of 'structuration'. Structuration theory incorporates a 'decentering of the subject' in which human beings become people through drawing on structural properties to generate social practices. Thus structure becomes real only when instantiated by agency. However, as we have argued (following Marshall), at the level of the social, gendered institutions have a reality that is experienced as such by individuals.

6. Our discussion will focus largely on Europe and the Scandinavian countries.

7. Ireland is exceptional, in that divorce is still not legal and state restrictions on fertility controls remain.

8. TABLE 1.1. *Total fertility rates, selected European countries, 1960–1995*

Country	1960	1970	1980	1992	1995
Germany	2.37	2.03	1.56	1.33	1.25
France	2.73	2.47	1.95	1.73	1.70
Italy	2.41	2.42	1.64	1.28	1.17
Netherlands	3.12	2.57	1.60	1.59	1.53
UK	2.72	2.43	1.90	1.79	1.70
Finland	2.72	1.83	1.63	1.85	1.81
Norway	2.91	2.50	1.72	1.88	1.87
EU12[a]	2.61	2.40	1.82	1.48	1.43

[a] 15 in 1995.
Sources: Eurostat (1996); demographic statistics, 1997.

9. TABLE 1.2. *Crude divorce rates, selected European countries, 1960–1995*

Country	1960	1970	1980	1990	1995
Germany	1.0	1.3	1.8	2.0	2.1
France	0.7	0.8	1.5	1.9	2.0
Italy	—	—	0.2	0.5	0.5
Netherlands	0.5	0.8	1.8	1.9	2.2
UK	0.5	1.1	2.8	2.9	2.9
Finland	0.8	1.3	2.0	2.6	2.7
Norway	0.7	0.9	1.6	2.4	2.4
EU12[a]	0.5	0.7	1.4	1.6	1.8

[a] 15 in 1995.
Sources: as Table 1.1.

10. However, it is not identical with a gender-systems approach, in that there is more of a stress on societal *uniqueness*.

11. For example, in France, a country that is discussed extensively in this book, women have historically received a range of maternity-related benefits in their capacities as employees, rather than as wives. As has been noted in respect of women's employment, the French case lies outside the corporatist location indicated by Esping-Andersen's original classification of regimes. (See Lewis 1992; Hantrais 1993; Lane 1996.)

12. It may be noted that there are parallels between the criticisms developed of Giddens and Beck and those which have already been made of post-structuralist/postmodernist feminist theories. Both Giddens and Beck have rejected the 'postmodern' label, referring instead to 'reflexive' modernity. However, as Kumar (1995) has noted, much of their work is indicative of a 'closet postmodernity'.

13. It is true that Beck emphasizes that biographical choices are 'standardized' via 'fashions, social policy, economic cycles and markets' (1992: 131). Nevertheless, the explanatory emphasis remains upon the individual, rather than on the structuring of these 'choices'.

14. This last category is not taken from Esping-Andersen's framework. The ex-state-socialist countries are an interesting comparative case in that their regimes had formally espoused women's equality in the public sphere—which included full employment for women—whilst gender relations in the private sphere remained highly conventional. See Buckley (1989).

15. The ISSP is an ongoing programme of cross-national attitudinal research, which fields (in addition to a set of core questions) module(s) relating to different topics each year, using a suite of mutually agreed questions (Davis *et al.* 1989). Advance copies of the ISSP Family and Gender Roles Module, gathered in 1994–5, were obtained for Britain, Norway, and the Czech Republic. Many thanks to Social and Community Planning Research (SCPR), London; The Gender Studies Centre, Institute of Sociology, Academy of Sciences, Prague; and Norwegian Social Science Data Services, Bergen, for their assistance in obtaining advance copies of the Family and Gender Roles data sets.

16. Interviews have been carried out by Elena Mezentseva, Irina Aristakheva, Marie Cermakova, Irena Hradecka, Jaroslava Stastna, Gunn Birkelund, Merete Helle, N. Le Feuvre, Florence Benoit, Rosemary Crompton, and Fiona Harris.

2

Obligations and Autonomy in Social Welfare

JANE MILLAR

INTRODUCTION

Looking to the post-war future, in which the British state would take on responsibility for the welfare of citizens from the 'cradle to the grave', William Beveridge was very clear that this meant quite different things for men and for women. Full employment would mean that men would always be able to support at least 'a wife and one child' and it would be their responsibility to do so. Women would withdraw from the labour market on marriage to take up their other duties as mothers to the new generation. The provisions of the post-war British welfare state thus rested on a very strongly gender-differentiated model of family life, in which men were full-time workers and women were full-time carers. Men were responsible for the financial support of their wives and children and therefore acted as the main point of contact between the family and state income-maintenance provisions: they received the tax allowances and social-security benefits. Women were responsible for family care and therefore acted as the main point of contact between the family and state services: they were the ones mostly seen by health visitors, doctors, teachers, and social workers. State benefits provided a back-up to men's provider role, while state services provided a back-up to women's caring role.

This gender-differentiated model was very clear in the post-war British welfare state, both in language (the Beveridge report itself is full of quotable 'soundbites', and examples of taken-for-granted assumptions about gender difference were, and often still are, very easy to find in official publications), and in actual policy provisions (where examples run almost from the cradle to the grave, from differences in the educational curriculum for girls and boys to old-age pensions that offer very different types and levels of support to women and men). And perhaps because this gendered model was so strong and so visible, it has also had a profound impact on the way in which the welfare state has been interpreted and analysed by feminist scholars in Britain. To simplify, feminist analyses of welfare in Britain have been characterized by two key features. The first is that state welfare has been seen as contributing to the reproduction of gender inequality, creating and sustaining differences in the rights of women and men, and granting women less than full social citizenship. Wilson's (1977) book *Women and the Welfare State* was one of the first British texts to address the issue of gender and welfare, and her approach illustrates this clearly: 'the welfare state is more than a set of services, it is also a set of ideas about society, about the family . . . about women . . . social welfare policies amount to no less than state control over women's lives.' The second key feature of much feminist analysis of the British welfare state is that the male-breadwinner model has been a central part of the framework used for analysing and understanding the nature of welfare provisions. Pascall (1997: 25) notes that: 'A continuing theme through feminist critiques of social policy . . . has been the dependent position of women within the family and the impact of social policies in sustaining it . . . Support for the breadwinner/dependent form of the family has entrenched the dependency of women within marriage.'

However, cross-national variations in state welfare policy and practice challenge both of these assumptions. As Orloff (1996*a*) points out, in contrast to the view that state welfare acts to reproduce gender equality, there is an alternative view that state welfare acts to ameliorate social inequality, including gender inequality. Rather than reproducing patriarchy, state action has the capacity to undermine it and to promote woman-friendly policies, which set out deliberately to promote gender equality. The Scandinavian welfare states, and Sweden in particular, have been analysed in this way by some authors (e.g. Hernes 1988; Duncan 1995). In addition, the capacity of the male-breadwinner model to capture cross-national variations in welfare states has come under increasing scrutiny. This is well summed up by Sainsbury (1996: 49):

An underlying assumption in earlier feminist theorizing about the welfare state was that the gendered division of labour, as typified by the male bread-winner model or the family wage, has been encoded in the social legislation of the industrial nations, and that public provision of welfare reflected and maintained traditional gender roles. Only as feminists have adopted a comparative perspective have they considered the possibility that the bread-winner model has varied in strength across countries . . . The assumption of the pervasiveness of the breadwinner model, which has underpinned much feminist scholarship, has not been subject to systematic comparison.

The most influential attempt to apply the male-breadwinner concept to cross-national analysis of welfare states can be found in the work of Jane Lewis (Lewis 1992, 1997; Lewis with Hobson 1997). Lewis and Hobson (1997: 6) define the male-breadwinner model in the following terms:

In its pure form, we would expect to find married women excluded from the labour market, firmly subordinated to their husbands for the purposes of social security entitlements and tax, and expected to undertake the work of caring (for children and other dependants) at home without public support. No country has ever matched such a model completely, but some have come much closer than others.

Thus welfare states can be classified as strong male breadwinner (for example, Ireland), modified male breadwinner (for example, France), and weak male breadwinner (for example, Sweden). This highlights some key differences in policy approach and outcomes but, as Lewis herself points out, does not entirely account for variations in the social rights of one particular group of women—lone mothers. Their access to state support, and the living standards they are able to achieve, vary widely across countries within the 'strong' breadwinner category—for example Germany, the Netherlands, and the UK (Hobson 1994). Duncan (1995: 268) argues that the bread-winner model is purely descriptive, providing nothing more than 'a colourful, but detheoreticized term for patriarchy'. Others, however, maintain that the concept is of explanatory value when comparing the different nature of welfare states (both cross-nationally and historically), but that it requires further and more systematic elaboration. In my own cross-national comparison of policies towards lone mothers (Millar 1996: 111–12) I argued that more attention should be paid to 'the way in which the earnings of the male breadwinner are replaced, in particular whether this is by means of social insurance or social assistance', and to whether women's claims to welfare 'are on the basis of status as wives, mothers or workers'. Sainsbury (1996: 72) provides a similar analysis but goes further:

a major shortcoming of the breadwinner model is its concentration on the husband as the principal beneficiary and the main source of women's social entitlements. The model fails to distinguish between women's entitlement as wives and as mothers . . . [there is a] necessity to rethink the male bread-winner model and to consider a female caregiver model focusing on mother-hood . . .

Thus she is arguing that the male-breadwinner model has tended to conflate two different situations: one in which women are treated as wives and receive social entitlements indirectly through their hus-bands; and the other in which women are treated as mothers and receive social entitlements directly and in their own right. Different welfare states mix these two approaches in different ways.

Another critique of the applicability of the male-breadwinner model has also started to emerge from some studies of the nature of welfare provisions in countries outside the northern European and the English-speaking countries (that is, USA, Canada, Australia, and New Zealand). Countries of southern Europe have often been seen as rather undeveloped or 'rudimentary' welfare states (Leibfried 1992), in which welfare is provided outside the state, through the vol-untary sector (especially religious institutions) and through the household and family. However, Trifiletti (1995: 3) argues that such an approach 'underestimates the coherent historical differences of the Mediterranean model' and, further, that neither can the male-breadwinner model readily be applied to these countries: 'in Italy . . . the traditional family role of the non-working mother was not, originally, particularly protected *as such* through additional benefits given to the male breadwinner in charge of her . . . keeping poor women at home was a luxury we never had, and this was not even perceived as particularly harmful by social reformers'. Thus there was no breadwinner through whom support was channelled. Instead, she argues that the family, and especially the extended family, was the unit that brought together a 'cumulation of breadcrumbs'—from market, state, and voluntary-sector sources—to meet their social and economic needs. This is not to say that gender roles are neutral within the family unit or 'enterprise', but that state benefits and ser-vices have not generally been based on the assumption that a family would have a single breadwinner and nor have state provisions been structured to support such a role. Bimbi (1997) points to the com-plexity of the Italian situation with significant regional variations and argues that 'the system is one where dependence is intergenera-tional rather than between men and women . . . Italian familialism prevails over the male-breadwinner model' (p. 196).

What these various critiques suggest is that the male-bread-winner/female-dependant concept may not be sufficiently differenti-ated to pick up the various dimensions across which welfare states may affect gender relations and created gendered outcomes. In par-ticular, the way in which the male-breadwinner model implies a contrast between 'independence' (the preserve of men through their position in the labour market) and 'dependence' (the preserve of women through their position in the family) has been challenged. Two concepts—autonomy and care—have been seen as particularly important in this. Orloff (1993, 1997) focuses on the capacity to form and maintain an autonomous household and argues that autonomy in these terms 'implies more than individual independence—it also gets at whether women can support families, thus including some of the legal issues around women heading households and also reflects the character of laws regulating sexuality, marriage and household formation' (1997: 196). This focus on legal regulation, and not just social-welfare provisions or labour-market policy, is also important to the way in which McLaughlin and Glendinning (1994) formulate the concept of 'defamilialization', or the conditions under which individuals enter into, and exit from, families. These conditions are shaped by both family law and social-welfare provisions. The differ-ences in the extent to which women, compared with men, can opt into, or out of, care work in the family is central to the gendered out-comes of state policy. Lewis (1997: 173), in her reflection on her own use of the male-breadwinner model, suggests that more attention needs to be paid to both 'cash and care, and how and why they are combined for different groups of the population'. And others, such as Knijn and Kremer (1997), put 'the right to care' and 'the right to be cared for' at the centre of their comparative analysis.

Sainsbury (1996) offers an analysis that focuses on the basis of claims to state support. She argues that mainstream analyses have often differentiated between different national approaches according to how far three different sorts of claims have been accepted as justified: claims on the basis of need, claims on the basis of labour-market status, and claims on the basis of citizenship. These broadly correspond to Esping-Andersen's (1990) three 'worlds of welfare capitalism' (need in the liberal regime, labour-market status in the conservative regime, and citizenship in the social-democratic regime), but, she argues, they are incomplete because they do not capture the main ways in which women's claims to welfare have been justified. She, therefore, adds two further dimensions: claims made on the principle of maintenance (that is, claims made on the grounds of supporting someone else) and claims made on the principle of care (that is, claims made on the grounds of caring for someone else). She concludes that entitlements on the basis of citizenship are particularly important to women, because they 'neutralize the impact of marriage on social rights . . . maternal rights based on citizenship undermine the principle of maintenance and the family wage ideal' (Sainsbury 1996: 45).

OBLIGATIONS AND AUTONOMY

In a recent study undertaken with Andrea Warman, in which we looked at family obligations in Europe (Millar and Warman 1996), we were grappling with some of the same sorts of issues—how to describe and compare cross-national variations in the ways in which dependency is constructed in law and policy. This research developed out of some observations about policy change in the UK, where, towards the end of the 1980s, there were a number of policy developments that seemed to be shifting the boundaries between the family and the state, and placing on families wider obligations for both financial support and care. For example, there was the withdrawal of social-security benefits for 16–17 year-olds, the payment of lower rates of benefit for under-25 year olds, and the shift from grants to loans for students in higher education (all measures prolonging family dependency for young people); the 1989 Children Act and the 1990 Child Support Act (both of which defined parental responsibilities towards their children, the latter very controversially); the implementation of the 1990 Health and Community Care Act (which includes access to informal, often family, care in the assessment of need for public services); and the growing importance of means-testing for social-security benefits (which reduce individual entitlement in favour of family-based assessments).

These policy developments seemed to step in the direction of less state/more family and to raise a number of questions or issues. First, to what extent are changes such as these part of a more general restructuring of the welfare state? Such restructuring was the avowed goal of the British conservative governments during the 1980s and 1990s, and encompasses not only reductions in levels of expenditure but also qualitative changes in the nature of social welfare (Pierson 1994; Esping-Andersen 1996). If the state withdraws from meeting certain needs, then these needs must either go unmet or be picked up somewhere else. Increasing family obligations could provide one route to reducing state provisions. Secondly, how far is it possible to go in redefining family obligations? Finch (1989*a*) has argued that, if policy gets out of step with normative views about what family members should do for each other, strong opposition can be generated. People will resist taking on obligations that they feel are unfair or illegitimate. The reaction to the child-support legislation in the UK can be interpreted in this way—the protests from separated parents, mainly fathers, have been not only against the higher levels of financial support involved but also against the definition of their financial obligations as unconditional and not dependent upon circumstances (Millar 1997). Thirdly, what is the likely impact on women and on women's social rights? A male-breadwinner/female-carer division of roles may be reinforced, or reconstructed, through developments such as these. And, finally, on a more comparative note, do different ways of defining family obligations reveal something about the defining characteristics of different welfare states? Definitions of family obligations spring from views about what is 'natural'—that women care for small children, for example, or that old people should be cared for by their daughters or sons—and such views, and the state policies that follow, may show considerable cross-national variation.

The research project involved sixteen European countries, the EU member states plus Norway, and data were collected from national respondents in each of those countries (see Warman and Millar 1996 for discussion of the methodology, and Millar and Warman 1996 for the main report). The data were in the form of national reports describing law and policy in each country on the basis of a common framework. This broadly followed a life-cycle approach, covering the obligations of couples to each other, of parents to children, of couples following separation or divorce, of adult children to elderly parents, of families to adults with specific care needs such as disability. Information was also collected on the extent to which social-security benefits and income-tax regimes were individual, family, or household based. This was, therefore, a very broad project: it included quite a large number of countries; it covered family law, particularly in relation to marriage, cohabitation, and divorce;

social-care policy, including childcare and care of dependent adults; and income-support policy, including tax and social security.

The focus was on the definition of obligations in law and policy and not on what actually happened in practice. For example, we wanted to know whether or not adult children had an obligation to care for their elderly parents, not whether they did actually provide such care. There can, of course, be quite a gap between policy and practice, but our interest was in the former and not the latter.[1] We were also more interested in the nature and objectives of policy rather than directly in levels of support, except in so far as the latter were indications of the former (for example, when we looked at various social-security benefits we were more interested in who was eligible for these than in how much they were eligible for). 'Obligations' were defined to include both cash—that is, the obligation to support another person financially; and care—that is, the obligation to look after another person (these broadly correspond to Sainsbury's 'principle of maintenance' and 'principle of care', discussed above). Alongside legal obligations, we also tried to get some sense of the more implicit expectations that can influence the shape of provisions. By looking at obligations we were hoping to be able to build up a picture of differences and similarities in the ways in which autonomy and dependency are constructed, and to explore the place of gender in this.

ANALYSING OBLIGATIONS

Looking across such a broad range of policy areas highlights the degree of difference that can be found within countries, and this is especially true when looking at provisions that are determined and delivered locally, which is often the case for social-care services. This creates caution in describing a national model and even more so in describing cross-national models. But, drawing all the various indicators together, we divided the sixteen countries into three clusters or, to borrow Castles's (1993) phrase, 'families of nations'. This is not to say that the countries we placed within each 'family' are similar in all respects—sometimes the relationship is close (like a sibling) and sometimes more distant (more like a cousin or perhaps a step-sibling). The aim is to cluster the countries according to the extent to which they share similar expectations about family obligations.

Individual Autonomy

In the Scandinavian countries—Denmark, Finland, Norway, and Sweden—the emphasis is on individual entitlements and citizenship rights available to all. Those in need expect and receive state, rather than family, provision and there are rarely any legal requirements for families to provide support. Care of the elderly is not seen as a family obligation and, although care services are not entirely rights based, they are more likely to be so than in other countries. Cash benefits and tax systems are mainly individual in character and rarely include dependants' additions. Marriage is less important than parenthood as a relationship giving rise to ongoing rights and obligations. There is limited regulation of marriage and divorce and recognition of non-marital sexual relationships, heterosexual and homosexual. Divorce almost always severs any obligations between the former spouses, and ongoing maintenance for a ex-spouse would be very rare. Children have some rights as autonomous individuals and not simply through their parents.

Extended Families

At the other extreme, in southern Europe—Greece, Italy, Portugal, and Spain—the extended family plays a more important role. Although there are clear obligations within the nuclear family (from spouses to each other and from parents to children), these obligations are embedded within a much wider set of familial obligations that brings in grandparents, siblings, uncles, and aunts. Families are legally obliged to support one another across a broad range of relationships and someone in need is expected to look first to his or her family for support. The type and level of support expected from family members will usually depend on the closeness of the relationship, with more expected from immediate family than from wider kin. Cash benefits recognize not only spouses but also in some cases a wider range of dependants. Survivors' benefits, for example, recognize other dependency relationships apart from widowhood. Divorce is uncommon and does not end financial obligations between spouses. State provision of childcare for young children is relatively low and children would be separated from their parents only in cases of abuse or neglect. 'Non-family' relationships, such as cohabitation, are unlikely to be perceived as giving rise to either rights or obligations in the same way as kin relationships. Opting out of providing family care is difficult, since services are mainly only for those without family.

Nuclear Families

The nuclear family—spouses and parents and children—is the basic unit in most European countries. In the UK and Ireland this is usually defined as parents and their dependent children in both family law and social-welfare provisions. In Austria, Belgium, France, Germany, Luxembourg, and the Netherlands family law and civil codes continue to specify 'upward' as well as 'downward' obligations (that is, from adult children to their parents as well as from parents to dependent children), although in practice social-welfare provisions often focus more on the obligations spouses owe to each other and parents owe to dependent children. In most of these countries individualization in taxes and benefits is relatively undeveloped. Services are intended to support family care, and access to these may include a significant degree of discretion, where family support may or may not be taken into account (in contrast with the individual countries, where family support will not be taken into account, and the extended-family countries, where family support will be taken into account). Marriage confers rights that are not generally extended to those who cohabit, although some of the obligations of marriage may also be imposed on cohabiting couples (so, for example, cohabiting couples may be treated as a single unit for social-assistance benefits but not for survivors' benefits). Divorce does not necessarily end the obligations of spouses to each other, although this is increasingly the case in many of these countries.

WHAT ROLE DOES GENDER PLAY?

These three broad models of family obligations are likely to have different implications for women and for gender autonomy. The countries with more individualized systems of support and where rights extend into the arena of care and not just cash allow women more choices and thus more autonomy. In the countries with a more extended family focus, assumptions of dependency are pervasive in respect of both cash and care. This limits the possibilities of opting out for both men (whose financial obligations to spouses continue after divorce, for example) and women (who cannot easily opt out of care, except perhaps by refusing to take on care in the first place—which is one interpretation that has been placed on the very low birth rates found in these southern European countries). However, the nuclear family group seems rather undifferentiated with regard to gender autonomy, since it includes, for example, countries like Ireland (a strong breadwinner country (see Lewis 1992)) and France (a modified breadwinner country).

One way to look at this is to consider the likely impact on women of changing policies within the different countries and clusters of countries. We found two main examples of apparent policy convergence among these sixteen countries. One was the declining importance of marriage and the increasing importance of parenthood as a relationship giving rise to unconditional and lifelong obligations. The other was the widespread introduction of cash benefits or payments to support individuals carrying out caring roles, including parental care of children. Such care has traditionally been seen as outside the range of government policy and within the range of family support, and thus the creation of these schemes does seem to reflect a shared shift in the definition of what is legitimate activity for the state. As Ungerson (1995) has argued, care is becoming increasingly 'commodified' across Europe. Evidence from our study supports this observation. For example, in ten of the countries there are now schemes of paid parental leave, and all but one (Luxembourg) have some form of social-security payment for adults with care needs. These latter take two main forms: as payments made to the 'caregivers' (to compensate for their earnings loss while caring or simply to recognize their caring contribution) or payments made to 'care-receivers' (to allow them to buy in their own support, possibly from family members).

Payments for 'caregivers' exist in five of these countries (Belgium, Denmark, Ireland, Italy, and Norway), for 'care-receivers' in six (Austria, Germany, Netherlands, Portugal, Spain, and Greece), and four countries have both sorts of scheme (Finland, France, Sweden, and the UK). Thus caregivers are less likely to receive payments in those countries where family care is expected and assumed (the extended-family countries and the less gender autonomous nuclear-family countries). Furthermore, where caregiver benefits are made, these vary in nature, with a contrast between schemes that involve formal contracts of employment and make payments at levels that could financially support the carer (for example, France, Norway, Sweden, and Finland) and those which are more 'symbolic', where payments tend to be low and make a small contribution to costs but would not be enough for carers to live on in the absence of other income (for example, Ireland, Italy, and the UK). Such payments are also likely to have a different impact in countries with high and low levels of service provision. Thus payments for care in Ireland, where service provision is low, are intended to encourage family members to care for their older relatives and thus reduce the need to develop public-sector provisions. In Sweden such payments are more about compensating family carers, if they choose to provide such care. These different types of care payments illustrate the ways in which different assumptions about families and gender roles influence the nature, and thus outcomes, of policy change.

CONCLUSION: REDEFINING OBLIGATIONS AND RESTRUCTURING WELFARE STATES?

Finally, this last section returns to the questions of whether there are limits to redefining family obligations and what role such redefinitions might play in the restructuring of welfare states. The two are linked. As Pierson (1994) has argued, retrenchment in social policy is very difficult to achieve because it involves losers who will try and resist loss of their benefits or entitlements. If the losers are politically weak, they may not have the power to resist. Other strategies to reduce opposition include obfuscation (keeping real policy objectives under wraps), divide and rule (preventing alliances from emerging), and compensating losers (and thus not taking retrenchment as far as planned). All this seems very relevant to understanding shifts between family and state. Redrawing the state/family boundary may be very controversial if made visible and the policy goals are clearly spelt out. But it is difficult to resist if introduced in an incremental way and at a local rather than a national level.

Thus the visible policy changes—for example, child support in the UK, care insurance in Austria and Germany, changes to community care in Finland and Sweden—have been controversial and concern has been expressed about the gendered implications of these. Changes that are more invisible have generated less attention and therefore less opposition. One example of this is the way in which the age at which 'children' are deemed to be financially independent of their parents has been creeping upward in a number of countries. The 'long' family, in which young adults remain and are treated as dependants of their parents, is common in southern Europe and very much part of their family-based model of welfare. Other countries—for example, Austria, Luxembourg, and Belgium—pay family allowances for young people into their mid-twenties; and some countries with minimum income schemes (for example, France, and Luxembourg) also pay these only to people in their mid-twenties and above. The long family may become a more widespread model in the future. In many countries it is probably more acceptable than trying to convince adults that they have an obligation to pay for their elderly parents, since it appears that the dependence of children on parents is seen as more 'natural' than the dependence of parents on children. It is well suited to a low-waged labour market in which individuals do not earn enough to support themselves independently but must pool with others to achieve adequate incomes. It can be achieved in a relatively silent and invisible way.

Other relatively silent policy changes include tighter eligibility for social-insurance benefits that exclude more people and hence increase the importance of social assistance. Social assistance is always family or household based and so individual entitlement is reduced almost by default. In the area of social care, the lack of legal rights to services in most countries means that the boundaries between state provisions and family support can be moved through the use of existing discretionary powers and without the need for new legislation. Furthermore, the use of discretion in the allocation of services can give more space for attitudes and beliefs about what can and should be expected of family members to have more influence on these decisions. And, where they exist, the support obligations that are outlined in civil codes can potentially be invoked more often across a wider range of areas. When analysing welfare-state restructuring, it is, therefore, important to examine these much less visible and more often local changes, as well as the more upfront changes at a national level. This, of course, has particular implications for women, who in many countries are politically weaker as a group than men and more affected by changes in social-care provisions. The 'women's welfare state' of social care and social assistance may be easier to restructure than the 'men's welfare state' of social insurance and fiscal support.

Sassoon (1997: 183) has argued that 'the male breadwinner model is weak but the female caregiver model is hegemonic'. Women bear the main responsibility for caring wherever we look, but there are nevertheless substantial differences in the conditions under which women care and the impact such caring has upon their individual autonomy. Viewing countries through a male-breadwinner model lens identifies these differences to some extent. But a focus on the concepts underlying the model—autonomy, care, dependency—may provide a more powerful way of analysing the different ways in which state provisions, in law and social welfare, produce particular forms of gendered outcomes.

NOTE

1. There is a parallel here with the model-families approach to cross-national comparison, where the outcomes of different systems are measured by their impact on the incomes of families of pre-specified types (as in, for example, Bradshaw *et al.* 1993). These studies focus on what would happen if each system worked perfectly in practice and not on what actually happens. They give, as does our approach, a picture of what is intended in national policy, not necessarily what is delivered.

3

Dual Breadwinners between State and Market

ANNE LISE ELLINGSÆTER

INTRODUCTION

A profound reorganization of contemporary work and family life is
taking place in all advanced capitalist societies: 'More women—and
also more men—are facing dual and often conflicting labour market
and family responsibilities. Ensuring the compatibility of employment
and family commitments within individual lives is a major challenge
emerging from the process of structural change' (OECD 1994: 1). A
major problem is that modern dual-breadwinner practices generate
tensions when they confront structures and cultures in work life built
around the traditional male-breadwinner model and the industrial time
regime. Structural and social reform is widely regarded as essential to
modify these problems. Adjustment policies recommended generally
include social infrastructures, such as childcare services, flexible work
hours, and measures to prevent the negative effects of career breaks
(OECD 1994).

The role of state policies in shaping new worker and carer practices
is a much debated issue. The impact of policies is often measured by
correlating particular national policies with national-level data
aggregates of practices. However, macro-level change is generated by
complex processes, and national reforms are contextualized in space
and time. State policies interact with structures and cultures in the
labour market; a particular set of national policies may generate different responses in different segments of the labour market. Thus, in
understanding the possibilities and limitations of policies, it is crucial
to examine what happens when politics meet the market. Further, a
dynamic perspective on policy models is essential, as policies are
shaped and reshaped over time, through varying degrees of consensus, conflicts, and compromises. A gender perspective including men

is also important, as policies shape not only mother worker–carer practices, but also men's.

In the Scandinavian welfare states the work–family tensions arising from the erosion of the male-breadwinner model have been modified by state policies. The present analysis of the role of policies in the construction of worker–carer practices is based on Scandinavian experiences, taking Norway as the main case. The main focus is on flexibility in time off work to care for children, as this practice is most likely to be in conflict with the worker role. One of the interesting features of the Norwegian policy model is the systematic difference in time flexibility generated between women and men, and between the public and the private sectors. Thus sectoral location, following the public/private division, is an interesting entry point for studying how policies interact with structures and cultures in the labour market in generating change.

First, the principal constituents and the historical legacy of reform policies regarding work and care in Norway are outlined. Secondly, structures and cultures in public versus private work organizations that may be conducive to, or in conflict with, a worker–carer model, are considered. Thirdly, gender and sectoral differences in the worker–carer practices generated in the labour market are examined. Finally, the future prospects of the Norwegian worker–carer model are discussed.

WORKER–CARERS AND THE STATE

In general there are several policy models for modifying the tensions between employment and childcare. Three policy elements are central: (1) time to care, (2) money for care, and (3) care services. These elements appear in different mixes in national welfare-state policy models (see Bettio *et al.*, forthcoming), they may change over time, and they have different implications for the transformation of gender relations in the restructuring of provider models.

In Scandinavia, there have been different national mixes of policy elements. Sweden has a pioneering history in both extensive public childcare services and time to care for children through generous parental-leave schemes. Denmark has a solid reputation as the provider of the most extensive child-care services in Europe, particularly for very young children, but parental-leave schemes have been modest compared to Sweden. Historically, Norway has been lagging behind both Sweden and Denmark in terms of services, and behind Sweden in terms of parental-leave schemes, but has spent comparatively more on monetary transfers to parents (Ellingsæter and Hedlund 1998).

The Scandinavian countries have taken considerable steps away from a traditional male-breadwinner model towards dual breadwinning. Employment rates among mothers are high. For example, 73 per cent of Norwegian mothers of preschool children were employed in 1995 (Ellingsæter and Wiers-Jenssen 1997). Political commitment to women's right to work and the recognition of mothers as earners, and legislation and services to support this commitment, are present to a considerable degree. The large majority of women are employed for a substantial part of their lives, and the majority of Scandinavian employed parents support an egalitarian provider model. However, there are important differences in policies, and in practices and preferences, reflecting peculiarities in the national modernization processes in which the transformation of gender relations have taken place. There is no doubt that 'politics matter' in the structuring of provider models, but the ways in which welfare-state policies interact with other structural and cultural mechanisms in generating change are complex (Ellingsæter 1998a).

Economic crisis and welfare-state restructuring have been accompanied by both similar and different policy trends in Scandinavia (Kuhnle 1996). Social reform is likely to be patterned by its historical legacy. In Sweden, during the severe economic recession in the 1990s, the generosity of leave schemes has been subject to retrenchments, yet benefits are still comparatively high. Moreover, a new requirement that local authorities have to provide childcare when parents are working or studying has been introduced. In Denmark, new parental-leave schemes have been launched (1992), but interestingly their main political rationale was not the reconciliation problems of working parents, as in Sweden and Norway, but unemployment and job sharing. In Norway, childcare services, and particularly parental-leave arrangements, have expanded significantly, despite a quite severe recession (involving rising unemployment) from 1988 to 1993. However, a new reform paying cash to parents not using public childcare might possibly reverse the growth trend in public childcare. In contrast to most other countries, Norwegian oil revenues increase the state's freedom of action in a situation of external pressures.

The Norwegian Worker–Carer Model

Norwegian family policies have been directed primarily at changing the institutional structures of parenthood. Policies have been based on a model of a symmetric family of two worker–carers, in which time to care for children has a high priority among both working mothers and fathers. The worker–carer model of shared employment and family responsibilities implies a departure from the traditional male norm of full-time, lifelong continuous employment, towards more flexible employment models. A main principle of the policies supporting the model is the opportunity to pursue parenthood within the work contract, and time flexibility is crucial. Policy measures such as access to reduced work hours and parental-leave schemes, including innovative measures such as a father quota and a time account system, are central to the model (for an overview of policies, see Ellingsæter and Hedlund 1998).

Parental leave of absence in connection with childbirth was significantly extended in the 1980s and 1990s. Currently, the leave consists of fifty-two weeks with 80 per cent compensation, or forty-two weeks with 100 per cent compensation. This leave has a *mother quota*, which is directed at protecting biological motherhood: altogether three weeks before and six weeks after birth. There is a *father quota* of four weeks, which will be lost to the parents if not taken by the father. The rest of the leave may be shared between the parents as they prefer. The rights of fathers are linked to the mothers' employment relations prior to birth: women must have worked 50 per cent or more (Likestillingsrådet 1996). In addition there are two weeks of unpaid 'daddy leave' in connection with the birth, which aims at establishing the social father–child relationship as early as possible. The parental leave can be taken according to a time account system, which in principle gives a high degree of time flexibility.

In general, parental-leave rights apply to both the private and the public sector, but the public-sector employees enjoy extra benefits in connection with childbirth and childcare. Mothers in the public sector (both state and municipalities) receive full wage compensation in connection with paid leaves. They are also entitled to extra unpaid leave (maximum of three years) before the child is 12 years old. There are differences between the public and private sectors concerning the father quota. Fathers in the private sector are compensated economically only up to a certain threshold, and compensation beyond this level depends on negotiations with the employer. Moreover, 'daddy leave' is paid in the public sector.

Parents have the right to return to their jobs after parental leave. Parents with small children have the right to reduced working hours without compensation, if this is not a disadvantage to the employer. Moreover, parents have the right to leave of absence to care for sick children of ten days per parent per year (for children younger than 12 years old).

The other main policy measure is access to high-quality public childcare. Public day care plays an important part in the everyday life of parents, although mothers entered the labour market long before the supply of public day care had expanded sufficiently to affect their employment decisions (Leira 1992). Still the supply is short of the demand, particularly among the youngest children: 31 per cent of children 1–2 years old, and 72 per cent of those aged 3–6, were enrolled in publicly supported day care in 1995 (Statistics Norway 1996). From 1997 6-year-old children have been enrolled in the primary-school system, creating more capacity for younger children in childcare institutions.

Politicizing Motherhood and Fatherhood

The concern for working mothers in the welfare state has historically been centred around protection of what may be called *biological motherhood* (Eisenstein 1983); pregnancy, birth, and breastfeeding. Protective rights for working mothers can reduce their market capacity, and there is legislation to prevent discrimination because of this (Dahl 1991). These activities are seen as naturally given, and can never be equalized between women and men. However, biological motherhood also has elements of social construction, evidenced by historically contingent practices. In Norway, the 'good mother' is subject to many expectations about proper pregnancy behaviour; related to nutrition, smoking, and alcohol. The prolonged duration of breastfeeding recommended in recent years (now about one year) happens to be the maximum duration of paid leave. Prolonged breastfeeding has clear temporal implications for the division of care work between mothers and fathers, and thus for the organization of employment in the early stages of parenthood. These 'rules' are legitimated by the medical profession, but some of them are scientifically unfounded (Eskild 1994). The boundaries between nature and culture are not fixed.

Political motherhood is all the other care work mothers do in connection with children (including economic provision, physical and
psychological care), and its content is defined politically and socially,
by prevailing practices and ideas. The issue of working mothers
became an important question for second-wave feminism in Norway,
which claimed the right of women to have both children and paid
work. Shared work and family responsibilities for both women and
men have been a core idea of Norwegian feminism. However, working mothers have been a controversial issue in Norwegian politics.
Gender equality and family reforms have been brought forward by a
series of political compromises, and not by the strong consensus
across political parties found in the other Scandinavian countries on
this issue (Leira 1993; Ellingsæter 1998*a*). While the main argument
in favour of expanding public childcare in Denmark and Sweden was
the concern for working mothers, for a long time the benefit of children was the political rationale of public childcare in Norway (Leira
1992). Norwegian policies have been characterized by reluctant
reforms, influenced by the persistence of traditional family values.
Ambivalence concerning working mothers is reflected in the expectations that Norwegian parents feel are directed at them. The majority
believe that most *other* people think that fathers should be sole
providers when children are young, while their *own* preferences are
characterized by gender equality (Ellingsæter 1998*a*).

An interesting element of Norwegian policies is that it has put
political fatherhood on the agenda. While employment for women
was the main issue of policies in the 1980s, criticized by some as a
masculinization of women, the caring father, and thus the domesti-
cation of men, is the new issue of the 1990s. The father quota is based
on the assumption that, in order to change the care practices of men,
they have to be subjected to (mild) structural coercion. The element
of coercion in the father quota, and the allocation of reproductive
rights as 'fathers' only' entitlements, and not as mother's or gender
neutral rights, is a new construction. The quota is argued partly as a
family policy concern: to strengthen the father–child relationship, by
expanding the physical and psychological childcare of fathers. It
provides opportunities for fathers to include aspects other than
economic provision in their care for children. Partly it is a gender-
equality policy concern; mothers' expanding involvement in the
labour market needs to be followed by changes in men's family
involvement.

Norwegian gender-equality policies and family policies have been intertwined, which is reflected both in institutional arrangements and in political thinking. The coordination and implementation of gender-equality policies have been placed in the Ministry of Children and Family Affairs (previously the Ministry of Family and Consumer Affairs) since 1972. A recent government policy document states that: 'Family policies and gender equality belong together' (St.prp. nr. 1 1994–5: 26). The idea underlying the close link between gender equality and family affairs is that the family is a unit of *common* interests. Arguments in favour of separation suggest that the family is a unit of *differing* interests, and that these two policy areas might have conflicting interests (NOU 1995). The integrated gender-equality/family-policy model unites policy areas with potentially conflicting aims. For example, policies aimed at increasing women's autonomy, on the one hand, and policies supporting the family as a collective and the needs of children, on the other, might represent conflicting interests. Some scholars see the parental-leave reforms and their motivations as representing a shift from a gender-equality focus to an emphasis on family values and the concern for children; a shift from 'state-feminism' to 'state-familism' (Leira 1996). The new cash reform (see below) is mainly argued from the needs of children.

The development of the worker–carer model has been strongly influenced by a long period of social-democratic governments. However, family–work policies are a contested terrain in the modernization of gender relations in Norway. There is a historical legacy of a lack of political consensus and continuous pressures from political quarters supporting traditional values or liberal anti-state interventionism. The most disputed issue has been subsidized public childcare. As a result of a change of government in 1997, when a centre minority government came into power, an extensive cash-benefit reform was introduced in 1998. Parents with small children who do not use public childcare get paid in cash the amount equivalent to the state subsidy to a place in the services. The reform diverges from the main principle in the worker–carer model in that benefits are not tied to the employment contract. The proponents argue that the reform increases the flexibility of individual choice in childcare and fairness in distribution of state subsidies to families with children. The reform has also been framed very much as a 'time issue', claiming that this reform is giving parents 'back their time'. Arguments against the reform are related to the potential weakening of women's labour-market relations, the limitation of choice when there is still an unmet demand for public services, and a potential increase in the unregulated informal market of private childminders.

WORKER-CARERS AND THE MARKET

State policies interact with labour-market structures and cultures in shaping worker–carer practices. There are two important reasons for studying the significance of sectoral location in generating flexibility. One is the importance of the public sector in Norwegian employment in general, and in women's employment in particular, and several other structural differences between the sectors. The other is the theoretical claim that the public sector is a different type of labour market from the private sector.

It is necessary to clarify the concept of flexibility and its different contents and meanings. Different types of flexibility have very different meanings for workers and implications for gender relations. One can distinguish between at least three types of flexibility in employment relations (see Yeandle, Chapter 5 in this volume). First, arrangements that enable individuals to tailor their employment to their family and personal circumstances varying over the life course—a flexibility which is mainly supply based; this is the type of flexibility ideally implied in the Norwegian worker–carer model. Secondly, a more limited version of flexibility, covering specific female accommodation patterns, which might be either supply or demand led. Thirdly, flexibility corresponding to the paradigm dominating current economic and political debates, in which flexibility represents a disruption of the traditional industrial economic system, implying flexibility in both production methods and the use of labour; this type of flexibility is demand led.

In most countries flexible employment models have been established among women, but these new forms of work have been categorized as atypical, and are often perceived to be at the bottom of the hierarchy of jobs. The prevalence and consequences of various flexible employment models may vary between countries and within national labour-market sectors, however. The single most important form of flexible working among women—part-time work—may be classified under each of the three flexibility forms, depending on the specific national conditions regulating this type of work.

Sectoral Structures

In most countries the public sector creates more jobs for women than
the private sector, jobs which are associated with better employment
protection and social security, and a lower gender differential in
earnings (Schmid 1991). The Scandinavian countries have had the
highest growth rates in the public sector, and the state is the single
most important employer (Hagen 1991). In Norway, employment is
characterized by a high public-sector dependency: 33 per cent of all
employees work in the public sector; 46 per cent of all women and 22
per cent of all men (Statistics Norway 1998). Public-sector dependency is even stronger among mothers, and 56 per cent of all
employed mothers work in the public sector (Survey of Working Life
1993, see Statistics Norway 1995; author's calculation). Women are
the numerically dominant group in the public sector, and 64 per cent
of employees are female. In the private sector about one-third are
women. Moreover, state and municipal employers are likely to feel
more obligated to adjust to public policy measures. The Ministry of
Children and Family Affairs takes a particular responsibility for
integrating gender-equality concerns in the state and municipal
sector.

Public-sector employment started to grow markedly at the end of
the 1960s, and has continued to increase ever since. During the recession of 1988–93 public-sector employment, and particularly local
state employment (municipalities), continued to grow. The number
of persons employed in government producing services increased by
14 per cent, and 92 per cent of the increase was found in local government services. Thus, although the recession intensified the pressure on government budgets, it did not seriously affect public
employment. Cutbacks were directed at subsidies and transfers to
individuals, households, and private industries, while spending on
government services, such as education, public childcare and care for
the elderly, which have the most direct impact on employment, was
expanding. During strong employment growth since 1993, the private sector has increased most rapidly. However, while women
increased their numbers in the public sector, the number of men actually declined (Statistics Norway 1998).

There are several other structures distinguishing between workers
in the public and the private sector, and conditions are generally
the least favourable for women in the private sector, including skill

levels, gender differentials in earnings, union density, and vertical gender segregation. Moreover, compared to public-sector work-places, Norwegian private businesses are relatively small, which might make it more difficult to accommodate flexible time patterns. Small company size increases the vulnerability in relation to absent employees.

The public sector is a high-skill sector. Gender-equality practices tend to increase by educational levels, and will thus tend to generate more flexible worker–carer practices in the public sector, among both men and women. For example, only 15 per cent of women in the private sector had university-level education, compared to 39 per cent of women in the public sector (Survey of Working Life 1993, see Statistics Norway 1995; author's calculations). Nearly half of the fathers in the private sector work in blue-collar occupations, which are often more traditional in their practices and ideals (see Ellingsæter 1998). In contrast, 40 per cent of the fathers in the public sector are top professionals. Mothers in the private sector are con-centrated among low- (31 per cent) and middle- (35 per cent) level salaried employees, while the concentration at the middle level is high in the public sector (48 per cent).

A longitudinal cohort study shows that the majority of highly edu-cated women in the postwar birth cohorts found employment in the public sector (Ellingsæter *et al.* 1997). While about 93 per cent of women with high educational level born in 1945 worked in the pub-lic sector at the age of 33, the corresponding proportion of women with the lowest educational level was 21. This is changing among younger women, and a substantially higher proportion of those with high educational levels are recruited to the private sector (24 per cent among those born in 1960). However, the majority still work in the public sector.

Differences in earnings (including gender differences) are the largest in private-sector jobs (Barth and Mastekaasa 1993). In the public sector workers are well organized. While gender differentials in union density are disappearing, sectoral differences remain large. About 80 per cent are union members in the public sector, compared to less than 50 per cent in the private sector (Ellingsæter 1995*a*).

Vertical gender segregation is most resistant in the private sector. In the last decade, the relative gender difference in the proportion of managers was reduced in the public sector, while there was no gen-der equalizing effect in the vertical segregation in the private sector.

The difference between the sectors is largest among top-level managers, where the proportion of women is very low (Kjeldstad and Lyngstad 1993: 71). Top professionals constitute a somewhat lower proportion among mothers in the private sector (9 per cent), compared to mothers in the public sector (17 per cent). The increasing number of female public-sector top bureaucrats, the 'femocrats', might be influential agents in promoting and monitoring gender-equality interests, constructing a positive normative climate for the worker–carer model.

Sectoral Cultures

One important question is how the public versus the private labour market should be conceptualized. It has been argued that only the private sector of the labour market is a market in a conventional sense, in which market principles, such as a profit motive and a productivity logic, operate (Esping-Andersen 1990). The motivating factor in the market is self-interest; economic relations are governed by a 'spirit of gain' (Sejersted 1995). The market and the economic sphere have been subject to a continuous process of rationalization in Western societies. Rationalization of the economy makes the individual the most relevant unit of action, and individualism becomes a societal ideology (Buchmann 1989). Rational economic action is purposive; means and ends are calculated. Rational economic action is not restricted to the service of particular needs, and any end is pursued using the most efficient means. The rationalization of the economic sphere presupposes production factors and economic exchange relations that are not restricted by traditional norms defining and regulating economic transactions.

It has been argued that particular expectations are directed at the state as employer, and the state has the reputation of being a 'good employer' (Beechey and Perkins 1987; Esping-Andersen 1990). This needs modifications, however. First, one can argue that employment conditions in the public sector are to a large extent determined by the social contract shaping different types of welfare states (Schmid 1991). Secondly, although the market logic is most articulated in the private sector, the sharp distinction between the public and the private labour market is becoming blurred. Some would argue that there is a shift from the state as a 'good' employer to an 'efficient' one. A general cult of efficiency is spreading (Hochschild 1997). Elements of a market logic, such as efficiency and productivity, have been invading the public sector. Activities that can hardly be measured by conventional economic criteria are forced into this logic. The belief in the market's regulatory capacity has been fluctuating historically, but the 1980s represented a strong revival of the belief in the market as the best regulator of economic relations, which is obviously connected to the collapse of Keynesian economic policies (Sejersted 1995). However, the privatization of the public sector has been very modest in Norway. Moreover, the private market does not operate as an autonomous economic system, but is restricted by state and organized labour.

Despite the increasing influence of traditional market criteria, there is still relatively less emphasis on conventional efficiency and cost-benefit criteria in the public sector. Thus, supply-led flexible work–family arrangements are assumed to meet most resistance in the private sector. Working time is an important component in the operationalization of efficiency and productivity. Various types of 'absence' and 'presence' have different cultural meanings, and are implicitly associated with different degrees of efficiency and productivity, ideas that again are connected with perceptions of women and men as workers. Time for care is time directed at aims other than the organization's.

WORKER–CARER PRACTICES

Gender Difference

The expansion of the worker–carer model has had a major impact in increasing the continuity in Norwegian mothers' employment practices in connection with births. The significant increase in the late 1980s in mothers returning to work after giving birth is clearly affected by the extension of parental-leave schemes. In the late 1980s, 62 per cent of mothers were employed one year after the birth (Ellingsæter and Rønsen 1996). The speeding-up of mothers' return to work involves an increase in both full-time and part-time work. The possibility of part-time work is an important reason for many mothers returning to work. Access to public childcare does not have the same direct impact on how soon mothers go back to work after giving birth (Rønsen 1993).

Parental leave is mainly taken up by women. In 1996, 73 per cent of mothers were entitled to paid parental leave; of those, 67 per cent chose fifty-two weeks' leave with 80 per cent compensation (Ellingsæter and Hedlund 1998). About one in every three mothers receives only a lump-sum parental grant, as they are not eligible for parental benefits. Those not eligible belong to households with much lower incomes and higher levels of social assistance than mothers receiving paid leave benefits. Parental-leave benefits contribute to equalize women's and men's incomes, but do increase differences between families.

About 80 per cent of fathers have the right to paid leave in families where mothers are entitled to leave (Ellingsæter and Hedlund 1998). In 1996, close to 80 per cent of the entitled fathers took up some leave; in 1995 and 1994, the corresponding rates were 70 and 45 per cent. Among the leave-takers in 1996, most fathers (68 per cent) took up one month, 'the father quota'. Only 9 per cent took up two months or more. Before the 'father quota' was introduced, less than 4 per cent of all fathers took some of the parental leave (Brandth and Kvande 1992). Interestingly, the main factor explaining the practices among these few men taking up leave was not the father's work situation, but the mother's income and educational level (Brandth and Kvande 1992). Parents sharing leave of absence included a high proportion of couples in which both had high social status. The father quota has institutionalized new norms for the time use of a large group of fathers. The earlier socio-economic bias is significantly weakened, although there is still significant variation by educational level. Among fathers with university education, 83 per cent used the father quota, compared to 71 per cent among fathers with compulsory primary and secondary education (Brandth and Øverli 1998).

Fathers are generally positive towards taking up leave (Brandth and Øverli 1998). Some fathers taking up leave report some negative reactions from employers, but the general picture is that the reform is widely accepted. Among fathers, 61 per cent want an extension of the paternity quota to eight weeks, and 72 per cent think that fathers' leave entitlements should be derived from their own employment record and not their spouse's (Brandth and Øverli 1998). Obviously, the father quota is not only something that is forced upon fathers; it is also a right they want to use.

An equalization of working time among mothers and fathers is the new trend of the 1990s, as fathers' work time declined slightly and mothers' increased somewhat through more full-time work (Ellingsæter and Hedlund 1998). While the proportion of fathers working excessively long hours increased simultaneously with mothers' increasing employment rates in the 1980s, this trend has been somewhat reversed in the 1990s. There was a decline in the proportion with long work hours (forty-five hours per week or more) from 1991 to 1995 (Kitterød and Roalsø 1996). Whether this was a mere effect of the economic recession, or a more consistent trend remains to be seen. Yet, while only 5 per cent of mothers of preschool-age children have weekly work hours of forty-five or more, 34 per cent of fathers work these hours. A substantial proportion of mothers work part-time (although this is declining); 52 per cent of those employed in 1995 (Ellingsæter and Wiers-Jenssen 1997). However, there are large differences in work hours among women by mothers' educational levels. Full-time work is the dominant practice of highly educated mothers. Access to part-time work is an ambiguous indicator as far as gender equality is concerned. It is clearly family friendly, but does not promote gender equality as long as this is a 'mother-only' adjustment.

Changing attitudes towards work hours might indicate a shift in the normative climate. From 1991 to 1996 there was an increasing share of employed parents wanting shorter work hours (provided that wages were proportionally reduced). The strongest increase was among mothers of preschool children and among single mothers, the two groups in which work hours actually increased in this period. In particular, mothers in full-time work preferred shorter work hours (50 per cent of those working thirty-five hours per week or more NOU 1996)). Among fathers, those working long weekly hours (more than forty-five hours) would most often like to reduce their work hours (one in three). The right to stay home with sick children is used extensively by parents, but women are twice as likely as men to stay at home. The likelihood of absence decreases with the increasing age of children (Mastekaasa 1992). Absence because of sick children is lowest among part-time workers and increases with increasing work hours, suggesting that unplanned absence in connection with children's illness is reduced for men by their partners' working-time flexibility. It is likely that men are less absent because they more often have jobs that are considered more difficult to stay away from, as men often have jobs of higher status than their partners. For example, Leiulfsrud and Woodward's (1989) study of

Swedish cross-class families found that men stayed at home with sick children when their wives had higher-status jobs. Women's absence thus is at least in part an effect of their structural position in the labour market, as they are over-represented in part-time work and low-status jobs.

Sectoral Difference

It has been argued that, in the current debate about labour-market restructuring and flexibility, the focus has been on the private sector, while the public sector has been virtually invisible (Fairbrother 1991). In general, the prevalence of flexible work contracts in Norway indicates that most flexibility is actually generated in the public sector. Part-time work is most prevalent in the public sector: 44 per cent of women in the public sector work part-time, compared to 32 per cent among private-sector women. In both sectors part-time work is most prevalent among salaried employees with low skill levels. Part-time work in Norway has been considered as mainly supply led, although in recent years the increasing proportion of underemployed among part-time workers suggests that particular types of part-time work are increasingly employer led. Under-employment among part-time workers seems to be growing most in welfare-sector jobs (Ellingsæter and Wiers-Jenssen 1997).

Temporary work contracts are more frequent in the public than in the private sector. This is in part the price for the flexibility granted to permanent employees. The more generous leave-of-absence rights in the public sector creates a higher demand for temporary employees (Torp 1990). Thus generous rights for one group of women require that other groups of women have to work on less favourable contracts.

However, there are also significant variations in flexibility *within* the two sectors. In the private sector it is particularly the male-dominated manufacturing industries that exhibit very traditional work-time patterns. In the public sector it is the welfare sector, rather than the government bureaucracy, where part-time jobs and tempo-rary work contracts are found (Ellingsæter and Wiers-Jenssen 1997). This might in part be explained by access to different types of time flexibility in welfare-care jobs as compared to jobs in welfare bureau-cracies. Care occupations generally have little daily flexibility, while access to reduced work hours is extensive. This might indicate that there is a trade-off between the two types of flexibility.

Flexibility in parents' worker–carer practices varies by sector, both among women and men. Mothers' new flexible and continuous employment patterns are less prevalent in the private sector. Having a job in the public sector is shown to speed up the return to work after birth, all other things being equal (Ellingsæter and Rønsen 1996). An interesting finding is that mothers who are manual workers in the private sector have lower levels of part-time work than mothers who are professionals in the public sector. A significantly higher proportion of fathers take up the father quota in the public than in the private sector: 83 versus 77 per cent in 1995 (Brandth and Øverli 1998). Mother's sectoral employment affects father's leave patterns in a similar direction. Fathers who have the longest work hours have the lowest share of paternity-quota users, and fathers in the private sector are more likely to work long hours than men in the public sector (Ellingsæter 1990; Brandth and Øverli 1998). High income tends to reduce the take-up of parental leave or the father quota. But the fathers' employment contract is particularly important: fathers who have permanent employment have significantly higher take-up rates than those on temporary work contracts or self-employed.

There are indications that women's time flexibility is 'punished' more in the private than in the public sector. Hansen (1995) concludes that there is a 'care deduction' in the private sector—that is, women who reduce their work hours are punished in terms of wages and promotion over time. Thus the public sector is a better employer for mothers than the private sector. However, this study includes only the oldest postwar cohorts of women, who went into the labour market as mothers in the 1970s, when women had fairly traditional employment patterns in connection with childbirth. Demographic research shows that the new patterns of family formation and employment were first clearly established among women born after 1960 (Blom *et al.* 1993), characterized by delayed births and increasing differences between educational groups. Moreover, these trends are supported by more recent data. A study of career trajectories in the public sector indicates that absence from work does not affect earnings (Barth and Yin 1996). A case study of a large private company suggests, on the other hand, that working reduced hours and having taken up parental leave have a strong negative effect on the probability of promotion (Longva 1997). However, another study found that work hours and stability in employment relations were

significant in explaining promotion in both the private and the public sector (Hoel 1995). A traditional female pattern was 'punished'
both in male-dominated occupations in the private sector and in
female-dominated occupations in the public sector.

However, having a career position restricts the proportion of
women who go into part-time work, independently of their family
situation (Hoel 1995). While the work-time reduction in connection
with childbirth does not necessarily differ much, the ways time reductions are arranged may vary: part-time work is most frequent in the
female-dominated occupations in the public sector, while women in
male-dominated occupations in the private sector more often leave
their jobs temporarily. The total reduction in work time thus might
not be that different, but the reduction is differently organized tem-
porally (Hoel 1995). This might indicate that structural differences in
the access to part-time work in the two sectors partly explain the patterns, rather than differences in preferences.

THE WORKER–CARER MODEL IN THE FUTURE

The Norwegian worker–carer model has facilitated a flexible combination of employment and care among parents. Public policies have
been implemented in employment, and flexible practices have
increased significantly over a quite short time span. This suggests
that there is a considerable potential for expanding time flexibility.
The expansion in the parental-leave arrangements demonstrates how
policies have contributed to the institutionalization of new time
norms for both mothers and fathers. However, the dominant pattern
is a two-tier model of parenthood in work life—one model for
mothers and one for fathers. The shared worker–carer practice
remains largely a women-only practice, thus cementing gender
difference. If time flexibility remains a mother-only practice, the conception of women workers as a group with a less than full labour-
market capacity will persist.

The flexible worker–carer model is more seldom practised, and
more often 'punished', in the private than in the public sector of the
labour market. It has been argued that this is why the public sector is
preferred by women. The public sector accommodates the greatest
flexibility in its workforce, a flexibility used extensively by large
groups of mothers. Accordingly, a large, flexible public sector has

been of significant importance in enhancing the new flexible worker–carer model. Sectoral difference is generated by structural, institutional, and cultural factors. The public-sector workforce is composed of a relatively high proportion of well-educated and well-organized women. Parents' reproductive rights are more extensive than in the private sector. There is also the still relatively lower emphasis on conventional efficiency and cost-benefit criteria associated with labour in the public sector, in combination with an institutionalized concern for gender equality. A crucial question is whether it is possible to improve the Norwegian worker–carer model in the future—and particularly the scope for expanding the model among men and in the private sector. Of particular importance to the future development of gender and sectoral divisions are the direction of labour-market restructuring, and the development of time politics and workplace time norms.

Labour-market demand and supply influence the relative pull and push of employment versus care. The access to jobs in the public versus the private sector, and the temporal organization of jobs and reward structures, will play a vital role. Work forms that strengthen the individual's relation to the workplace may become more important in both sectors. Upgrading the qualifications of workers, and new incentive systems, may make work increasingly more attractive and de-alienated, shifting the relative pull from family to work (Hochschild 1997). Increasing unemployment may also reinforce the individual's involvement in his or her work. Job insecurity—for example, in the form of temporary work contracts—is likely to have a negative impact on flexible worker–carer practices.

Rights to parental leave are not equally extensive for men and women, or for private- and public-sector employees. The father's right to parental leave, and level of compensation, is tied to the mother's employment situation, producing disincentives to the father's taking up leave. The father is thus considered to be the mother's 'helper', and not an independent care person for the child (Ellingsæter and Hedlund 1998). An expansion of the father's own rights, and of the father quota, might increase fathers' caring time. The new cash-benefit reform might increase the duration of women's absence from work. This might create a new re-entering problem for groups of women, particularly if unemployment increases. In Denmark a significant number of women who have been on extensive parental leave have problems re-entering the labour market.

Many of these women have little education and began leave as unemployed (Ligestillingsrådet 1998).

The worker–carer model has been developed by the state largely as a response to demands from second-wave feminism. Further expansion of time flexibility to the private sector will also depend on the role of time politics in the strategies of the labour-market actors. Norwegian unions have traditionally focused most on wages. Welfare in terms of more time (time welfare) is an alternative route to more welfare, but it requires a reversing of the relative value attached to time versus money (Hörning *et al.* 1995). There are signs that the perception of the relative utility of money over time may be shifting. Norway's largest employee federation (LO) has been dominated by men and is strongly class based in its interest profile. However, women are the fastest-growing group of new members, and women have recently made their ways into positions as elected representatives in the top of the organization. LO's programme (1997–2001) focuses on the need for new flexible working-time reforms—that is, a flexibility that accommodates individual needs over the life course. Growing diversity in working-time regimes and schedules may, however, undermine the power of unions. Further, employers' resistance has been much stronger to reductions in standard working time than to increases in wages, because these involve complex issues of reorganization (Hinrichs *et al.* 1991).

More flexibility seems to be a pressing need in the private sector. The private sector loses out to the public sector in the competition for well-educated women. Women are now the majority in higher-level education in Norway, and the federal employers' organization (NHO) realizes that women comprise an increasing share of the most attractive workers of the future workforce, as high human capital is seen as the most important success criterion for enterprises. The danger is that this flexibility will be offered only to the most attractive workers, leading to increasing inequalities in women's opportunities to combine employment and children in the private sector. Thus time flexibility might act as a new source of inequality.

In the Norwegian labour market there has been an increasing tendency towards a widening gap between formal regulations and actual practices. For example, while paid overtime is formally restricted, unpaid overtime has increased. Practices may generate informal norms about time use outside the institutionalized framework. A crucial point concerns the development of organizational time cultures. Time norms governing working life have differed between the public and the private sector, but this might change in the future. In large segments of work life, long work hours and visibility through presence at work are likely to be equated with company commitment. Long work hours among men have previously been most prevalent in the private sector. High-commitment time regimes transform an instrumental contractual relation into an open-ended moral bond, making claims on private feelings such as total commitment, eroding the boundary between the public and the private (Bailyn 1993). The conflict between the company's temporal claim on the worker and the child's temporal claim on its father seems to be less acute regarding a limited number of weeks away from the job than regarding usual work hours. Absence of short durations does not question an individual's job commitment in the same way as reduced time over longer periods. The father quota makes fairly limited claims on fathers' time, in contrast to women's longer leaves and part-time working.

Some argue that the boundaries between work time and personal time are being blurred, particularly in jobs where competence and knowledge are personified (Sørhaug 1996). This type of job is increasing most in the knowledge-based service industries in Norway, and there are more men than women in these jobs (Ellingsæter and Wiers-Jenssen 1997). In an increasingly individualistic society where autonomy is highly valued, time autonomy is likely to be tied to social status in different ways. The potential for self-managed flexibility is the greatest in the types of 'good' jobs that men hold—that is, jobs relatively independent of customers and clients. There are indications that time flexibility is used as a reward for the most time committed workers. However, this is a type of time flexibility that is unlikely to expand the practice of combining employment and caring work.

4

The Modernization of Family and Motherhood in Western Europe

BIRGIT PFAU-EFFINGER

INTRODUCTION

In the last decades the social practices of motherhood have changed substantially in Europe. Women have to an increasing degree entered the labour market, particularly in the phase of 'active motherhood'—that is, when their children are still young. As a result, the employed mother has become a new norm in Europe. These changes are reflected in the experiences of childhood. In many European countries, young children in particular are cared for to a greater extent by public institutions. These developments are part and parcel of the social processes of individualization that emerged after the Second World War (Beck 1986) and have contributed to the erosion of traditional forms of the family.[1] However, the outcome has not been one uniform type of 'new European mother'. Rather, practices of motherhood differ considerably between European countries, with respect to basic dimensions of motherhood. These include the extent and degree to which mothers participate in waged work, and childcare arrangements. This chapter deals with the question as to how such cross-national differences in the way the family and practices of motherhood have changed can be explained.[2] In feminist discourse, the explanation has often been attributed to differences in policies of welfare states. I argue, instead, that cross-national differences in practices of motherhood can be explained adequately only by examining differences in the complex interrelations of institutions, culture, and social actors. The theoretical framework of the 'gender arrangement' will be developed for the cross-national analyses of gender, work, and the family.

In the next section I discuss how the development of motherhood in European societies can be described and classified. In the third section, two major types of approaches to the explanation of differences are identified. In the fourth section, a theoretical framework for the explanation of these differences is introduced. In the last two sections it will be demonstrated how this approach can be used to explain cross-national differences in the development of the family and motherhood in West Germany, the Netherlands, and Finland. Finally, I will briefly summarize the central arguments.

ANALYSES OF THE PROCESSES OF MODERNIZATION OF MOTHERHOOD IN EUROPE

In feminist thinking gender and motherhood in European societies have been conceptualized within the framework of the male-breadwinner model of the family. The basic idea behind this approach is that in each country the social practices of motherhood may be described by a more or less strong male-breadwinner model of the family that is reflected in national welfare states (Lewis 1992). However, there are two problems with the breadwinner concept. The first is that the status of the concept is not always clear. Does it characterize social practices, or does it refer to the cultural ideals behind social action? A range of empirical research has demonstrated that the social practices of motherhood often did not conform to the cultural ideal of housewife marriage, even at times when this ideal apparently had a strong normative influence, as for instance in West Germany (see e.g. Born *et al.* 1996). The second problem is that, in Western Europe, other cultural models of motherhood have played an important role that cannot be described within the framework of the male-breadwinner family model. A broader theoretical framework, therefore, is needed to classify and analyse cultural ideals relating to motherhood. Leira (1992) has argued that the policies of welfare states are based on different 'models of motherhood', which refer to cultural ideals about motherhood and employment. Using the example of Norway, Leira has also shown that women in their everyday life are oriented towards 'models of motherhood' that are not, however, necessarily the same as those reflected in state policies.

I suggest a broader framework for the analyses of the cultural basis of motherhood (Pfau-Effinger 1998*a*, *b*, *c*). I define the gender culture as those norms and values that refer to the desirable, 'normal' form of gender relations and of the division of labour between women and men. Cultural models of motherhood form a central element of gender cultural models—that is, cultural ideals about gender, the family, and motherhood. Gender cultural models have four dimensions:

1. the social ideal relating to the societal spheres through which women and men should be integrated into society, and the way the interrelationship of these spheres is constructed (symmetry versus complementarity);
2. the way dependencies between women and men are constructed (autonomy versus one-sided/mutual dependency)
3. the cultural construction of the relationship between generations, and
4. the main social sphere for caring (in modern Western societies: family, state, market, or intermediary sector).

There are numerous possible combinations of these four variables that form different 'gender cultural models'. They prescribe patterns of behaviour and life plans related to the different social roles and relations within gender relations and the family.

Viewing Western European development in the decades after the Second World War, at least five different gender cultural models may be identified. Two of these—the family economic model and the male-breadwinner/female-carer model—represent traditional models; the others are more modern. Only two of these models are versions of the male-breadwinner/female-carer model of the family. The different models can be characterized as follows (Pfau-Effinger 1998*a*):

1. The family economic gender model. This model is based on the cooperation of women and men in their own family business (farm or craft business), in which both sexes contribute substantially to the survival of the family economy. Children are treated as members of the family economic unit—that is, as workers—as soon as they are physically able to contribute. There may exist a strong sexual division of labour within the family economy, which in fact varies according to the context of time and space (Honnegger and Heintz 1981). Within the family economy, the work of women is seen as important for the survival of the family as that of men, and women and men are substantially dependent on each other. Motherhood is not constructed here as a long phase of life in which special tasks of caring absorb a substantial proportion of women's capacity for work.

2. The male-breadwinner/female-home-carer model. This model conforms to the idea of the basic differentiation of society into public and private spheres. Women and men are seen to be complementarily competent for one of these spheres: men are regarded as breadwinners who earn the income for the family in the public sphere with waged work, whereas women are primarily regarded as being responsible for the work in the private household including childcare. This model is also based on a social construction of childhood according to which children need special care to be supported comprehensively as an individual.

3. The male-breadwinner/female-part-time-carer model. This is a modernized version of the male-breadwinner model. Women and men are to an equal degree integrated into waged work as long as there are no dependent children in the household. During the phases of active motherhood, however, it is seen as adequate for women to combine waged work and caring by working part-time, whereas the role of fathers is the breadwinner role.

4. The dual-breadwinner/state-carer model. This model conforms to the idea of the 'completed labour market society' (Beck 1986), with full-time integration of both sexes into the employment system. Women and men are seen as individuals, who in marriage are both breadwinners who earn income for their own living and that of their children. As in the male-breadwinner/female-carer model, childhood is constructed as a phase of life with its own worth, in which the individual needs much care and support. It is different, however, in that caring for children is primarily seen not as the task of the family, but to a considerable extent as the task of the welfare state. The state is regarded as more competent for fulfilling this task than private households are.

5. The dual-breadwinner/dual-carer model. This model reflects the notion of a symmetrical and equitable integration of both sexes into society. In contrast to the preceding model, child-rearing is to a large extent seen as a responsibility of the family. The basic idea is that the family economy consists of an equal distribution of domestic—meaning, in particular, childminding—and waged labour between a female and a male head-of-household. This is possible only because the labour market is organized in such a manner that structurally allows for parents to fulfill a 'dual responsibility'. Such a model requires domestic labour to be financed on the basis of a family wage or on the basis of a state transfer system.

Whereas models (1) and (2) represent more traditional types of gender and the family, models (3)–(5) are more modern versions. Within these modernized versions, motherhood is located in different ways within the public/private division, as 'public' motherhood or as a public/private mix of motherhood. An extension of the analysis to Central and Eastern European societies and societies outside Europe would, of course, extend the range of gender cultural models.

INSTITUTIONAL AND IDEATIONAL APPROACHES TO THE EXPLANATION OF DIFFERENCES

In feminist discourse, cross-national differences in practices of motherhood—in the labour-force participation of mothers and in childcare arrangements—have often been explained by differences in welfare state policies (see e.g. Lewis 1992; Orloff 1993). This explanation is too limited, however, as it neglects the orientations of women towards motherhood and waged work (Pfau-Effinger 1998*a*). Often it is assumed that the orientations of women towards motherhood and waged work should conform to their objective interests to be economically independent from a male breadwinner and the state, and that women therefore in general pursue the aim to be in full-time employment. There is empirical evidence, however, that women often do not wish to be in full-time employment during motherhood (Geissler and Oechsle 1996). Thus Hakim (1997) has argued that at least two groups of women can be distinguished, which differ in the quality of their orientation towards waged work. One group of women, she argues, orient towards full-time work and a professional career, and the other group of women orient towards motherhood, the family, and part-time work.[3] Although Hakim's work may be criticized (Crompton and Harris 1998*a*), she has made an important contribution to the analyses of motherhood insofar as she considers that women are competent actors who pursue their own life plans with respect to the way they combine waged work and motherhood.

What is not clear in Hakim's argument is why women choose different strategies in combining waged work and a family. It is not clear why these two distinctly different groups of women have developed, and what are the reasons why an individual woman decides for one or the other. In contrast, I would argue that differences in the work orientations of women are connected with cultural ideals about gender, the family, and motherhood at the macro-level of society, and can be understood only by analyses of these interrelations.

I would doubt, however, if part-time work of mothers in general is connected to life plans that one-sidedly refer to a 'marriage career' (Hakim 1997: 43) and not a professional career. A temporary phase of part-time work during active motherhood can be an element of a professional career biography of women, as is often the case in professional service jobs of women in West Germany (Baumeister *et al.* 1990; Quack 1993). The role of part-time work of mothers varies with the societal context, the cultural and institutional framework for motherhood and waged work.

Hakim is correct to criticize approaches to women's behaviour with respect to waged work that are one-sidedly institutionalist. It is important to consider the importance that the orientations of women towards waged work have for their labour-market behaviour. These include general cultural ideals about the family and motherhood at the macro-level of society. I would argue that a theoretical framework for the explanation of cross-national differences in practices of motherhood should include the complex interplay of important differing dimensions in the theoretical framework for analyses: the interrelations of institutions, culture, and social action.

THE CULTURAL AND INSTITUTIONAL FRAMEWORK FOR SOCIAL PRACTICES OF MOTHERHOOD WITHIN THE GENDER ARRANGEMENT

I propose to explain cross-national differences in the social practices of motherhood using a gender-arrangements approach as a broader theoretical framework for cross-national analyses of gender relations, the waged work of women, and the family (Pfau-Effinger 1996*a*, 1998*a*, *b*). The approach consists of three central concepts: the gender system, the gender culture, and the gender arrangement. Social practices of gender and motherhood are conceptualized as the result of the complex interplay of gender culture, institutions, and social actors.

The *gender system* comprises the pertinent structures of gender relationships as well as the relations between different societal institutions with reference to the gender structures.[4] The structures and policies of the welfare state are particularly important, for they produce a substantial part of the regulatory framework for the gendered division of labour and social practices of motherhood. At the level of *gender culture*, the dominant gender cultural model/s in a society is/are the result of former interaction processes of social actors and are a main reference point for policies of institutions and behaviour of individuals. Although there is usually a set of dominant cultural values and ideals, it cannot be assumed that there is cultural coherence in society. Alternative and competing cultural value systems may exist (see also Archer 1996*a*).

The duality of culture and social system is an important element of sociological theory. Seminal works of political and sociological thinkers such as Max Weber, Karl Marx, Talcott Parsons, and Jürgen Habermas have demonstrated the explanatory power of these analytical dimensions. Theories using a feminist perspective have, however, too often tended to neglect the differentiation between these dimensions in their analysis. The theoretical differentiation between gender culture and gender system helps to uncover and explain important aspects of the manifold connections and interweavings as well as of the tensions, breakings, and time lags in the relationship of cultural ideals and societal practice.

The respective *gender arrangement* forms the frame produced by gender culture and gender system. The gender arrangement includes binding contents of gender culture and gender structures that are, so to speak, the result of societal negotiations. I refer here to the 'gender-contract' approach of Hirdman (1988, 1990; see also Duncan 1995; Pfau-Effinger 1994). In Hirdman's approach, the way culture and social system are interrelated is left as an open question. The gender-arrangement approach stresses the importance of negotiations between actors for social order and social change, even though the negotiations may be based on an unequal distribution of power. 'Negotiation is not merely one specific human activity or process . . . social orders are, in some sense, always negotiated orders' (Strauss 1978: 234–5). It should be noted here that actors enter the arenas for negotiation with different resources and different abilities to use power.

The necessity for the analysis of the dynamics of change in the gender arrangement will be emphasized. Contradictions that develop at the level of the gender culture or in the gender system, and conflicts, struggles, and negotiation processes between social actors, can result in cultural and social change within gender arrangements. Cultural change is interconnected with structural change by the behaviour of social actors and the policies of institutions, but is in part also autonomous from it. There may be time lags and discrepancies in the development between both levels. This can increase existing tensions and contradictions or create new ones.

To summarize, it is possible to explain cross-national differences in the practices of motherhood, in the extent and forms in which women are integrated into the labour market, and in childcare arrangements more adequately if these are placed in the context of the respective gender arrangement and gender culture. Within the gender arrangement, different gender cultural models can dominate. It is important to treat this classification as a dynamic one, which includes processes of change and transformation.

According to this approach, 'motherhood' has different dimensions. It is a cultural construction, a type of social practice and of social relations, and is influenced by social relations. It refers to the position of women in the relationship between generations and between sexes. Practices of motherhood in each time and space, as I would argue, can be seen as an outcome of cultural ideals with respect to motherhood within the respective gender arrangement, as well as a response to institutional regulation and a result of creativity and reflexivity of individuals who are able to change practices and create new ones. During the processes of the modernization of motherhood, contradictions between the cultural level and the level of institutions may develop as well as between the gender arrangement and the cultural ideals about the life phases of childhood.

WEST GERMANY, THE NETHERLANDS, AND FINLAND: TWO MODERNIZATION PATHS OF MOTHERHOOD AND THE FAMILY

In the following section I will carry out a cross-national analysis of differences in the way social practices of motherhood have changed in West Germany, the Netherlands, and Finland. This will be used to show how the theoretical framework described above can be used to explain cross-national differences in the modernization of practices of motherhood. I analyse the cultural and structural development of

motherhood and the way it was embedded in the modernization of
the gender arrangement in West Germany, the Netherlands, and
Finland in the decades since the 1950s. These represent examples of
the modernization of motherhood within two different modernization paths of gender arrangements: the modernization of the male-
breadwinner/female-carer model and the transformation of a family
economic model to a dual breadwinner/dual carer model.

The basic features of the cultural images of motherhood and the
family already differed from each other at the point of departure of
this analysis—that is, during the period following the Second World
War. Whereas in West Germany, and even more in the Netherlands,
the housewife model of the family was dominant, in Finland even
during the process of industrialization a family economic model had
survived in an egalitarian variant. The dominant cultural model of
motherhood in each of these countries in the 1950s had a comprehensive validity and a high normative strength. Women in their life
plans as well as institutions and firms referred to these ideals in their
social practices to a high degree. In the following decades, in all three
countries processes of renegotiation of the gender arrangement
between social actors and a change in cultural ideals of the family
and motherhood took place that were primarily initiated by women.
The new ideals are more than before based on the cultural construction of the 'employed mother'. Cultural change was based on different cultural traditions, proceeded with a different dynamic of
change, and took different pathways. In those countries in which the
tradition of the male-breadwinner/female-home-carer family had
prevailed, the idea of private motherhood and childhood survived at
least in part. At the institutional level, restrictions and options for
women to realize their orientations are different in the gender systems of all three countries. Differences in welfare-state policies contributed substantially to this variation of opportunities.

*West Germany and the Netherlands: From the Housewife-and-
Mother to the Part-Time Mother*

In West Germany in the 1950s the gender cultural model of the male-
breadwinner/female-home-carer was dominant; motherhood was
constructed in this framework as housewife/mother (see Ostner
1993). However, in social practices the waged work of mothers
played a considerable role, particularly amongst wives of blue-collar

workers. The welfare state did not provide the financial resources for these families to live on the income of one single breadwinner (Krüger 1995). The outcome of cultural change in West Germany was the male-breadwinner/female-part-time-carer model, which characterizes also the orientations of the majority of women of the younger generations (Pfau-Effinger 1993, 1999). In a 1996 survey, women were asked which life situation they would like best. The great majority of women said that they would prefer to be a mother (83 per cent). About half (52 per cent) of these women said that they would most like to do this by combining caring and waged work by working part-time, whereas the second largest group, mostly older women, said that they would like best to be a housewife and mother (37 per cent). It is likely that the orientation towards the housewife-and-mother model will be marginalized when the older generation dies out. The 'career' model—to be a full-time employed mother—in West Germany has nearly no relevance at all, and was preferred only by a rather small group (8 per cent of all women) (Institut für Demoskopie Allensbach 1996). The male-breadwinner model of the family is not questioned by a high proportion of West German women. It is still accepted also by the great majority of younger women (Geissler and Oechsle 1996).

Within the new gender cultural model, cultural ideals about a more equal-gendered division of labour, on the one hand, and about childhood, on the other, overlap in a somewhat contradictory way. On the one hand, the waged work of mothers is accepted much more than before, and waged work has gained much more importance in the lives of women. Public childcare is accepted within the population to a substantially higher degree than it was some decades ago. This is linked to an image of childhood in which the idea that it is best for children to be supervised by their mother at home plays an important role. The majority of people accept only part-time public childcare, and full-time nursery schools are rather unpopular. Most people think that children should be cared for at least part-time at home. Only 24 per cent agree that mothers of pre-school children should be employed, women in the same proportion as men, and only 51 per cent are in favour of waged work for mothers of schoolchildren (Höllinger 1991: 769). Children are seen as a central element of a good life for their parents, as individuals who need much personal care, supervision, and education within the family. Particularly in the middle classes it is seen as the task of mothers to provide their daughters and sons individually with enough cultural and social capital for a good starting position in the competition of the adult society. Therefore it is common for middle-class mothers to take their children by car to activities which are seen as necessary, such as ballet schools, tennis training, or music lessons (Zeiher and Zeiher 1991).

Mainly because of these new cultural ideals about childhood, the part-time work of mothers has been an important element of the modernization of the male-breadwinner family model (see also Pfau-Effinger and Geissler 1992). Though in part precarious, part-time work turned out to be a new form of employment of women in the biographical phases of active motherhood.[5] This new orientation is only in part reflected in social practices of motherhood, however. The share of women who want to work full-time (35 per cent) and those who are really working full-time (35 per cent) matches rather well. However, because of institutional lags in development, the share of women who want to work part-time (35 per cent) is much higher than that of women who are in fact working part-time (15 per cent). Particularly among the non-employed and unemployed, a high proportion of women would prefer part-time employment to staying at home (Schupp 1991, from the 'Sozioökonomischen Panel' of 1988).

The policies of the welfare state contributed substantially to these discrepancies between cultural orientations and the social practices of motherhood. The West German welfare state was reconstructed after the Second World War as a conservative-corporatist welfare state. Social provision was organized according to the social status of different social groups and thus reproduced existing hierarchies (Leibfried and Tennstedt 1985; Kaufmann 1989*b*; Esping-Andersen 1990). The principles of welfare-state policies were combined with the promotion of the housewife marriage. The expansion of the welfare state in the following decades was shaped by the principles of the male-breadwinner family. The standard biography of the male breadwinner became the main reference point for the employment relationship and for social insurance. As a consequence, women were disadvantaged within the employment system (Pfau-Effinger 1990, 1993; Plantenga 1992*b*). State policies are still lagging way behind women's emancipation efforts. Neither the possibility for mothers to stay home and care for their children independently of a family breadwinner, nor the integration of mothers into the labour market has been actively promoted (Pfau-Effinger and Geissler 1992; Quack 1993; Ostner 1995). Even if the number of places in public childcare were to be increased, the timetable of elementary schools does not match even with part-time employment of mothers. This is because public childcare is seen as part and parcel of the system of education and not in the first place as a measure to promote the labour-force participation of mothers (Kaufmann 1989*a*). Market solutions like hiring private childminders are used as an alternative, particularly by middle-class women, who use in particular the cheap labour of highly qualified migrants from East European countries. This creates new problems of inequality among women (Friese 1996; Rerrich 1996).

The part-time work of mothers has not been promoted, and this is still a form of employment that is discriminated against in relation to the social-security system and future career prospects in firms. This is to a considerable extent also due to the policies of the unions, which have been oriented towards the security of the standard employment relationships of their male members (Wiesenthal 1987). The policies of the feminist movement also contributed to the problems connected to part-time work. Many feminists wanted the full-time integration of all women into waged work and the expansion of part-time jobs was never a political aim of the feminist movement (Pfau-Effinger and Geissler 1992).

To conclude: the new cultural model of motherhood that is shared by a broad majority of people including women in West Germany is based on a private/public mix of motherhood and childhood in the framework of the male-breadwinner marriage. The main idea of gender equality is based not on the ideal of an equal sharing of waged work and family work of women and men, but on 'equality within difference'.

In the 1950s in the Netherlands a very strong housewife model of the family was still dominant. Nearly all women stayed at home when they were married—the employment rate of married women was only 6 per cent, compared to 33 per cent of West German women after marriage (Pott-Buter 1993: 200). In contrast to West Germany, single mothers were included in the general cultural ideal of the caring housewife. Since 1965 the state has substituted for the male breadwinner as provider and developed generous social benefits for one-parent families that allowed them to stay at home until their children were adults (Bussemaker 1994).

As a substantial part of a 'cultural revolution' in the Netherlands, an egalitarian dual-breadwinner/dual-carer model has been developed, even if it has been realized only in part in social practice. The waged work of mothers is much more accepted than in West Germany: 46 per cent vote positively for the employment of mothers of pre-school children and 86 per cent for mothers of schoolchildren. Höllinger (1991) concludes that the Netherlands belongs to those few countries in which a more 'modern' type of attitude towards employment of mothers prevails, whereas West Germany belongs to the more 'traditional' camp. The new cultural model of motherhood is related to an image of a part-time caring father and a public–private mix of caring within a relatively egalitarian form of the family. Part-time work is a central element of this model and was even more central for the modernization of motherhood and the family than in West Germany.

Even if the share of employed women who work part-time is much higher (67 per cent compared to 34 per cent in West Germany (OECD 1996: 192)), a recent survey suggested that there is still a considerable mismatch with respect to the proportions of those women who want to work part-time and those who do work part-time, whereas the rate of those women who would like to work full-time and those who in practice work full-time matches rather well (12 per cent versus 16 per cent) (van der Putte and Pelzer 1993). Here, there is a 'double mismatch': on one hand, there is a high surplus of women in the sample who said they would prefer a part-time job compared with those women who are working part-time. On the other hand, there is also a high rate of women who are involuntarily working part-time: nearly one-quarter of part-time working women would prefer full-time employment and are in effect 'involuntary' part-time workers.[6] In most cases these are mothers in the biographical phase of the 'empty nest' who did not succeed in changing from part-time to full-time employment after their grown-up children left home (Plantenga and van Velzen 1994).

For a long time the welfare state in the Netherlands contributed to the mismatch between cultural orientations and social practices with respect to motherhood (Knijn 1994). Though the state was constructed as a social-democratic welfare state, based upon the cultural principles of solidarity and equality, its gender policies strongly promoted the housewife model of the male-breadwinner family until the beginning of the 1980s. This contributed to the special characteristics of this welfare regime.[7] In the 1970s and in the beginning of the 1980s, the policies of the state reacted hardly at all to the dramatic increase in the employment orientation of women. There was no expansion of the—nearly non-existent—public childcare system (see Bussemaker 1994). During the 1980s, however, the gender policies of the state were transformed substantially. Within two sequential equality programmes, gender equality and the financial autonomy of women, as well as a just division of caring and housework, were proclaimed as new political aims. At the highest political level, a commission for the promotion of gender equality was founded (Emancipatieraad), in which representatives of the feminist movement worked together with representatives of the government, of unions, and of employers (Bussemaker 1994).[8]

The promotion and protection of part-time work for women and men was part and parcel of this gender policy (Plantenga 1992: 84). This can be seen, among others, as a response to claims of the feminist movement. In contrast to the situation in West Germany, mainstream feminists in the Netherlands were relatively homogenous in their political aims. They struggled for a fundamental restructuring of paid and unpaid work according to which men and women could distribute their working time equally to caring and waged work (Plantenga and van Velzen 1994). The unions, in cooperation with representatives of the state and the women's movement, participated in developing a strong policy for the promotion of part-time work, which has, as a consequence, a relatively high standard of working conditions and social security. In sum, welfare-state policies in the Netherlands have promoted developments leading to a more egalitarian dual-breadwinner/dual-carer model based on part-time work of mothers and fathers much more strongly than in West Germany. Time lags and contradictions within welfare-state policies, however, even now contribute to the fact that social practices of motherhood, but even more those of fatherhood, still lag behind the new cultural ideas about gender and the family.

Finland: From the Full-Time Female Farmer to the Full-Time Employed Mother

Until the 1950s, in Finland a family economic model was dominant at the cultural level and in social practices. During the industrialization processes developing since the end of nineteenth century, women contributed substantially to the survival of the family farms. Childhood was not seen as a life phase of its own in which children are individually promoted and cared for, rather children were supervised alongside, and were expected to contribute to, the farmwork as early as they were able. The behaviour of women contributed substantially to the fact that the agrarian sector survived such a long time in Finland. Since the 1960s, when the modern sector of industry and services increased dramatically, women entered to an increasing degree the modern employment system, mainly in the service sector. As a consequence of work outside the home, it was impossible for mothers to supervise their children. There was a public debate on this problem in the 1960s, and the consensus that was found between the main social actors was based on a model of public childhood and caring.

A dual-breadwinner/state-carer model is the new, uniform cultural model, which has also been realized in social practice. Motherhood is constructed within this framework as 'public motherhood': the caring of children is done here by women whose jobs are considered to be of a relatively high quality. In contrast to the other two societies under discussion, the male-breadwinner/female-carer model was never dominant in Finalnd, the ideal of full participation of women in the production sphere was maintained during the modernization process, and part-time work of mothers did not play any role in the new gender cultural model. Therefore the rate of women working part-time has always been low, at about 11 per cent (OECD 1996).

There is a relatively strong correspondence of part-time orientations and part-time employment of women in Finland. The proportion of women working full-time who said that they would prefer a part-time job (1–29 hours) is only 4 per cent (Nätti 1995: 20, and author's own calculations); moreover, amongst the un- and non-employed there is only a very low proportion of women who want to work part-time (Nätti 1995). In contrast, the rate of women involuntarily working part-time is relatively high, at 49 per cent (see Annual Labour Force Survey 1993, cited in Nätti 1995: 17).

Finland's welfare state has contributed considerably to changes in the social practices of motherhood. It was organized as social-democratic welfare regime (see also Esping-Andersen 1990). Cultural values and regulatory principles based on solidarity and the principle that all citizens should have equal access to welfare benefits and services play a central role here. This regime is also based on the idea of full employment integration of women and public childhood. Since the beginning of the 1970s, married women and men have been treated as individuals, not as couples in social insurance and in the tax system. A comprehensive public childcare system was developed that allows both parents to work full-time. The state also promoted the waged work of women in its role as employer, largely by extending the number of service jobs in welfare administration, so that it was possible for women to work continuously in full-time employment (Korppi-Tommola 1991). Because of this individualization in terms of social security and income, and because of full integration of all adults into the employment system, single mothers are not discriminated against in terms of income and social security.

The 'women-friendly' policies of the welfare state were substantially influenced by women as a social group; they form the major proportion of staff in the public-welfare service sector. The social mobilization of women within civil society already had a long tradition in Finland, and women's federations had to a great degree contributed to the building of the welfare state (Anttonen 1990; Simonen 1990).

EXPLAINING CROSS-NATIONAL DIFFERENCES IN THE MODERNIZATION OF MOTHERHOOD

What explains the differences in the direction of cultural modernization? Differences in the way motherhood was culturally reconstructed can be attributed primarily to the fact that cultural change was based on different cultural traditions. In those countries in which the tradition of the male-breadwinner/female-home-carer family had prevailed beforehand, the idea of private childhood survived at least in parts. As a consequence a private–public mix of caring and part-time work of mothers were substantial elements of the modernization of the male-breadwinner family model. This private element is particularly important in the Netherlands, where the tradition of the 'home-caring society' and the housewife marriage was much deeper rooted than in West Germany (Pfau-Effinger 1996a). Institutional regulation has in part stabilized the orientation of mothers towards part-time work in these countries. In contrast, in Finland, where the male-breadwinner/female-carer model never was dominant, the tradition of full participation of mothers in the production sphere was maintained during the modernization process. The welfare state was given a new, strong role for the provision of caring facilities and a cultural construction of 'public' motherhood was developed and comprehensively realized.

What explains the differences in the relation of cultural and institutional change? At the beginning of post-war development the cultural norms and values with reference to the gendered division of labour were still stable and formed an important framework for the policies of the state and of firms. Through this, social practices that corresponded with the cultural ideals were promoted in principle. During processes of change in the gender arrangement, asynchronies and contradictions in the gender cultural foundations of the policies of institutions and of the individuals developed. This was the reason that new cultural ideals were realized in practice only incompletely or with considerable time lags. The question of the general cultural foundation of welfare-state policies (referred to by Esping-Andersen's concept of welfare regime) played an important role in the extent to which change in the gender culture accompanied corresponding changes at the level of gender system. A gender policy that was more favourable for the integration of women into the labour market according to their own orientations or preferences developed more in those societies that are based on a social-democratic welfare regime, in Finland and—with certain limitations and a substantial delay—in the Netherlands.[9] The conservative-corporatist welfare regime of West Germany, which was combined with a gender policy that reflects the male-breadwinner/female-home-carer family, was the least in favour of the labour-market integration of women.

The way and degree to which the labour market reacted to changes in the cultural orientation and labour-market behaviour of women were substantially influenced by the way and degree the welfare state intervened in the labour market to promote the realization of new cultural models for women. The innovative potential of the labour market in favour of women was also dependent on the negotiation processes and policies of social actors in the system of industrial relations. The innovative capacities of the German labour market and system of industrial relations were rather limited, in contrast to the Netherlands and Finland, and the promotion of the integration of those who are responsible for private caring as well as waged work was low.

The role of the feminist movement is another explanatory factor. A feminist movement with a policy based more or less on a consensus among feminists, which is integrated into the decision-making process of welfare-state institutions, as in the Netherlands and Finland, seems to promote the realization of new cultural models of motherhood more than a feminist movement that is split within itself and fails to integrate into welfare-state institutions (as in Germany). In all three countries the establishment of a feminist movement can be seen as the result of the increase of a female faction of the middle classes. In societies with a male-breadwinner tradition this faction developed its own interests. Traditionally, when their social practices were in most cases still based on the housewife-and-mother model of motherhood, the interests of middle-class women were to a substantial degree reflected by the social position of their husbands. However, women of these classes have increasingly developed particular interests that are based on their education and professional status and differ in part from those of men of these classes. These groups of women were the driving forces in the processes of modernization of motherhood and formed also the grassroots of the feminist movements. In Finland in particular, a broad coalition of women of the small urban middle classes and women of the agrarian classes was a strong societal force and played a central role in state policies and the making of the welfare state.[10]

A substantial precondition for the feminist movement to influence the policies of the state is its unity. In contrast to the position in Finland and the Netherlands, where feminists were able to unify on common aims, the feminist movement in West Germany was split culturally between those groups that stressed the idea of gender equality and full integration of women into waged work—the hegemonous fraction—and those groups that stressed the idea of gender difference with the political aim to revaluate femininity.

The way in which the feminist movement approached the cultural orientations of the social group it represented was also important. In Finland and the Netherlands feminists stressed the idea of the societal importance of maternity and used it as a cultural resource to improve the situation of women. In the Netherlands feminists used maternity to promote a policy of the state in favour of the dual-breadwinner/dual-carer model, whereas Finnish feminists used it as a central value to promote the dual-breadwinner/state-carer model with its principle of public motherhood and childhood.[11] West German feminists, in contrast, never used this argument; they even contributed substantially to the cultural devaluation of motherhood.

A majority of feminists for a long time favoured a model of 'mother-hood without children', a dual-breadwinner/state-carer model, where the state as an anonymous power cares for the children, in contrast to the Finnish version of this cultural model, where the idea of 'public motherhood' is given a high valuation. By favouring this model, West German feminists ignored the orientation of the major-ity of West German mothers, even within the group they themselves represented, the professional middle class women. This contributed to the political weakness of the movement.

CONCLUSIONS

Motherhood is a complex cultural and social construction that should be analysed at different theoretical levels: at the level of cul-tural ideals, at the level of institutional regulations with respect to gender relations and childhood, and at the level of social practices. The practices of motherhood do not in general change within the framework of the male-breadwinner family model. Since the 1950s in Europe, a broader variety of gender cultural models has been important and has changed along different modernization paths. Within more recent gender cultural models, motherhood is con-structed either as public motherhood or as a kind of public–private mix of motherhood. The new models differ also in that motherhood is not connected to the same kind of cultural ideal of gender equal-ity in all of them: gender equality is constructed either, as in Finland and the Netherlands, as uniformity in the tasks of women and men (though in the Netherlands social practices are still more character-ized by difference with respect to the participation of women and men in waged work), or as 'equality within difference', as in West Germany. The realization of new gender cultural models and mod-els of motherhood in social practices of women often lags behind cultural change.

   The comparison of the change of practices of motherhood in West Germany, the Netherlands, and Finland demonstrates that the dif-ferences cannot be explained one-sidedly by differences in the poli-cies of welfare states or of orientations of women towards waged work, but rather by the complex interrelations of culture, institu-tions, and social actors within the framework of the respective gen-der arrangements.

NOTES

1. The individualized mother in a way is a paradox, however, for motherhood itself is culturally defined by dependency and a caring relationship, whereas the individual is defined as autonomous.
2. This is a revised version of a paper presented at the International Conference 'The Restructuring of Gender Relations and Employment: A Cross-National Perspective, University of Bergen, 25–6 Apr. 1997.
3. Hakim's original classification included a third group, the 'drifters', who have recently been given more prominence in her work and relabelled 'adaptives'.
4. I refer here in part to the approach of the 'gender order' of Connell (1987).
5. This is different in Eastern Germany; see, for a comparison, O'Reilly (1996) and Quack and Maier (1994).
6. The proportion of women working part-time 'voluntarily' of all employed women according to the OECD definition is 46%—still a much higher rate than the rate of women working part-time in other West European countries (OECD 1990: 181, and author's own calculations).
7. Also in other respects the policies of the Dutch welfare state are different from those of the Scandinavian welfare regimes that have been described by Esping-Andersen (1990). Social citizenship is based here much more on universal social rights rather than on social rights based on employment. The Dutch welfare system is considered one of the most generous of all Western industrial countries (Heiligers 1992; Bussemaker 1994: 9).
8. Trudi Knijn (1994) describes this as a process that was not only favourable to women but also had as a consequence a loss of security the welfare state had offered to women (see also Heiligers 1992).
9. Also the domestic division of labour in the Netherlands and in Finland is more egalitarian than in West Germany. As empirical research has shown, in Finland and the Netherlands a modern 'father' also exists. Men contribute much more to caring and household labour than men in West Germany where the domstic division of labour is still rather traditional (Nikander 1992; Künzler 1995). West German mothers thus get less help from their husbands to facilitate their employment than mothers in the other two countries.
10. Women had also contributed substantially to the welfare-state development in Germany and the Netherlands but in more subordinate positions, with less political influence (cf. Chamberlayne 1993).
11. The first wave of women's movement also dealt in part with maternity in this way; see the comparative historical analysis of Koven and Michel (1990).

5

Women, Men and Non-Standard Employment: Breadwinning and Caregiving in Germany, Italy, and the UK

SUE YEANDLE

INTRODUCTION

This chapter draws on a number of statistical and survey sources to explore recent changes in the sexual division of labour in three European countries: Germany, Italy, and the UK. It reviews the evidence on the growth of non-standard employment in these countries, and explores some aspects of the relationship between the changes in women's and men's employment behaviour and social policy, cultural and attitudinal factors. The discussion draws on a growing literature offering theoretical and empirical insights into the differences and similarities between countries in the contemporary development of gender relations. Analysis of welfare regimes[1] has recently been enhanced by more complex analysis of the detailed composition of social policies and their origins (Lane 1993; Millar and Warman 1996; Gornick *et al.* 1997) and by attempts to incorporate theorizing about gender (especially Connell 1987) into an explanatory model capable of offering insight into the gender arrangements and trajectories of European societies (Lane 1993; Pfau-Effinger 1996*b*).

The first part of the chapter presents the context for caregiving and breadwinning in the selected countries. This provides background to the empirical data on non-standard working (drawn mainly from the European Labour Force Survey 1985–95), in the second part of the chapter. In the third part, the question of whether the sexual division of breadwinning and caregiving work is being reorganized is addressed, and three different interpretations of the debate on non-standard working are explored. Briefly, developments in non-standard working are considered: (i) as supports to established male-breadwinner arrangements; (ii) as a form of disruption to established economic systems, linked to broader processes of social and economic polarization; and (iii) as an increasingly tailored and potentially equitable distribution of labour, which, consistent with other developments in 'late modernity', produces greater 'individualization' and is part of a more flexible response to the demands arising at different stages of the life course. Here, particular attention is given to how Pfau-Effinger's conceptualization of a 'gender arrangement' may be applied in the three countries, and some additional evidence relating to the role of culture is offered.

Within Western capitalist and late modern societies some universality is sometimes claimed for changes in the organization of labour forces, with post-fordist working arrangements, technologically driven shifts, and the impact of globalization being most frequently cited (Esping-Andersen 1993*a*: 227). This chapter examines the inter-relationship between family life, labour-force participation, welfare arrangements, and dominant cultural practices and attitudes in an attempt to gain insight into important contemporary developments in the sexual division of labour.

THE BREADWINNING AND CAREGIVING CONTEXT: GERMANY, ITALY, AND THE UK

There are important differences between the three countries in terms of family life and behaviour, as a variety of standardized measures confirms (see Tables 5.1 and 5.2). Italy has the lowest rates of fertility, divorce, extramarital births, cohabitation, single-person households, and 'no-child' families, while the UK measures highest of the three countries on all these indicators. Italy has the highest marriage rate, more families with two or more children, and more households containing several adults.

Publicly funded childcare provision for very young children is limited in all three countries, with approximately 6 per cent of 0–3 year olds having places in Italy (1991), 2 per cent in West Germany (1990),[2] and 1 per cent in the UK. By contrast, for children aged from 3 years to compulsory school age, Italy had places for 91 per cent in 1991, Germany for 78 per cent (100 per cent in former East Germany), and the UK 53 per cent. Provision for the out-of-hours

TABLE 5.1. *Measures of family behaviour, Germany, Italy, and the UK*

Measures of family behaviour	Germany	Italy	UK
Population, 1992 (millions)	78.0	57.0	57.0
Total period fertility rate, 1993 (average number of children over a lifetime)	1.3	1.2	1.8
Extramarital births, 1992 (as % of all live births)	11.6	6.7	31.0
Marriage, 1992 (total first marriage rate for women below age 50)	0.64	0.66	0.58
Divorce, 1992 (per 1,000 population)	1.9	0.4	4.3
Cohabitation, 1985* (non-marital unions among 25–29 year olds, %s)	6.2	1.8	12.8
Living alone, 1995 (single person households as a % of all households)	34.4	22.7	28.3
Adult-only households, 1995 (several adults, no children, as % of all households)	42.7	50.4	42.9
2-adult, 2-children households, 1995 (as % of all households)	16.0	18.2	18.4

Sources: Snyder (1992); Eurostat (1995); Millar and Warman (1996).

TABLE 5.2. *Family change Germany, Italy, and UK, 1981–1991 (%)*

Percentage of families	Germany		Italy		UK	
	1981	1991	1981	1991	1981	1991
With no child	21	38	23	24	35	39
With one child	36	32	32	34	25	26
With two children	28	23	29	31	26	24
With three or more children	14	7	16	11	14	11

Source: Eurostat (1995).

care of school-aged children was small, though developing, in the UK (Department of Health 1997) and in Germany, and patchy in Italy (Snyder 1992: 210; European Commission Network on Childcare 1995). However, school hours are shorter in Germany and Italy (typically mornings only) than in the UK, where school normally finishes between 3 and 4 p.m. (Gornick *et al.* 1997). There are some regional variations, especially in Italy. In Germany, childcare has been seen as a primarily maternal responsibility, and women's employment patterns since the mid-1960s have reflected this. In Italy, wider kin group responsibilities have been more readily invoked, with grandmothers and sisters-in-law, for example, playing a key role in supporting mothers. This has been a feature of some parts of the UK also, mainly in stable working-class communities, although the 1980s and 1990s have seen a stronger UK trend towards private childcare arrangements outside the family, and until 1997 public policy firmly placed responsibility for the care of pre-school children with parents, in practice with mothers.

Cultural traditions and established social/welfare policies place different obligations upon family members to provide care and support for elderly and disabled persons in the three countries. In Italy, there are legal obligations on extended family members to provide financial support, and strong expectations, becoming somewhat eroded in recent years and especially in the north of Italy, that families will provide daily physical care and support where needed. This 'traditional family self-sufficiency' is becoming increasingly untenable with smaller family size, increased female labour-force participation, and migration from rural to urban areas. In Germany, most care services for elderly persons are delivered to them at home. Adult children are legally obliged to provide assistance in the first instance, although community services are fairly widespread, as the welfare system has developed complementary informal and professional elements in recognition of the support needs of family carers. The UK places no legal obligation on kin to provide care, but since the 1980s the 'care-in-the-community' policy has involved continued reliance on informal family care, with some support from social services. Individual elderly persons in the UK are increasingly expected to contribute to the costs of their care, and financial support is also delivered via the social-security system (Millar and Warman 1996).

Millar and Warman's (1996: 12) report identifies three broad groupings of countries according to 'patterns of partnership': a 'Scandinavian/Anglo' model, where cohabitation is increasingly common, and marriage plays a less central role (the UK features in this group); a 'Mediterranean/Irish' model, in which by strong contrast long-standing marriage remains a central aspect (Italy is included here); and a 'Central' model, which falls somewhat between the other two, where, notwithstanding the continuing importance of marriage, living alone has become a common phenomenon (e.g. Germany).

As the above suggests, Germany, Italy, and the UK each has distinctive welfare arrangements, the UK most often being categorized as having an essentially 'liberal/residual' welfare state, Germany as having a 'conservative/corporatist' welfare state (strongly linked to labour-market participation, and despite some changes imposed by German unification), while Italy falls into the 'Latin-rim' category (Leibfried and Ostner 1991), where welfare systems remain in a state of development, and where traditional arrangements rooted in religious and family systems remain important. Lewis (1992: 16) has stressed the historical importance in some European systems of 'the strong male breadwinner welfare state'. This applied particularly to countries such as Germany and the UK, and to some extent to Italy. In these states, past arrangements have included prohibitions on married women's employment, institutionalized wage inequalities favouring men's employment, and a variety of elements in welfare and social-security policy designed to keep mothers out of the labour market, devoting full-time effort to the care of their families and to the well-being of their children. Women's own social protection was often most effectively assured through their husbands' work and national insurance records. However, modifications to the strong male-breadwinner model have been made in all three countries, particularly during the last quarter of the twentieth century. Here feminist politics have played no small part, in tandem with European policies aimed at equalizing some aspects of social protection (Pillinger 1992).

The situation of mothers bringing up children alone outside marriage or after divorce differs in important ways between the three countries, illustrating some important points of contact between cultural practices, employment behaviour, and welfare systems. In the UK, the state has been slow to support married women in their employment role (Lewis 1993: 16), and has until recently been concerned to provide social-security arrangements enabling lone mothers to remain outside the labour force. In Germany, with citizenship rights derived mainly through male employment, and with husbands empowered to prevent their wives' employment until as late as 1977, women's social protection was best assured through marriage (Ostner 1993: 99). Without the support of a husband, however, women, including mothers, have found it more advantageous, and more in tune with the welfare system, to engage in paid employment. In Italy, welfare provision has emerged under complex pressures, including an influential feminist movement, particularly in the 1970s, the enduring power of the Catholic Church, and the demands of trade unions and the Communist Party. Bimbi (1993: 156) particularly emphasizes the importance of feminist trade unionists within the expanding social-services sector in putting women's citizenship onto the Italian political agenda and in pushing forward reforms such as the 1977 'gender parity of employment conditions' reform.

These aspects, which can only be briefly touched on here, offer some context for the trends in non-standard working discussed below. Germany and Italy both retain relatively 'traditional' family arrangements, with the emphasis in Germany on the marital relationship and on a sexual division of labour between married couples in which women's labour-force participation is inhibited by the emphasis on a housekeeping and childcare role for mothers, and German mothers have been encouraged by a range of public policies to remain outside the labour market when they have a child under the age of 3 years (Scheiwe 1994). Nevertheless, smaller families, childlessness, and lower marriage rates mean many German women have found alternatives to this situation. In Italy, the wider kin group and family remain a crucial support in providing for the care needs of children and others. Italian women's fertility has declined very significantly in recent decades, resulting in a significant drop in family size, and the emergence of employment opportunities for women, especially in public-sector service occupations, has been important. A further aspect of the Italian situation concerns the large informal employment sector: by definition this cannot be precisely measured, but expert commentators suggest it is both particularly important and strongly feminized in Italy, with informal employment partly a response to labour-movement gains after 1968 (Pinnarò and Pugliese 1985: 240; Saraceno 1992: 227; Chamberlayne 1993: 177).

Because of the role of the EU in regulating employment, particularly with regard to maternity rights and the status of part-time and temporary workers, some harmonization is developing between the three countries. Earlier arrangements differed markedly, however, and some important differences remain. Employment protection in relation to maternity and provision for parental leaves from work were introduced or strengthened in all three countries in the 1970s: in the UK through the 1976 Employment Protection Act and through the 1975 Sex Discrimination Act; in Italy through legislation on maternity leave in 1971 (Chamberlayne 1993) as well as some earlier but less comprehensive legislation (Bimbi 1993). In Germany women's employment rights were enhanced by the *Erziehungsurlaub* (parental leave) introduced in 1986 (*Employment Observatory* 1993), although fourteen weeks' maternity leave (including six weeks during pregnancy) had been established as early as 1952 (Frevert 1989: 284). Part-time workers in Italy have *pro rata* benefits with full-timers, and those working more than twenty-four hours per week receive maximum child-benefit payments (Snyder 1992: 214; Chamberlayne 1993: 176). Perhaps because of the level of protection offered (making such employees relatively more expensive), the level of 'official' part-time working amongst women in Italy is low, whereas over a third of working women in Germany are part-time, and the UK has the highest rate of all (Tables 5.3 and 5.4).

TABLE 5.3. *Average hours worked by employees per week, Germany, Italy, and the UK, 1997 (hours)*

Type of employee	Germany	Italy	UK
Full-time			
men	40.4	39.8	45.8
women	39.3	36.4	40.6
Part-time			
men	16.5	29.8	16.2
women	19.1	22.6	18.0

Source: *Social Trends* (1998).

TABLE 5.4. *Changes in part-time employment, Germany, Italy, and the UK, 1985–1995 (%)*

	Germany		Italy		UK	
	1985	1995	1985	1995	1985	1995
Women employed part-time as a percentage of all part-time employees	90.5	87.4	61.6	70.6	88.0	82.3
Men employed part-time as a percentage of all employed men[a]	2.0	3.6	3.0	2.9	4.4	7.7
Women employed part-time as a percentage of all employed women[a]	29.6	33.8	10.1	12.7	44.8	44.3

[a] Figures for Germany 1985 refer to West Germany only.
Source: OECD (1997).

A further analysis of 'usual weekly hours worked' in the EU (Table 5.5) shows that UK employees were more likely to work both short and long hours than those in Germany and Italy, where there was significant standardization, in recorded employment, around a working week of between thirty-five and forty-four hours. By contrast, one in ten UK workers works fewer than sixteen hours per week, while more than one in four works forty-five hours or more. This is a very different distribution from that found in either of the other countries.

TABLE 5.5. *Employees working specified average weekly hours, Germany, Italy, and the UK, 1990* (percentages working specified hours)

Average weekly hours	Germany	Italy	UK
Fewer than 16	4.2	1.7	9.7
16–24	6.9	6.7	8.2
25–34	4.3	3.5	6.9
35–39	53.3	25.8	25.6
40–44	24.3	52.2	22.6
45–50	4.3	8.5	16.0
more than 50	2.9	1.6	11.2

Source: ELFS, derived from Watson (1992: 554–5).

Pay differentials between men and women are greater in the UK and Germany, where collective bargaining efforts have historically been geared to protecting male access to a 'family wage' (Frevert 1989: 279; Chamberlayne 1993: 178), compared with Italy, where trade unions have pursued equal pay over a longer period as a means of preventing 'undercutting'. Snyder's comparative assessment (1992) reports women's manual hourly earnings as a percentage of men's, for all industries, as West Germany 73.4 per cent(1988); Italy 82.7 per cent (1985); and UK 68.9 per cent (1987).

TRENDS IN NON-STANDARD WORKING IN GERMANY, ITALY, AND THE UK

The emergence of 'non-standard' employment arrangements in Western capitalist societies has been much discussed in recent years. It has at times been accorded a sociological importance akin to the extension of individual wage labour during the Industrial

Revolution, and it has been particularly noted as impacting upon male-breadwinner social norms—either (1) as a limited support enabling those arrangements to continue essentially unchallenged, with men retaining the majority of economic power, or (2) as a disruption to established economic distribution systems—invariably favouring men—that has links to social and economic polarization and to the emergence of new forms of class division. A third possibility is (3) that the emergence of non-standard employment heralds a potentially more equitable distribution of work and its rewards between the sexes, enabling individuals to tailor their labour-force attachment to their family and personal circumstances, and to life-course stages. This third possibility would be consistent with claims about 'individualization', such as have been made by Beck (1992). Non-standard working in the past decade has been a phenomenon predominantly affecting female participants in the labour force, and one linked to women's family status. However, men's labour-market situation has also been affected, and there are important emergent trends towards more male non-standard working, and towards participation patterns that extend non-standard work to groups of both sexes at the younger and older ends of the working life.[3] The evidence summarized in this chapter relates to part-time employment, to fixed-term/temporary working, and to self-employment and family working.

Changes in Part-Time Working

Among female German employees, part-time employment rose to almost 34 per cent by 1990, and remained at a high level in the 1995 figures. Across the decade, part-time working increased markedly for 25–49 year olds (from 2.2 m. to 3.8 m.): almost two-thirds of all German part-timers are in this age group. It also increased sharply for 50–64 year olds, almost doubling over the decade to 1.5 m. in 1995. Compared with Italy and the UK, part-time employment was less important among young Germans, although this again increased, from 180,000 to 281,000. These low figures may reflect the established practice of prolonged full-time education into the 20+ age group in the German educational system (Rainbird 1993[4]), in which one-third of German university students 'support themselves' (Wallace 1994), as well as the relative affluence over much of the decade of German youth and their parents. However, recent analysis of German service-sector employment found little evidence of 'youthful stop-gap jobs' (Bloßfeld *et al.* 1993), with considerable heterogeneity among unskilled service workers. Part-time employment has also increased among UK 25–49 year olds (from 2.9 million to 3.4 million), but in the UK the rate of increase has been faster among the under 25s (from 700,000 to over 1 million) and among 50–64 year olds (1.2 million to 1.5 million). In Italy, part-time employment is a less important feature of the economy, occurring at a low level among 14–25 year olds (182,000 in 1985, 173,000 in 1995), and decreasing slightly among older workers (by 1995, 214,000 50–64 year olds and 46,000 aged 65 or above). There has been an increase, however, from approximately half a million to 850,000 among Italian 25–49 year olds, of whom 640,000 are women.

When these trends are broken down by sex, some important differences emerge. Trends towards more part-time employment have been particularly marked for German men, with percentage changes of +130 per cent or more in all age groups under 65 years. Percentage changes have also been large for German women (almost +100 per cent among 50–64 year olds and +63 per cent among 25–49 year olds). In the UK, percentage changes over the decade for women have been more modest (around +12 per cent for 25–64 year olds), in marked contrast with the trend for men, which has been +80 per cent(14–25 year olds), +145 per cent (25–49 year olds), and +130 per cent (50–64 year olds). The Italian situation offers a very different picture, with a minus percentage change for men in all age groups (except 25–49 year olds (+28 per cent)), and among women aged 50 and over, and only a modest upward trend among young women (+7 per cent). However, among 25–49-year-old Italian women, a sharper increase, similar to the trend in Germany, occurred (+60 per cent).

Of the three countries, then, Italy has the smallest part-time workforce, by a considerable margin. Almost all of the increase in part-time working in Italy has occurred in the service sector (and for women also in the industrial sector), although overall these upward trends have been offset by a decline in part-time working for both sexes in the agricultural sector, and for men in the industrial sector. As in Germany, very few young Italians combine attendance at school/college with employment (less than or just over 3 per cent for males and females aged 18, 22, and 26 in 1994 (OECD 1996: 132)). The UK has a strong established pattern of maternal part-time employment, reflected in the fact that over 44 per cent of employed women in the UK were part-timers in 1995. The growth of this type of part-time employment in the UK became visible after 1945 and accelerated during the following decades. The 1995 figure (44 per cent) represents over 3 million women aged 25–49 and over 1 million women aged 50–64, and there were also significant numbers of part-time women workers in younger and older age groups. Between 1985 and 1995, all of the increase in part-time employment was in the service sector, and indeed the strong upward trend here was partly off-set by a downward trend in the industrial and agricultural sectors. Some of the change in the German picture in 1985–1995 suggests that maternal part-time employment is also a strengthening feature of the German labour market. However, as in the UK, male part-time working has been emerging—not, it would seem, to enhance men's capacity to contribute to caregiving activities and in response to women's greater earning capacity, but more in response to structural changes in the labour market, which have made continuous full-time employment throughout the working life increasingly difficult for men.

Moss (1996) has calculated patterns of full and part-time employment for mothers and fathers of a child aged under 10 years in European countries (Table 5.6). This focuses on a population group with clear caregiving responsibilities. It reveals remarkable consistency in the 'volume' of paid work undertaken by men in all three countries, and shows that this is at a level more than double the 'volume' for women, with the disparity between male and female volumes most marked in the UK, where fathers in full-time work averaged 47.6 hour per week in 1993, with German and Italian fathers working 41.7 and 41.6 hours respectively.

In summary, then, and taking all three countries, a much larger proportion of female than male workers work part-time. While the normal caveats about actual numbers of women working part-time apply (for example, one person may hold two or more part-time contracts[5]), it is clear that contracting women (and some men) to work part-time is a very significant employment practice in Germany and the UK, although one used less in formally recorded employment in Italy. This may reflect a tendency for part-time work to take place in the informal economy in Italy, as suggested in the first section of this chapter. By 1995, Germany and the UK had more than 5 million officially recorded part-time workers. The influence of patterns of education and vocational training for younger women, and of support

TABLE 5.6. *Employment rates and hours usually worked per week, employees with a child under 10, Germany, Italy, the UK, and EU12, 1993*

| Country | Employment rate (%) | | Usual working week (average hours) | | |
Volume[a]	Full-time	Part-time	Full-time	Part-time	All employed
Germany					
men	90.8	1.4	41.7	20.6	41.4	38.2
women	26.3	24.8	40.6	19.2	30.2	15.4
East Germany					
men	89.5	0.6	n.a.	n.a.	n.a.	n.a.
women	55.1	14.2	n.a.	n.a.	n.a.	n.a.
West Germany					
men	91.2	1.6	n.a.	n.a.	n.a.	n.a.
women	18.3	27.8	n.a.	n.a.	n.a.	n.a.
Italy					
men	91.4	1.4	41.6	33.4	41.4	38.4
women	36.4	6.3	36.0	23.3	34.2	14.7
UK					
men	82.3	1.8	47.6	19.2	47.0	39.6
women	17.7	34.8	40.2	16.5	24.5	12.9
EU12					
men	88.0	1.7	43.6	24.6	42.7	38.3
women	30.3	20.2	39.2	19.2	31.2	15.8

[a] Volume is the total hours of paid work undertaken by men/women with a child aged under 10 years divided by the total number of men/women with a child aged under 10, whether employed or not.

Note: n.a. = data not available.

Source: Moss (1996).

with childcare for women of parental age, are clearly influential factors, although the significance of employment regulation and employer demand (together with its sectoral distribution), as well as the prevalence of other forms of employment, such as self-employment, also need to be taken into account. The chapter now turns to some of these alternative forms of employment.

INCREASES IN SELF-EMPLOYMENT AND FIXED-TERM CONTRACTS

These two forms of employment are particularly important in relation to the theoretical aspects outlined above. Self-employment is suggestive of worker autonomy and self-actualization, yet may also be involuntary (among workers who would otherwise be unemployed) or 'bogus' (where the worker is dependent upon a single client, or working on a subcontracted basis). It may be economically advantageous, if the worker is able to establish a portfolio of flexible clients requiring his or her varied skills, or economically precarious, leaving the worker with no income security and vulnerable to business collapse/bankruptcy. Fixed-term contracts may also be viewed both as a form of worker exploitation, with employees denied employment security and protection, and especially vulnerable in sickness, lean times, and so on, or as offering workers the opportunity to exploit demand for their skills/labour in ways that relieve them of long-term commitment and obligation, and enable them to focus on their own career/professional development or to fit their paid work around other commitments and activities.

Self-employment is most important, in relative terms, in Italy, where more than a quarter of economically active males, and more than one in eight economically active females, works on this basis. Trends in this area of employment are related to the sectoral distribution of employment, although the significance of kin networks in Italian culture is another important influence. Therborn has noted the 'distinctively petit-bourgeois flavour to (the Italian) class structure', where 'there are four self-employed and family workers for every ten workers/employees' (1995: 78). The proportion of the economically active Italian population who are self-employed has remained remarkably stable for both men and women over the ten-year period.

The UK witnessed a rather marked increase in male self-employment between 1985 and 1990, although this levelled off in the years to 1995, and the trend was very much more muted for women. In both the UK and Germany, but not Italy, public policy has introduced special schemes to assist the unemployed into self-employment (Teague 1989).

Temporary or fixed-term contract working affects a small (approximately 6–8 per cent) proportion of workers in Italy and the UK, and has been fairly stable for the working population as a whole in these countries over the period 1983–1994 (OECD 1996: 10–11). In Germany, this type of employment contract affects a larger, but again apparently[6] stable proportion of the working population (between 10 and 12 per cent). When broken down by sex, it can be seen that, in all three countries, fixed-term contracts are more common for women than for men, although the difference between the sexes is not large. There is important variation between states in the way fixed-term contracts are regulated: German law specifies rather closely the circumstances in which fixed-term employment is possible, and sets a limit of eighteen months on the contract in most cases under the Employment Promotion Act 1985;[7] Italy permits the conclusion of a fixed-term contract only if one of nine legally defined conditions applies; while the UK 'has no statutory restrictions . . . on entering into fixed term contracts of employment' (Schömann et al. 1994: 34). These, and other, variations in employment regulation are linked to the prevalence of self-employment and, particularly, fixed-term contracts. Labour-market regulation is weaker in the UK than in most of the rest of Europe (Beatson 1995), and in Germany, even since the 1985 Employment Promotion Act, which relaxed the rules governing fixed-term contract work (Cousins 1997: 7), the use of 'permanent' contracts remains the norm. We can also note that 1991 data showed a notable concentration of fixed-term contracts in the agricultural sector in Italy, but a much wider spread across industrial sectors in the other countries, with significant use of such contracts in services, construction, and the distributive trades.

Family Workers

Family working[8] may be viewed: (i) as part of an essentially pre/non-industrial division of labour; (ii) as a particular form of worker exploitation, consistent with patriarchal social systems; or (iii) as an essentially equitable, partnership approach to business organization, in which individuals can exploit ties of kinship and affect to give them greater satisfaction or market power.

Italy has by far the strongest tradition of family working of the three countries studied, and, although this way of organizing work has declined for Italian women since 1985, from 9 per cent of the economically active female population to just over 6 per cent, it is still the case that about one in twenty-five of the economically active population in Italy works on this basis. In the UK, family working is relatively insignificant, at under 0.5 per cent of the economically active population, while in Germany the figures are well under 2 per cent. The changes visible here reflect declining employment in agriculture, together with trends away from family stability and towards greater female autonomy in some countries. Both of these trends would support the first or second interpretations of the role of family working, rather than the third. A far greater proportion of women are family workers (respectively 3.2, 6.3, and 0.8 per cent of economically active females in Germany, Italy, and the UK) while among men, family working is relatively insignificant, except in Italy (Germany 0.6 per cent, Italy 2.5 per cent, UK 0.3 per cent of those economically active). Further emphasis may be given to this interpretation, as Italian male family working has been strongly linked to raised levels of unemployment in the economy and to problems of insertion into the labour market for young workers.

Technological and Other Changes Affecting the Organization of Employment

This chapter can allude only briefly to changes in this sphere, which are discussed elsewhere in debates about home-working, teleworking, and home-based working. Most observers have concluded that, while the potential for significant change in the organization of employment is large, most economies have to date made relatively little use of technology to shift production to the home, although there has been important change in the organization of work in parts of the service sector (for example, banking and retail) and in manufacturing.

Another important development is the re-emergence of private domestic work (Yeandle 1996). This has been carefully documented for some regions of the UK (Gregson and Lowe 1994), and has emerged as an important empirical finding in at least one German study (Rerrich 1996). I have argued that the use of the paid labour of women outside the family to provide childcare, cleaning, and other domestic services by families that have dual earners, usually both in professional or managerial jobs, is an especially important source of polarization between women in societies where the state has not accepted responsibility for enabling parents to participate in the labour force. For Germany, Rerrich suggests that it is often women who are non-German nationals who take on such work; in the UK the work is very frequently undertaken by poor women in families that are in some way dependent on state benefit, as well as by young women who lack alternative employment opportunities, some of whom may be non-EU nationals working as *au pairs* (Gregson and Lowe 1994). This point is taken up again in the discussion of gender arrangements below.

BREADWINNING AND CAREGIVING:
WHAT KIND OF RESTRUCTURING, AND WHY?

Families and households of all types access economic resources through the wages of their members or through access to welfare benefits. In modern societies, the ability to generate economic resources—to 'win the bread'—is related to the labour-force partici-pation of adults in the family/household, and to the number of such adults and their labour-market skills. Within families, individuals also provide significant amounts of labour on an unpaid basis in the form of housework and provisioning, and care for dependent mem-bers, be they children, or adults with care needs. This section consid-ers the differences and similarities between the patterns of employment (wage earning) and caring/domestic labour of men and women in the three countries. Since hours of work are related to earnings, the variation in men's and women's hours of employment is taken into account. Sources of evidence here are patchy and the discussion is reliant upon published statistics and recent studies of parental employment and of family obligations and commitment, including some attitudinal and time-budget data. The broader con-text for the developments discussed in this last part of the chapter has already been outlined in the first section above.

Germany

During the period 1983–93, Germany experienced declining fertility rates and declining marriage rates. However, births outside marriage remained stable at 15 per cent of all live births, and by 1993 approximately one in five households with a child aged under 18 was headed by a lone parent. The divorce rate was 1.7 per 1,000 people and approximately one-third of all households comprised individuals living alone. On average, women entered motherhood at 27 years of age, and approximately 15 per cent of the population was aged over 65 years. The unification of Germany in 1991 presents challenges for comparative social analysis, although it is clear that social practices established in the former West Germany are likely to become dominant within a relatively short time (Ostner 1993). The 'institutional conservatism' of social policy in the former West Germany (Rerrich 1996) has been widely discussed. The strong link between labour-market position and citizenship and welfare rights (which tended to benefit men and offered women the best possibility of security through lifelong marriage) encouraged women to select a housewife role. This has discouraged the development of maternal and part-time female employment, as has the structure of educational provision[9] and childcare and the strong cultural valorization of full-time and devoted motherhood.

Rerrich (1996: 28) has emphasized the wealth of evidence showing that 'the traditional division of labour between men and women within families in Germany has not changed to any considerable extent'. Yet she also stresses that there are important 'processes of redistribution of reproductive work currently taking place'. These processes take the form of a redistribution *between* women: 'other women . . . are lessening employed women's (and men's) family workload, thus setting them free for work outside the home' (ibid.). Rerrich stresses that for three-quarters of (West) German employees, working hours do not conform to a standard morning to evening, Monday to Friday model. Shift, weekend, flexible, and part-time working are their experience. The mismatch between this variability and the rigidity of what Rerrich calls the 'structure of German public time' is striking. Hours of schooling, widespread childcare practices, and other activities related to family life means that 'the social construction of family life in families with working mothers often involves a whole group of people in complex patterns of cooperation' (1996: 30). The notable characteristics of these 'scenarios of cooperation' are that men are rarely involved; that the establishment of cooperative support arrangements is part and parcel of women's accepted family work; that class-specific patterns of cooperation can be discerned, which involve significant developments in the informal economy; and that those paid to perform private domestic work in or for family households are often non-German, migrant workers.

Italy

Italy has seen a rapid decline in fertility rates in recent years, and in 1993 total fertility stood at 1.21, much lower than in either the UK or Germany. Italy is also notable for its low divorce rate (0.4 per 1,000 people in 1993), reflecting comparatively recent legalisation on divorce and its low level of extramarital births (7 per cent in 1993). Only one in five Italian households is a single-person household, and there are relatively few lone-parent families (in 1993, 6 per cent of all families with a child aged under 18 years) (Eurostat 1995). The extended family plays an important part in the enactment of family life and obligations (Finch 1989*a*; Millar and Warman 1996) and is an important component of an essentially non-interventionist social policy. Nevertheless, marriage rates are low (5.1 per 1,000 population in 1993), and average first childbearing is, similar to Germany and the UK, in the late twenties (27 years).

Italy offers relatively high levels of nursery/kindergarten provision (Millar and Warman 1996: 30–1), although this is intended to support rather than to replace parental and family care. There is no statutory paternity leave for Italian fathers, and no state child or lone-parent benefits are paid (ibid.). More than two-thirds of young Italians are still attending school or college at age 18 (1994 figures, OECD 1996) and nearly 30 per cent are doing so at age 22.

The Catholic Church had an important influence on family policy and thus on the status of women in Italian society until at least the 1960s: however, in recent decades feminist ideas have had an important influence, and arguably the mismatch between the family system and the emergent modernized educational system, offering opportunities for qualification to girls yet providing little welfare support to those wanting to combine motherhood and career, has been an important reason for the flight from parenthood. As one observer noted:

While Italian society moves on, government support structures, the health system and Italy's over-cosseted men and the older generation of women who brought them up have remained stuck in a 1950s time-warp of paternalistic family values, strict cultural codes and high aspirations for children that derive from the post-war economic boom, but have long since become misguided and misplaced.   (Gumbel 1997)

The UK

In the UK in the 1990s, diversity in family living is widespread despite rather ineffectual resistance by government and policy-makers. Approximately one-third of children are born outside marriage, and 21 per cent of families containing a child under 18 years are headed by lone parents. This last figure is expected to continue rising (Haskey 1998). There is growing recognition that family structure is fluid and variable across the life course, but this has not prevented a moralistic public debate about the risks of family diversity: the absence and fecklessness of fathers, the 'dependency culture' and 'babies on benefit'. The development of a Murrayesque underclass and a concern with the high cost of benefits to a growing category of poor, single-parent families led Conservative governments to very significant policy developments (for example, the Child Support Act 1990), accompanied by extensive vilification of women in this group in media and political debate. The Labour government (from 1997) claims to be seeking to support all families, with a particular emphasis on encouraging lone mothers to obtain paid work, but is seen by many commentators as critical of non-nuclear family arrangements.

Throughout the period 1985–1995, the UK had the lowest levels of pre-school childcare provision in Europe, and lone parents of young children found extreme difficulty in accessing employment, with childcare costs frequently an insurmountable barrier. Historically by comparison with other European countries, the UK education system has discouraged extended education (only 38 per cent of 18-year-old women and 32 per cent of 18-year-old men were attending school or college in 1993 (OECD 1996)), although there has been a small increase over the decade in the numbers in some form of apprenticeship scheme (8.7 per cent of 18-year-old women and 18.6 per cent of 18-year-old men in 1994 (ibid.)), and 'lifelong learning' has lately achieved some prominence on the public policy agenda.

The UK has come to terms with some measure of basic sex equality and anti-discrimination legislation (enacted in the 1970s, with some subsequent revisions), such that there is widespread lip-service to equality of opportunity between the sexes, although men's behaviour lags significantly behind the attitudes they express when it comes to the sexual division of domestic labour (Warde and Hetherington 1993). The breadwinning/caregiving divide has been explored in recent work on household time allocation (Horrell 1994) and on the domestic division of labour (Gershuny *et al.* 1994). Horrell's analysis shows that men put more time into routine aspects of housework when they have an employed spouse, whereas women employed full-time dramatically reduce the time they spend in housework compared to non-employed wives. Dual-full-time employment households allocated markedly less time overall to cleaning and tidying. Gershuny makes the important claim that there is a 'general social trend' towards (fairly small) increases in husbands' domestic labour, notably in cooking and routine housework, with households 'adapt(ing) gradually' to wives' entry into full-time employment, and argues that there is 'substantial growth' in men's proportional contribution to overall unpaid work, while men's share of total work (paid and unpaid) 'is in general decreasing' (1994: 183). This is claimed as evidence of a process of adaptation, and thereby of a significant shift in the overall sexual division of labour.

These issues affecting the division of breadwinning and caregiving can be placed in the context of theoretical claims about 'gender arrangements' (Pfau-Effinger 1996*b*). Such analysis follows Connell (1987) in regarding power (in its political and cultural dimensions), the division of labour (enacted through family, labour-market, and educational systems), and cathexis (personal relationships mediated by sexuality and/or emotion) as important. The gender-arrangement concept embraces the dynamics of gender relations in particular societies: it recognizes a dominant ideology of gender, but also that not all groups fully accept that ideology, or are (in terms of their structural and material position) able to enact these dominant social norms.

Pfau-Effinger (see Chapter 4) specifies four extant gender arrangements: the family economic model; the male-breadwinner/female-carer model; the dual-breadwinner/state-carer model; and the dual-breadwinner/dual-carer model. Over time, there can be shifts between the different models, and, within any given society, regional[10] and other sources of variation may occur. In the remainder of this chapter the usefulness of these 'ideal types' for analysing recent developments in the three countries is examined.

Germany: Gender Arrangement

Pfau-Effinger outlines the arrangement in Germany, noting the dominance of the housewife ideal since the beginning of the twentieth century, the increases in married women's employment, initially especially in maternal part-time working, in the quarter century after 1945, and the 'leap of modernization', which sharpened the contradiction between bourgeois (patriarchal) ideology and mid/late-twentieth-century notions of equality, particularly equality between the sexes. Attitudes towards maternal employment for a long time remained relatively conservative (1996*b*: 16) and 'traditional', with attitudes strongly influenced by an ideology of childrearing that prioritizes intense maternal involvement in the daily activities of children, both before and after they commence formal schooling. The gender arrangement in Germany is conceptualized as shifting from a *male-breadwinner/female-carer* model, with the expansion of women's part-time work an important element in the transition. The transition towards this model is incomplete, however, because women, not men, have taken steps towards change. Indeed, Rerrich suggests the shift towards a dual-breadwinner/dual-carer model may have been diverted or halted by men's inability/unwillingness to change. Perhaps what is emerging is a *dual-breadwinner/marketized-female-domestic-economy* model, in which domestic work becomes distributed across women and outside the kin network, creating new class divisions between women and new opportunities for mechanisms of exploitation for men.

Italy: Gender Arrangement

Using the same ideal types, Italy fits a *family economic* model throughout most of the twentieth century, with modernization (notably the introduction of ideals of equality and of aspects of feminist ideology into political and social life) heralding a (far from complete) shift towards an alternative gender arrangement: witness the relative importance of family working in Italy, and the extensive reliance upon networks of kin for the delivery of welfare. There is quite persuasive evidence of a shift towards a *male-breadwinner/ female-carer* model, supported by evidence of the involuntary nature of much part-time working in Italy. However, there are also indications suggesting a possible future shift towards a *dual-breadwinner/ state-carer* model. The marked decline in fertility in Italy suggests some younger Italian women may be selecting employment and the pursuit of a career rather than motherhood as currently constructed. The attitudes implicit here would be consistent with support for a shift towards state, rather than family, caring arrangements, although, on current evidence, such a conclusion can have only weak support. Important regional variation needs also to be noted in Italy, although the European Labour Force Survey (ELFS) statistics that have been used in the second section of this chapter are unable to render these differences.

The UK: Gender Arrangement

In the UK there has been a dominant ideology of male breadwinning since the end of the nineteenth century. Numerous analysts have emphasized this point (Lewis 1992), categorizing the UK as a 'strong' male-breadwinner state. The focus of policy and culture around the nuclear family was particularly strong in the UK up until about 1970, and there is extensive support for a dominant ideological emphasis (whatever the empirical reality for poorer families) on men's obligation to 'provide' in the literature on family life, education, and labour relations. Arguably, this gender arrangement was most dominant in the years between 1945 and 1960, a period in which, although part-time female employment began to be extensively used by employers, married women's earnings were widely viewed as 'pin money' and supports for 'life's little extras', rather than as serious contributions to family budgeting. Strong pressure towards a shift in attitudes to wives' earnings emerged in the second wave of feminism in the UK, but this was given a much sharper edge by consumerist ideology and, in the 1980s, to no small degree by the Conservative government's policy on housing, which edged many married couples into large mortgages requiring significant and continuous income from both spouses. The refusal of the state to accept the burden of care, especially since the mid-1970s, has forced other solutions on UK families. Among middle-income families there is now extensive use of private and often informal solutions to the burden of housework. Expansion in various parts of the service sector is also occurring to meet such needs (Yeandle *et al.* 1998). The UK, then, can be conceptualized as a *dual-breadwinner/dual-carer* model manqué. This is the direction in which the gender arrangement seemed to be moving in the 1960s and 1970s (Young and Willmott 1973). But the radical shift in the political agenda, away from public expenditure, pushed the gender contract back towards privatized solutions. Families faced with such dilemmas may take the route of equality and adaptation as argued by Gershuny: this would be the route to dual-breadwinner/dual-carer systems. But they may also invoke other priorities and other forms of power: and men's 'refusal' of a dual-paid/unpaid-work arrangement (men take part-time work only reluctantly and prefer a solution that does not reconfigure their place in the 'gender order') has led to the same privatized, feminised solutions as Rerrich has suggested for Germany. Here too, then, it may be a dual-earner/marketized-female-domestic economy model that emerges in the years ahead.

CONCLUSIONS

The above discussion of gender arrangements, and how they may have changed, indicates ways in which change in family structures and behaviour, and changes in attitudes and values (including those linked to feminist politics), may be reshaping men's and women's engagement with a changing labour market. Such developments, however, are cross-cut by patterns of class and social status. These patterns may be less rigidly structured than in the past from the perspective of the individual, whose capacity for social mobility (both upward and downward) has arguably become greater in the late twentieth century (Beck 1992). Nevertheless, the emergence of new class cleavages (Esping-Andersen 1993), perhaps closely linked to the emergence of 'bad' jobs (ibid. 239) or perhaps to barriers linked to skill and education, is already creating new divisions between women.

By comparison with the Scandinavian economies, the three countries examined here all have relatively undeveloped social and domestic services sectors. Jobs to deliver these services may emerge in the private sector, in the part-time, fixed-term, or self-employment sectors of the labour market, to meet the needs of the best-educated and skilled households whose capacity to provide caregiving to their members and their kin is limited by their careers and employment (Yeandle *et al.* 1998). Such a development, which seems most likely in the UK, but may well develop in Germany and Italy as well, will create new social divisions, and possibly greater polarization, between those dual-breadwinner households that can afford to purchase their own support services and avoid themselves giving care, and those households whose members are drawn into employment in the 'marketized female domestic economy' (notably lone mothers, unskilled women, and those women whose partners are unable to gain employment), whose social situation may be seriously disadvantaged to the extent that class closure results.

The evidence on non-standard working reveals that there are undoubtedly important shifts towards more variety in employment arrangements, with the standard, lifelong contract in full-time morning-to-evening employment encroached upon from many quarters. The data for 1985–95 discussed in this chapter show that some women are affected more than men by these changes, although there have been important developments in male working arrangements too. These changes are the product of: employer demand (not discussed here); of regulatory systems (which still vary considerably between EU member states); and of employee supply. The availability of workers is itself a product of a complex of factors that include family structure, educational and vocational training systems, and sectoral shifts in the structure of the labour market. All of these factors are encompassed within an overarching framework of gender relations.

This chapter has explored some of these factors for three countries. An attempt has been made to locate developments within a theoretical framework, using the concept of gender arrangement. The concept has been useful in explaining some of the observed developments in gender relations and employment, though the four ideal types developed by Pfau-Effinger (1996*b*) may require further elaboration or development. The role of marketized, but often informal and private domestic labour, performed almost exclusively by women, has been the focus for this suggestion. To assess how this element will develop in each of the countries considered in this chapter requires some information that is still unavailable on a comparative basis. Any judgement of how far polarization or class cleavages are developing will require information about the role of earnings and particularly about the relative contributions made by spouses and by state benefits to household budgets. At present, detailed information on the occupational distribution of workers engaged on non-standard contracts is also difficult to compare, and its value is reduced by very limited information about such employment in the informal sector of the three economies.

NOTES

1. Most recent conceptualizations of welfare regimes owe something to Esping-Andersen's analysis (1990). Useful developments of and correctives to this analysis have been offered by Leibfried and Ostner (1991), Lewis (1992), and Duncan (1995), among others.
2. Note, however, that 50% of these children had places in the former East Germany, with 98,000 places lost during 1990–1.
3. In the discussion which follows, the ten-year period 1985–95 is considered. This period has been chosen because ELFS data can be compared over this period.
4. Rainbird (1993) presents data on the share of young people in education by age group (14–18, 19–22, 23–24) in the EU member states in 1988. This shows a marked difference between those states, including Germany and Italy, where well over 20% of 19–22 year olds were in education, and around 20% of 23–24 year olds, compared with the UK, where the proportion of 23–24 year olds in education was less than 10%.
5. e.g. in the UK, 7.2% of part-time women and 7.8% of part-time men held a second job, while this was also true of 3.2 % of full-time men and 3.5% of full-time women (Watson 1992: 543).
6. Beck notes that in Germany 'illegal temporary work is estimated to be six to nine times higher in incidence (than legal work on temporary contract)' (1992: 148).
7. Cousins (1997) discusses the impact of the 1985 Employment Promotion Act.
8. There are some definitional difficulties with this category: for example, if husbands and wives establish a business partnership for tax purposes, this may disguise wives' family working, and it has recently been noted with respect particularly to the hotel and catering trade in the UK that some employers require their hotel and pub managers to be married men, with the implication that their wives' labour will be available, although contractual arrangements are made only with the men concerned (Adkins 1995: 68–91).
9. There is insufficient space here to discuss the German education and training system in any detail. However, note that Rubery and Fagan observe 'in Germany it is in the dual training system, in particular the allocation of women to training places in small firms and in female-dominated vocational areas, that the process of gender segregation takes hold' (1995: 227).
10. It is beyond the scope of this chapter to attempt any regional analysis. However, Duncan (1995) presents some interesting data relating to regions.

6

Attitudes, Women's Employment, and the Changing Domestic Division of Labour: A Cross-National Analysis

ROSEMARY CROMPTON
AND FIONA HARRIS

INTRODUCTION

As discussed in Chaper 1, Beck (1992) has described the broad outlines of the gender division of labour that emerged with the coming of industrialism as 'feudal'. Men were born to a lifetime of paid employment, whereas women were destined for a lifetime of household drudgery. This gender division of labour was reflected in the ideology of separate spheres of male and female activity, which was widely regarded as being somehow natural. The naturalness of separate-spheres ideology—and thus its utility as an explanation of the situation of women in the labour force—was extensively challenged by second-wave feminism. It was argued that patriarchal processes and institutions had operated so as both to exclude women from the labour force, and to ensure that they had access only to lower-level jobs when they were in employment. This arrangement kept women economically dependent on men as, unable to earn wages that might enable them to live independently, women were constrained to enter into relationships with male providers. Thus men's access to women's domestic labour was assured (Hartmann 1982; Walby 1990).

Men's economic advantage, therefore, looms large in feminist explanations of women's employment. These broadly materialist explanations have been paralleled in analyses of power relationships, and of the division of labour, between men and women within the household itself. The 'resource theory' of power within the household suggests that the person(s) with the greater power within the household are those who make the largest contributions to the resources of the unit (Blood and Wolfe 1960). On the basis of these arguments, in the 1970s it was assumed by some British sociologists that the rise in the number of working wives would be accompanied by a corresponding increase in the husband's input into domestic work (Young and Willmott 1973). That is, as women did more market work, so men would do more domestic work. Such arguments emphasized the importance of structural factors—in particular, the increase in women's employment and the significance of their material contribution to the household—in shaping the domestic division of labour.

However, a number of studies have demonstrated that, although men do take on more domestic work as a consequence of their female partner's paid employment, this increase does not equalize the amount of work (domestic and non-domestic) carried out by men and women. In her review of this literature, Morris (1990: 102) concluded that: 'none of the data seem to warrant any suggestion that the traditional female responsibility for household work has been substantially eroded, or that male participation has substantially increased'. Hochschild (1990) has described this as the 'stalled revolution'. Although women have increasingly moved into the previously male-dominated sphere of paid work, there has been no equivalent increase in the amount of unpaid work carried out by men—hence the gender revolution has been 'stalled': 'women have gone to work, but the workplace, the culture, and most of all, the men, have not adjusted themselves to the new reality.' Thus many women work a 'second shift'—of household work, as well as paid work. Part-time work, in particular, seems to have had little impact on men's domestic contribution, and even when women work full-time, this does not have an equivalent impact on men's work in the household (Kiernan and Wicks 1990; Morris 1990).

The persistence of women's identification with domestic work has been explained by some as reflecting the symbolic contribution of domestic work to the construction of feminine identity itself. 'Good women' are those who fulfill their domestic duties; conversely, domestic tasks are perceived as 'unmanly'. Women's and men's socialization, it is argued, incorporates a gendered attribution of task responsibilities that is virtually impossible to change, even in a context in which women's market work is on the increase. A powerful combination of persisting male material dominance, together with the effects of gender socialization, therefore, have been held to account for the relative lack of change in the gender division of labour within the household. Against these kinds of arguments, however, there is emerging a body of evidence and argument that suggests both that gradual changes in the direction of a more egalitarian domestic division of labour *are* in fact taking place, and, moreover, that these changes are closely associated with changing attitudes towards gender roles (Marx-Ferree 1991; Vogler and Pahl 1993; Gershuny *et al.* 1994; Benjamin and Sullivan, forthcoming).

We will be examining these issues via a cross-national comparison of gender-role attitudes, and the domestic division of labour, in three different countries: Norway, Britain, and the Czech Republic. This comparison includes one example of a national situation in which a historically rapid increase in women's participation in paid employment has had little impact upon the domestic division of labour. Women in the ex-state-socialist countries participated (and participate) in the labour force long term, and full-time (in some cases since the earlier decades of the twentieth century). The extent of their economic participation, however, was not matched by an increase in the domestic labour of East European men (Lapidus 1978).

CROSS-NATIONAL VARIATIONS IN GENDER-ROLE ATTITUDES

For the three countries under discussion, we have derived a measure of gender role attitudes (GRA) using data from the International Social Survey Programme's Family and Gender Relations module, which was fielded in 1994. Interviews were carried out with a stratified random sample of 2,087 respondents in Norway, 984 in Britain, and 1,024 in the Czech Republic.[1] A gender-role-attitude index was computed from individual responses to the three following statements:[2]

- A job is all right, but what most women really want is a home and children.
- A man's job is to earn the money, a woman's job is to look after the home and family.
- It is not good if the man stays at home and cares for the children and the woman goes out to work.

In Table 6.1, positive scores are indicative of greater gender role conservatism, negative scores of gender role liberalism.[3] As can be seen
from the table, gender-role attitudes are most conservative in the
Czech Republic, and most liberal in Norway, with Britain somewhere in between. These differences in gender-role attitudes, we
would argue, reflect in large part the impact of very different national
policies towards women's equality, women's employment, and the
family in the three countries under discussion.

TABLE 6.1. *Attitudes to gender roles and the gender division of labour, by country and sex*

Sex	Gender conservatism and liberalism scores		
	Norway	Britain	Czech Republic
Men	–0.50	–0.28	0.48
Women	–0.72	–0.45	0.40

These gender-role attitudes are reflected in the variation in the
nature of the domestic division of labour across all three countries.
The ISSP data include a series of questions relating to household
activities. We constructed a simple measure of 'traditional' and 'less
traditional' domestic divisions of labour from the answers to two
questions:[4]

  • In your household, who usually does the washing and ironing?
  • In your household, who usually cares for sick family members?

As is shown in Table 6.2, 60 per cent of the Norwegian respondents
fell into the non-traditional category, whereas 63 per cent of the
Czechs held to the traditional pattern. Again, the British respondents
fell in between the other two countries, but were closer to the pattern
in Norway than in the Czech Republic.

National Policies and Gender Attitudes

Historically, it has been women's role as mothers that has been the
major focus of state policy. Two, rather different, strategies have
been used by the state to try to ensure the reproduction of healthy
infants. First, the state may attempt to keep women in the home, by
cooperating in strategies that exclude them from paid work. Or the

TABLE 6.2. *Traditional and non-traditional domestic division of labour, by country (%)*

Domestic division of labour	Norway**	Britain**	Czech Republic**
Traditional	40	46	63
Non traditional	60	54	37
	100	100	100
N	*1284*	*545*	*637*

** sig. at 99.9%.

state may offer supports to women to make it less difficult for them to combine family life with paid employment, and thus better able to care for their children as well.

In Britain from the nineteenth century onwards experts in public health argued that the health of infants was to be best achieved by ensuring maternal care. Thus public-health efforts were focused upon, first, keeping mothers in the home, and, secondly, educating them in hygiene and childcare (Lewis 1980; Jenson 1986). The British state opposed paid maternity leaves and, 'even in the inter-war years, never ratified the International Labour Organization's . . . provision for (paid maternity leave) . . . As one policy maker argued then, such provisions would be wrong because they would usurp the father's responsibility for supporting the family and thus encourage family disintegration' (Jenson 1986: 21). Women were excluded from the labour market and the 'women's place' was firmly assigned to the home, where it was assumed that she would be supported by her husband.

The formal barriers to women's labour-force participation in Britain have been gradually removed, but, until recently, the state has done little actively to facilitate women's participation in the labour force. The extent of public childcare provision in Britain is the lowest in Europe (except Ireland) (Phillips and Moss 1988). Even when the British government has recognized the childcare needs of working mothers, it has argued that these needs should be met by the employers, rather than the state (Cmnd. 1988). So, whilst women in Britain are not now discouraged from becoming workers—indeed, at times of actual or potential labour shortage, women have been actively encouraged to join the labour force—working mothers or other women with caring and domestic responsibilities are expected to make their own arrangements for caring. In the 1990s the net result is that: 'Working parents (in Britain) with children under 3 must rely almost entirely on either the private market or their social networks' (Moss 1991:125) for childcare.[5]

The Czech Republic has a recent history of active pro-natalism, which was developed during the period of state socialism. In the 1960s, there was increasing concern at the declining birth rate. Concerns about the reproduction of the population led governments to begin to recognize the particular needs of women, which had been largely ignored in ideologies dominated by the image of the productive 'worker'. In 1971 a generous system of paid maternity leave was introduced (now three years), together with other inducements such as access to housing (only couples with a child had any chance at all of acquiring accommodation) and other benefits such as marriage loans for couples, with deductions from repayments following the birth of the first child (Mozny 1993). The level of state-provided childcare in Czechoslovakia was somewhat lower than in other state-socialist countries (Heitlinger 1979). Nevertheless, pro-natalist policies did give active support to motherhood, making paid employment for mothers somewhat easier. However, the distribution difficulties associated with state socialism, and the parallel developments in self-welfare locked Czech women firmly into extended caring roles and the domestic sphere.

In the Czech Republic, therefore, support for mothers and thus help with caring has been provided by the state largely as part of policies to persuade women to have more children: they have been directed at women as mothers, rather than women as workers. In Norway, however, debates around childcare have focused upon the needs of the child and preferred family forms, rather than the necessity for biological reproduction (see Chapter 3). Leira (1992; 1994) argues that preference for the gender-differentiated nuclear family was more pronounced in Norway than in the other Scandinavian countries, and that, in Norway, childcare policies were more oriented towards the needs of the child rather than the working mother. Thus the level of state-provided childcare has been relatively low in comparison to other Scandinavian countries. It has, however, increased recently and now 72 per cent of age 3 to school-age children have places in publicly funded childcare.[6] Women's equality is a major and explicit policy objective, as it is in other Scandinavian countries, and in Norway a feature of the debate around 'women's work' was that, to some extent, domestic caring is recognized as 'work'.

Governments in the three countries have also pursued rather different policies as far as women's equality is concerned. In general, liberal democracies have focused largely upon an equality of rights or condition and thus the removal of legal and other restrictions on women—for example, giving women the franchise, equal opportunities in education, access to employment, and so on. In relation to the market, therefore, men and women should receive the same treatment. Governments in Britain have largely restricted themselves to this liberal version of the equality agenda. For example, the government has passed equal-opportunities legislation and outlawed discrimination against women, but it has never considered 'affirmative action'—that is, special treatment for women or minorities to help them 'catch up'.

In the Czech Republic,[7] state socialism was associated with an equality agenda that privileged paid employment (Scott 1974). Following Engels's influential arguments, paid employment was seen as the major avenue through which women's equality should be achieved. State socialism gave women equal rights to education, to enter the professions, and so on. The demands of women's market work have been recognized in the state's provision of childcare for working mothers, but domestic work, and the division of labour in the household, was, ideologically, not seen as particularly important—although from the 1960s the 'double burden' of state-socialist women was increasingly recognized (Buckley 1989).

In contrast to the situation in Soviet-bloc countries, Scandinavian social-democratic socialism has, under the influence of second-wave feminism, also recognized the significance of caring work in the private sphere to the 'equality agenda', as well as equality in employment (Hernes 1987; Persson 1990). That is, it has been argued that moves towards equality have to include changing the gender division of labour in the domestic sphere. The state offers help to both parents in caring, particularly for children. As we have seen in Chapter 3, in Norway there are very generous maternity and paternity leaves together with caring allowances, and, most importantly, a proportion of childcare leave must be taken by the father. Both parents are entitled to leave to care for sick children.

In summary: there are important differences in policies towards women, and the family, in the three nation states under discussion. Britain may be described as a liberal welfare state, and it has also pursued liberal policies in relation to gender equality in employment.

Thus there are today few restrictions on the behaviour of individuals, but the state has not actively intervened to support women's equality, or to provide childcare. Under state socialism, the Czech Republic positively encouraged (indeed, some would argue, required) employment for women in promoting women's equality. Since the 1960s, pro-natalism has also resulted in some recognition of women's caring role, but, as was normal in the state-socialist countries, few efforts have been made to generate equality in the domestic sphere. In contrast, in Norway, equality for women has been seen to require not only equality in employment, but also the recognition of women's caring work and changes in the domestic sphere.

How do these differences between nation states help us to understand the differences in attitudes to gender roles described in Table 6.1? In Eastern Europe, the necessity for 'self-welfare' served to emphasize women's domestic role, despite an official ideology that privileged paid, rather than domestic or caring, work. Support for mothers was linked to the biological maternal role. The emphasis on paid work for women was resented as an element of discredited state socialism. We find, therefore, conservative attitudes relating both to the consequences of women's employment as well as to gender roles. Policies in Norway are characterized by a child-centred family emphasis, but, as we have seen in Chapter 3, in combination with a high-profile equality agenda much influenced by second-wave feminism. Norwegian respondents, therefore, emerge as most progressive in relation to gender roles. In Britain, it may be suggested that a pervasive ideological liberalism and an emphasis upon individual or family responsibility for caring, together with relatively high levels of women's employment brought about by economic necessity, have led to the acceptance of women's employment. However, governments have not attempted to influence the division of labour within the household (and thus the gender coding of caring and paid work), and gender-role ideologies in Britain are not as progressive as in Norway.

Attitudes and Behaviour

It is not too difficult, therefore, to develop plausible explanations for these cross-national variations in gender-role attitudes. To what extent, however, are these attitudes reflected in actual behaviour? As a first step, GRA was dichotomized and cross-tabulated with the domestic division of labour (DDL) measure to give the results reported in Table 6.3.[8] Table 6.3 shows that despite cross-national variations in GRA (demonstrated in Table 6.1 and summarized in the bottom row of Table 6.3), in all three countries, more liberal GRAs are more likely to be associated with a less traditional DDL. On the basis of this evidence, therefore, it would appear that attitudes to gender roles do have an impact on the domestic division of labour. Even though the domestic division of labour in the Czech Republic is extremely traditional (Table 6.2), nevertheless, respondents with liberal gender-role attitudes were more likely to be in households with a less traditional division of domestic labour.

This evidence of the significance of attitudes for the nature of the domestic division of labour is also supported by other empirical work. For example, Marx-Ferree (1991) has shown that, amongst dual-earner couples, the level of a couple's concern about gender equality is significantly related to men's hours of housework, and Vogler and Pahl (1993) have shown that the husband's attitudes (whether sexist or non-sexist) are the most important factor in determining the egalitarian management of money within marriage.

However, as was discussed in the Introduction, it is the impact of the level and extent of women's *employment* on the domestic division of labour that has most frequently been considered in Western debates. In fact, the level of women's employment is very similar in the three countries: women constitute 47 per cent of the labour force in the Czech Republic, 46 per cent of the Norwegian labour force, and 44 per cent of the British. It is apparent, therefore, that variations in the level of employment as such do not account for the national variations in gender-role attitudes, and the domestic division of labour, reported in this Chapter.

Gershuny and his colleagues (1994) argue that, over an extended period, the division of domestic labour is adapting to the changing circumstances of women's employment—a process they describe as 'lagged adaptation'. Many of the people who are having to adjust to the realities of women's paid employment themselves grew up and were socialized at a time when the division of labour in the household was more likely to be conventional. Normative attitudes acquired in childhood take time to change. This kind of argument, however,

TABLE 6.3. *GRA by DDL for Norway, Britain, and the Czech Republic* (%)

DDL	GRA					
	Norway**		Britain**		Czech Republic*	
	Liberal	Conservative	Liberal	Conservative	Liberal	Conservative
Traditional	35	51	41	56	57	66
Less traditional	65	49	59	44	43	34
	100	100	100	100	100	100
N	*877*	*387*	*342*	*196*	*218*	*403*
	(69%)	(31%)	(64%)	(36%)	(35%)	(65%)

* sig. at 95%.
** sig. at 99%.

Note: for couples who are married or living as married only.

really holds good only for Western Europe, as in the East the domestic division of labour has remained highly conventional, despite women's long-term labour-force participation. In the two Western countries under discussion here, (married) British women actually entered the labour force rather earlier than Norwegian women (90 per cent of married Norwegian women were still classified as 'housewives' in 1960), although, as we have seen, the domestic division of labour is rather less traditional in Norway, and attitudes to gender roles are more liberal.

However, even though the process of change may not be evenly spread, this does not mean that no changes are taking place. Gershuny *et al.*'s data (the results of a survey of UK households carried out in 1987) showed that men only did significantly more domestic work when their wives worked full-time. Non-employed wives with full-time husbands did approximately 83 per cent of unpaid household work, as compared to 82 per cent of part-time employed wives, but full-time employed wives of full-time employed husbands did 73 per cent—and the longer the wife had been in employment, the more domestic work the husband was likely to do.

Whether a woman works full-time, therefore, is clearly important. However, Gershuny *et al.*'s research also found that those couples who had parents with a relatively more egalitarian domestic division of labour were more likely to have a relatively egalitarian domestic division of labour themselves—suggesting that changes were taking place over time. They, therefore, compared the results of the 1987 survey with a similar survey carried out in 1975. This comparison showed that, in all household employment combinations (that is, whether the woman was not in employment, working full-time, or working part-time), the contribution of the husband to domestic work had increased. International comparisons also confirmed this general social trend. Gershuny *et al.* (1994: 184–5) conclude that:

With women's increasing entry into paid employment, so their total workload increases . . . But the increase is moderated, though not entirely offset, by the substitution of some male unpaid work for some female. The compensation is not complete, the women's paid work increases faster than the men's substitution of unpaid for paid work, but nevertheless a process of adaptation is clearly under way.

Gershuny *et al.*'s findings, therefore, suggest that the effect of women's employment *per se* on the domestic division of labour is becoming less important—although the process of change is very slow. Although we have (cross-sectional) longitudinal evidence only for Britain, the evidence in Table 6.4 lends support to this contention. Table 6.4 shows that, between 1988 and 1994, in Britain there has been a discernible increase in the extent to which these household tasks are reported as being shared between men and women, whatever the level of women's labour-force participation. Women's full-time work still makes a difference, but, nevertheless, there would seem to be a general trend in the direction of an increase in men's participation in domestic work. On the evidence of Table 6.3, it would seem that changing attitudes to gender roles are playing some part in this.

TABLE 6.4. *Distribution of household tasks, Britain, 1988 and 1994 (%)*

Task	Women's labour-force participation					
	Full-time		Part-time		Out of labour force	
Task	1988	1994	1988	1994	1988	1994
Washing and ironing						
mainly man	2	2	0	0	3	0
mainly woman	81	73	94	84	93	87
shared equally	17	24	6	16	4	14
Caring for sick member of family						
mainly man	2	0	3	0	2	0
mainly woman	58	51	66	55	82	54
shared equally	40	49	31	45	16	46

Note: for couples who are married or living as married only.

Source: ISSP data.

We would, however, emphasize that we are not arguing that the extent of a woman's material contribution does not have a considerable impact on the domestic division of labour. Table 6.5 shows that in all three countries, in households where the woman's earnings are equal to or more than those of the man, then the domestic division of labour is more likely to be less traditional—a finding that would broadly support the resource theory of power within marriage. As far as our cross-national comparisons are concerned, it is of interest that even in the Czech Republic, where the full-time employment of women has not had a substantial impact upon gender-role attitudes or the division of labour within the household, in situations where

TABLE 6.5. *Who earns more, the woman or the man, Norway, Britain, and the Czech Republic*

DDL	Norway*		Britain*		Czech Republic*	
	Man earns more	Equal/ woman earns more	Man earns more	Equal/ woman earns more	Man earns more	Equal/ woman earns more
Traditional	41	32	47	31	67	54
Less traditional	59	68	53	69	33	46
	100	100	100	100	100	100
N	862	260	230	62	428	114

* sig. at 95%

Note: for couples who are married or living as married only.

Source: ISSP data.

women earn more or equal salaries to those of men, then the domestic division of labour is likely to be less traditional.

In all three countries, therefore, both gender-role attitudes and the woman's economic contribution would seem to have an impact upon the domestic division of labour. The more liberal gender-role attitudes, the more likely the domestic division of labour is to be less traditional, and the more income a woman brings into the household (relative to the man), the less traditional the domestic division of labour.[9]

It would appear, therefore, that attitudinal changes (such as those that have been achieved in the Norwegian case) are of considerable significance in the reshaping the domestic division of labour. In order to assess the relative impact of material (women's employment, education level, and relative income), situational (age, sex, and family composition), and attitudinal factors, we carried out a logistic regression including GRA, with DDL as the dependent variable (Table 6.6). The logistic regression shows that there is a significant difference in the likelihood of a non-traditional division of labour in each of the three countries. Using Britain as our comparison, living in a Norwegian household raises chances of being in a household characterized by a non-traditional division of labour, by odds of 1.33. Conversely, in the

TABLE 6.6. *Logistic regression on DDL*

	Odds Ratio
Country (Britain is base case)	
Norway	1.33**
Czech Republic	0.55***
Age	0.97***
Child under 16 in household	0.58***
Sex: male	1.65***
Conservative gender-role attitudes	0.65***
Education (primary is base case)	
University (and incomplete university)	1.20
Secondary	1.12
Man earns more	0.77*
Woman earns more or equal	1.16
N	*2,408*
–2 Log likelihood of null hypothesis model	3,330.96
Model improvement	227.15***

* sig. at 95%.
** sig. at 99%.
*** sig. at 99.9%.

Czech Republic one is half as likely as in Britain (0.55) to experience an egalitarian division of labour in the household.

In all three countries, situational factors exert a major influence on the domestic division of labour. As one gets older, there is an incremental decrease in the likelihood of a non-traditional household division of labour, meaning that households of younger individuals are far more likely to be egalitarian than older people's households. This would support Gershuny *et al.*'s thesis that a process of lagged adaptation is under way, and that, as the younger age group moves through the life cycle, so gender-role attitudes will grow more liberal. Having a child under 16 in the household is another factor influencing a less equitable division of domestic tasks, reducing the likelihood of a non-traditional division of labour by odds of 0.58. The positive impact that being male has on the likelihood of having a non-traditional division of labour in the household (odds increase by 1.65) reflects the fact that, in the ISSP surveys, men are more likely than women to report a non-traditional division of labour.

While analyses and explanations of gendered inequalities within household division of labour have tended to focus on women's employment status, our analysis shows gender-role attitudes exerting an important influence as well as 'structural' factors. Holding conservative gender-role attitudes reduces the likelihood of a non-traditional household division of labour by odds of 0.65. This parallels the results of Benjamin and Sullivan (1997) and Marx-Feree (1991), who found attitudes to be an important determinant of a more equitable division of household labour.

A higher level of education is generally associated with an increased likelihood of a non-traditional domestic division of labour. In our initial cross-tabulations of education and the domestic division of labour, this association was significantly demonstrated in the case of Norway and the Czech Republic. However, in the UK case, there was no significant association between these two variables. In the logistic regression model, the odds ratios for the positive influence of higher levels of education on a non-traditional division of labour were not significant.

The model also shows that, where the male earns more than the female in a partnership, there is less likely to be a non-traditional division of household labour.[10] Perhaps rather surprisingly, given the emphasis that female employment status has been given in accounting for inequality in the domestic division of labour, this did not emerge as significant in our model and is excluded (the employment status variable is in fact rather unsatisfactory, so perhaps too much should not be read into this finding).[11]

The logistic regression demonstrated a significant country effect in explaining the domestic division of labour, in addition to situational, attitudinal and material effects. We ran the same model for each nation, rather than including country as an independent variable. It differs from the previous logistic regression in that women's employent status, which is not significant in the earlier model, is omitted. The results are shown in Table 6.7.

When the logistic regression is run separately for each country, situational factors continue to predominate. They are particularly important in the British case. Age exerts a very similar level of influence in the separate country models, as it did in the combined model: the greater one's age, the less likely one is to have a non-traditional household division of labour. Having a child under 16 in the household significantly reduces the odds of a more egalitarian division of labour, with this situational factor having the greatest impact in the UK. Conservative gender-role attitudes were found to reduce the likelihood of a non-traditional domestic division of labour in all three countries. In terms of material factors, a higher than primary-school level of education raises the likelihood of a non-traditional division of labour in Norway and the Czech Republic, while reducing its likelihood in the Britain.[12]

In respect of relative earnings within a couple, a man earning more than his female partner appears to be associated with a more traditional domestic division of labour in all three countries. Conversely, the ratios for a woman earning more or equal to her male partner are greater than 1, in both Norway and Britain, suggesting that this raises the chances of domestic labour being non-traditional. The ratios, however, are not significant.

The different performance of these material variables in country-specific logistic regression models, therefore, is suggestive of national variations in the impact of different factors on the domestic division of labour.

Occupational Variations

Our discussion so far has emphasized the importance of national differences in the shaping of gender-role attitudes, and their effects

TABLE 6.7. *Logistic Regression on DDL for each country*

	Odds ratios		
	Norway	Britain	Czech Republic
Age	0.97**	0.96***	0.98**
Child under 16 in household	0.63***	0.48**	0.51**
Sex: male	1.53***	2.08***	1.57**
Conservative gender-role attitudes	0.70**	0.57***	0.68*
Education (primary is base case)			
University (and incomplete university)	1.51**	0.78	0.96
Secondary	1.22	0.62*	1.48*
Man earns more	0.88	0.79	0.61*
Woman earns more or equal	1.23	1.36	0.99
N	*1,256*	*531*	*621*
−2 Log likelihood of null hypothesis model	1,691.10	732.30	815.60
Model improvement	78.40***	46.23***	32.26***

* sig. at 95%.
** sig. at 99%.
*** sig. at 99.9%.

upon the domestic division of labour. In each country, however, similar situational factors—particularly age, and the presence of children—also have an impact. In this section, we will present evidence that suggests that another important structural factor—the nature of a woman's occupation—also has an impact on the domestic division of labour, and that the nature of this impact is very similar across different nation states.

Our research included the collection of biographical interviews from thirty women in each of the three countries under discussion in this chapter, in two different occupations: medicine (qualified and registered doctors) and banking (managers) (that is, fifteen women in each occupation were interviewed in each country).[13] These occupations had been selected in order to highlight a number of employment contrasts, including rates of feminization, public versus private, and professional versus managerial employment. Table 6.8 shows that there are significant differences in both family building

TABLE 6.8. *Occupational variations in career intentions, children, and the domestic division of labour (%)*

	Doctors	Bankers
Early career/family intentions **		
Put career first, or 'just drifted'	42	76
Career decision shaped by anticipated family responsibilities	58	24
N	*43*	*45*
Children		
None, or only one child	41	62
More than one child	59	38
N	*44*	*47*
Own domestic division of labour *		
Traditional (respondent does most)	73	46
Other+	27	54
N	*41*	*41*
Childcare **		
Respondent main responsibility	74	38
Other+	26	62
N	*31*	*29*

* sig. at 95%.
** sig. at 99%.
+ includes shared with partner, partner does most, and help from others (paid/relative).

and the domestic division of labour between the women in the two occupations. In particular, women doctors have a considerably more traditional domestic division of labour than the bankers.

We would argue that the differences summarized in Table 6.8 derive from the contrast between 'professional' and 'managerial' occupations. The classic profession is characterized by a formal and extensive body of knowledge and expertise that is acquired through a long period of training. Professional standards are nationally (and usually internationally) recognized. Once the training and registration period has been completed, the professional is in possession of a 'licence to practise'. There has been a massive expansion of management training, but managers, unlike professionals, do not require a 'licence to practise'. Managerial careers are forged in an organizational context. In the classic bureaucratic model of organizations, the bureaucratic hierarchy provides a series of graded occupational slots to which managers can aspire. Trends, including 'delayering' and organizational 'downsizing', have had a considerable impact on the traditional bureaucratic career. However, this has not transformed the fundamental difference between classic professional and managerial occupations, which is that professional knowledge and expertise are regulated by an external standard, whereas managerial expertise is directly evaluated by the employing organization.

Once into their training, therefore, doctors know what to expect in career terms. We would suggest that the long period of training required of doctors has a tendency to be associated with the 'forward planning' of the domestic career as well, which is reflected in the choice of medical specialties. As we shall see in Chapter 9, in all countries, women doctors tend to opt for specialties (such as general practice, dermatology, etc.), that enable them to achieve some regularity in their working hours. In Chapter 7, we argue that this planning of medical and family careers is associated with 'satisficing' behaviour on the part of women doctors (that is, reaching a reasonably high level in respect of both employment and family goals rather than seeking to maximize either (see Chafetz and Hagan 1996)), through which conventional assumptions about domestic work (that is, that it will be organized by the woman) tend to be reproduced. This 'satisficing' strategy is reinforced by the wide availability of flexible and part-time work in medicine.[14] In contrast, in banking there is no long period of formal training before taking up employment, and expertise is acquired whilst in a job. Changes in the organization of banking services have (unlike medicine) changed the *content* of managerial jobs.[15] The rapidity of organizational change means that women in bank management have not, historically, been able to contemplate the long-term forward planning of their employment and family careers to the same extent as doctors. In the employment context of banking, a 'satisficing' strategy for women would normally be associated with a move to part-time working, found only amongst non-managerial staff. Thus employment flexibility is problematic for women managers, and, rather than merely 'satisfice', women managers with enhanced domestic responsibilities will seek to make changes in the organization of domestic work in their households.

In the 1970s and 80s, the masculinist 'sociology of work' tradition was criticized for its assumption that women's social position and attitudes were determined by their family and gender roles rather than their employment. As Feldberg and Glenn (1979) argued, in the industrial sociology of the 1950s, 1960s, and 1970s discussions of male workers used a 'job model', in which work as employment was seen as determining social position and socio-political behaviour, whereas studies of women workers assumed that social position and attitudes were determined, not by employment, but rather by family and gender roles. We have here inverted this critique by demonstrating that the nature of a woman's employment is significant in determining the nature of her family and gender roles. In a similar vein, Benjamin and Sullivan (1997) have demonstrated how different occupations are characterized by a differential access to therapeutic discourses (such as counselling and psychotherapy) that affects the level of a woman's relational resources, and thus her capacity to transform her interpersonal relationships. They found that women in occupations that facilitated access to such discourses (for example, social workers and marriage guidance counsellors) had developed greater relational resources than women in other occupations, such as accountancy—and had been more likely to renegotiate their domestic lives.

Conclusion

In making these contrasts between three rather different countries, we have shown that, as might have been anticipated, more liberal gender-role attitudes are associated with a less traditional domestic division of labour. Indeed, our data suggest that attitudes have a considerably greater impact on the domestic division of labour than women's employment *per se*. In national terms, it may be suggested that these attitudinal variations are reflected in the relative national impact of second-wave feminism and its impact on state policies. This has been most substantial in the woman-friendly Norwegian state, followed by the British government's acceptance of the equality agenda—but not affirmative action. In the case of the Czech Republic, second-wave feminism has not had an impact, and, indeed, 'feminist' ideas are seen to be associated with the recently rejected state-socialist past.

This emphasis upon the importance of attitudes in shaping behaviour does not mean that we are necessarily optimistic as to the continuing development of more liberal gender-role attitudes and a less traditional gender division of labour in the future, as is implied in Gershuny *et al.*'s thesis of lagged adaptation. Indeed, the very interdependence of attitudes and behaviour may be an indication of the underlying fragility of change in the area of gender roles and gender relations. Attitudes may become more conservative, as well as more liberal. For those supporting gender equality, therefore, the evidence discussed in this chapter does not necessarily give any grounds for complacency.

Neither does our emphasis on attitudes imply that we consider material factors to be unimportant. A woman's economic contribution to the household through employment is clearly likely to be linked to a less traditional division of labour within it. Even here, however, the pattern of causation is far from straightforward. Changes in gender relations, and in the domestic division of labour, are in the last instance a reflection of the negotiation and renegotiation of interpersonal relationships between men and women. Our occupational studies (as do those of Benjamin and Sullivan) suggest that the extent of these possibilities of renegotiation are systematically associated with particular occupations. Many women doctors appear to be 'tracked' into 'satisficing' behaviour at a relatively early stage of their career development, and thus locked into a relatively traditional division of domestic labour—despite the fact that they are holding down demanding jobs. In contrast, women bank managers who have managed to succeed in the rapidly changing organizational climate of the 1990s seem often to have changed their personal lives as well, and are characterized by a less traditional division of domestic labour. These kinds of occupational variations suggest that further research on this topic should continue to explore not only the interaction between the *extent* of women's paid work and the domestic division of labour, but also the more complex issue of how the *form* of the gendered restructuring of employment meshes with domestic work—both paid and unpaid.

NOTES

1. For a description of the ISSP programme, see Davis and Jowell (1989); also Jowell *et al.* (1993). Thanks are due to Social and Community Planning Research (SCPR), London; The Gender Studies Centre, Institute of Sociology, Academy of Sciences, Prague; and Norwegian Social Science Data Services, Bergen, for giving access to the data. The ESRC data archive has also given access to a (preliminary) spliced data set.
2. All of these responses were made via a five-point scale ranging from 'strongly agree' through 'neither agree nor disagree' to 'strongly disagree'. A simple gender conservatism–liberalism scale was constructed as follows: strongly agree 2, agree 1, disagree −1, strongly disagree −2. 'Neither agree nor disagree' and 'don't know' answers were scored 0. These scores were averaged. Thus the maximum gender conservatism score was 2, and the maximum gender liberalism score was −2. However, a zero score on any item will bring down the value disproportionately.
3. The original derivation of the index is discussed in Crompton and Harris (1996). This paper also demonstrates the robustness of the GRA index.
4. Answers could fall into three main categories: mainly women; mainly men; or shared equally. Those replying 'mainly women' on both items were classified as 'traditional', those answering 'mainly men' or 'shared' on either item were classified as 'less-traditional'. We are aware that this is a very generous measure of 'less traditional'. Other possible items that might have been used in constructing a measure included questions on shopping, deciding what to have for dinner, and domestic repairs. The answers to these questions reflected the rather different consumption (i.e. retail distribution) contexts in Western and Eastern Europe that prevailed at the time of the interviews, raising questions as to their suitability as a measure of the *domestic* division of labour. The items used both relate to activities carried out within the household.
5. The Labour government has recently (1998) introduced a series of measures to increase childcare provision, largely with the aim of facilitating the entry into the labour market of lone mothers.
6. It should also be pointed out that, despite the historically lower level of childcare, the labour-force participation rate of Norwegian women is one of the highest in Europe—70.9%—equal to that of Finland and less than 10% lower than Sweden and Denmark (see OECD 1994:192).
7. The Czech Republic was formed out of the division of Czechoslovakia into the Czech Republic and Slovenia, which took place at the end of 1994. The most recent data given are for the Czech Republic, but much of the information given here relates to the 'Czechoslovakian' period.

8. In dichotomizing GRA, a decision had to be made as to the allocation of neutral respondents—i.e. those with a zero score. Comparisons of GRA with the answers to other attitudinal questions suggested that, in fact, 'neutrals' in the West were conservative, whereas 'neutrals' in the East were liberal, and they were allocated accordingly.

9. It will be noted (Table 6.5) that the proportion in employment in the British sample was lower than in either the Czech Republic or Norway. This was due to the substantial proportion of British respondents over 50 who were out of the labour force or unemployed.

10. The data for 'who earns more' in a partnership had a large number of missing values, which drastically reduced the size of the sample. To maintain sample size, missing values for 'who earns more' were set as a dummy in the logistic regression model.

11. Accurate employment status data were available only for female respondents. For male respondents, information was available only as to whether their female partners were in employment or not and no other details were available.

12. However, cross-tabulation of the domestic division of labour against education levels shows that, as the level of education increases, so does the likelihood of a non-traditional division of labour, although the Chi square value is not significant, indicating that the trend may be random. The incompatibility between the cross-tabulation and the logistic regression result suggests that this is a maverick result, or one that may be explained by an interaction effect.

13. See the description of the Gender Relations project in Chapter 1. Table 6.8 draws upon the Norwegian, British, and Czech interviews only.

14. The point may be made that this generalization is valid only for the West, as part-time work was/is virtually unknown in Eastern Europe. However, our interviews suggest that considerable latitude was given to the mothers of small children—taking time off when they were sick, leaving early to collect them from school. Indeed, it was suggested that 'marketization' was going to make the combination of work and childcare more difficult, as these practices were likely to disappear.

15. For example, there is now much more of an emphasis upon the selling of financial services in the West. Changes in the organization of financial services in the East have been even greater.

7

Employment, Careers, and Families: The Significance of Choice and Constraint in Women's Lives

ROSEMARY CROMPTON
AND FIONA HARRIS

INTRODUCTION

In Chapter 1, it was emphasized that the complexity of the processes structuring gender relations and gender systems, and the divisions of labour associated with them, mean that it is important to take a position of theoretical and methodological pluralism. As Folbre (1994: 4) has argued, we need to develop an approach that 'emphasizes choice *and* constraint, co-operation *and* conflict, individual *and* group dynamics'.

In this chapter, we will develop these arguments through an in-depth investigation of the ways in which the women interviewed for the Gender Relations project had 'managed' their employment and family lives. We have already noted in Chapter 6 the differences in work–family arrangements as between professional and managerial occupations—a point that we will be exploring in the further analysis of our interview material. In our discussions, we will also address a recent version of the argument that the division of labour between men and women, and the occupational variations reflected in this division of labour, are to be seen largely as being a consequence of the innate differences between men and women. This essentialist argument lays particular emphasis on the choices made by different types of women and the weight that they place on domestic and employment careers (Hakim 1996).

This chapter draws upon the extensive coding exercises that we have undertaken in relation to the interview material. In the next section, therefore, we will raise a number of issues relating to methodology and interpretation.

GENDER RELATIONS AND EMPLOYMENT: SOME NOTES ON METHOD

In the Gender Relations project, the initial strategy of analysis was to identify and describe relevant structural factors that, so to speak, offered a 'gendered template' to the women in the different countries under investigation. It has been demonstrated that, at the macro-level, national differences in respect of crucial institutions—in particular, the development of the welfare state, family (reproductive) policies, and the approach to the liberal equality agenda instantiated by first-wave feminism—have had a significant and enduring impact on attitudes to gender relations (Crompton and Harris 1997*a*). Similar arguments have been elaborated and developed in Chapters 2–5 of this book. In Chapter 6, it was demonstrated that these variations in attitude are linked to behavioural differences in respect of the domestic division of labour (Crompton and Harris 1997*a*). Through an initial analysis of two feminizing occupations, medicine and banking, we have also suggested that the occupational structure plays an important role in shaping relatively more, or less, stereotyped gender divisions of labour and thus gender identities. Doctors have more children than bankers, and are also more likely to have a relatively conventional domestic division of labour (Crompton and Harris 1997*b*).

As described in Chapter 1, we have collected over 150 work-life biographies from women in two occupations—medicine and banking—in five countries. This strategy was adopted for methodological and theoretical reasons. The narrow focus has enabled us to achieve a measure of cross-national comparability, and the occupations were selected so as to illustrate particular trends relating to occupational feminization—in particular, the contrast between managerial and professional occupations. Previous research (Crompton and Sanderson 1990; Savage 1992) had suggested that women moving into higher-level occupations tended to be concentrated into 'professional niches' associated with high levels of expertise, but not managerial authority. One of our initial research objectives has always been, therefore, to explore this contrast and its consequences further. All interviewers used a common Topic Guide (see Appendix).[1] Relevant extracts of translated interviews were transcribed onto a common Recording Document.

The analysis of the data presented some practical problems. Consideration was given to the possibility of using a qualitative data-analysis package such as NUD*IST (Richards and Richards 1994). However, as NUD*IST essentially rests on a content analysis, there seemed to be serious problems in applying these techniques to translated texts (the linguistic idiosyncrasies of particular translators could lead to systematic 'findings' that might be artefacts of translation).

The first step in the analysis of the interview material, therefore, was a fine-grained coding exercise that recorded, for each interviewee, as much of the demographic and work-life history information on record as possible. This exercise, as we have described in the previous chapter, revealed a series of systematic differences between the doctors and the bankers. We will be discussing some further evidence from this first coding exercise in the next section of this chapter. As in all such analyses of qualitative research, we have also been able to draw upon sections of the transcripts that give a particularly apt illustration of the categories we identify and arguments we develop.

However, with over 150 interviews, it is difficult to capture the 'flavour' of the whole via selected quotes alone.[2] Although occupational contrasts had been brought out in the initial coding, this exercise nevertheless did not grasp the uniqueness of the individual biographies. This problem was addressed by developing a procedure that may be described as 'holistic' coding. The authors read every interview and wrote a paragraph giving biographical details, emphasizing the 'presentations of self' emerging from the Recording Documents. These focused both upon the interviewees' accounts of their management of their employment and family careers, and upon any turning points ('epiphanies' (Denzin 1989)) in either. This exercise was carried out several months after the initial coding exercise, and independently of it. Sixty pages of text resulted. We then developed coding frames relating to these focuses, and each researcher recoded independently, cross-checking the categories. The categories identified in the second round of coding were then analysed in relation to the first round of coding. As we shall see, these comparisons confirmed the reliability of the second-round 'holistic' coding (see Tables 7.1, 7.2, and 7.4).

The quantitative analysis of qualitative data raises a number of problems that are well known. First, there is the possibility that the researcher may effectively 'force' the cases in question into the researchers' own predetermined categories, thus reflecting the views of the researchers, rather than the respondents. Secondly, if such an exercise is carried out on a 'sample' that is too small, or non-random, the results of such quantification may in any case be spurious. We would suggest that the first problem has been to some extent met in the Gender Relations study by the cross-checking of two independent coding exercises, the first non-interpretative, the second 'holistic' (or interpretative). The second problem cannot be dealt with directly. Here our argument would rest upon the *consistency* of the direction of the findings (particularly as relating to occupational differences), as well as their magnitude. Before we develop the analysis of our findings, however, we will give a brief account of Hakim's recent arguments concerning the significance of women's choices in the management of their work and family lives, and the outcomes of these choices for the structure of female employment.

'GRATEFUL SLAVES' AND 'SELF-MADE' WOMEN: A VOLUNTARIST ACCOUNT OF OCCUPATIONAL SEGREGATION

Hakim (1991, 1995, 1996) has argued that women's employment patterns, as manifest in occupational segregation, part-time or non-standard working, and so on, are not a consequence of the institutional and/or structural disadvantages suffered by women, but rather, reflect the outcome of their varying choices. There are, she asserts, three 'qualitatively different' types of working woman, the 'committed', the 'uncommitted', and the 'drifters' or 'adaptives'. Committed women give priority to their employment careers; uncommitted women give priority to their domestic responsibilities. Adaptives or drifters have 'chaotically unplanned' careers and their activities 'probably defy explanation' (Hakim 1996). However, this latter grouping has recently acquired more prominence in her classification of female types in her development of 'preference theory'. She argues that they are probably the largest female category, and the most responsive to government policies.

Committed women work full-time; they are 'self-made' women in Hakim's terms; uncommitted women work part-time. The existence of these different orientations to employment, Hakim argues, explains the apparently contradictory finding that part-time workers (in Britain) express themselves as highly 'satisfied' with their low-level, poorly paid, employment (they are described by Hakim as 'grateful slaves'). Hakim goes on to argue that feminists have deliberately perpetrated 'fashionable but untrue' ideas concerning women's employment preferences (and related employment patterns) for overtly political reasons—that is, in order effectively to 'dictate . . . a narrow range of acceptable conclusions . . . that women are victims who have little or no responsibility for their situation' (1995: 448).

The deliberately provocative tenor of Hakim's recent commentaries has generated a number of critical replies (Bruegel 1996; Ginn *et al.* 1996). We would agree that she has set up straw feminists in constructing her arguments, and that it would be difficult to find academic feminists (none is actually identified by Hakim) who have claimed either that women are an undifferentiated mass in respect of their employment preferences, or that there are no differences at all between men and women as employees. We would also agree that some of her empirical procedures are highly questionable—for example, in treating hours worked as being more significant than numbers of jobs, and including a population group that was not actually asked a question in calculating an averaged 'response' to it.[3] Our purpose here, however, is not to extend these criticisms of the details of Hakim's arguments further. Rather, through an analysis of the *processes* through which women arrive at different combinations of employment and family biographies, we will demonstrate how both 'choice' and 'constraint' play their part. We will also show how women's intentions and actions change, and vary over time and with circumstances. This should make us cautious of using fixed categories in order to explain women's (or men's (see Crompton and Harris 1998*a*)) employment behaviour.

In contrast to our approach (which may be described as working from the 'bottom up'—that is, taking the individual as a starting point of the analysis), Hakim's argument moves directly from the macro-categories she identifies to the micro-level. Women in part-time employment, we are told, have 'chosen' to give priority to a marriage career, and no account is given of the mechanisms whereby this 'choice' of marriage career was arrived at.[4] Whilst asserting that 'Some women choose to be home-centred, with work a secondary activity', and 'Some women choose to be career-centred, with domestic activities a secondary consideration' (1996: 186), Hakim simultaneously holds that 'some women will switch between groups over their lifetime', thus contriving to have the argument all ways at once. Again, no suggestion is given as to why 'some women' might choose to change categories rather than remain in one or the other.

The existence of these different types of women lends support to both rational-choice and human-capital theories, argues Hakim. Uncommitted women make a rational decision to economize on the effort invested in employment, as this is not their main priority. In contrast, committed women, in line with the prescriptions of human-capital theory, will choose to invest in their employment careers. This fact of heterogeneous female preferences provides a link between psychological theories of male dominance and the concept of patriarchy (Hakim 1996: 212). Goldberg (1973; 1993, cited in Hakim 1996: 5) argues that hormonal differences between men and women make men more 'self-assertive, aggressive, dominant and competitive'. The fact that women are fundamentally divided within themselves, Hakim argues, serves to amplify the effect of these natural masculine characteristics, and men are, as a consequence, disproportionately successful.

In this chapter, therefore, we will be using the evidence of the work-life biographical interviews in order to focus upon the way in which different women, as gendered subjects, actively interpret their identities and 'work on' their lives. As we shall see, these processes have led to a diverse range of outcomes, even amongst women who, in Hakim's terms, might be considered highly committed to their employment. We shall also explore the extent to which women had changed the direction of their family or working lives, and the reasons for these changes.

MANAGING EMPLOYMENT AND FAMILY LIVES

In Chapter 5, using evidence from the first, non-interpretative, round of coding, we highlighted the differences in the employment—family biographies of the doctors and bankers. The doctors had had more children, taken a greater responsibility for childcare, and were more likely to live in partnerships with a relatively traditional division of domestic labour. We would link these differences in the work–family biographies between the two occupations to ideal-typical differences in professional and managerial career trajectories, and their characteristic interaction with the family life cycle. The classic profession is characterized by a formal and extensive body of knowledge and expertise, which is acquired through a long period of training. Once the training and registration period has been completed, the professional is in possession of a 'licence to practise'. Professional work such as medicine is largely concerned with the application of a recognized body of skills and expertise. As such, it may be purchased in flexible tranches as and when required. Managers, unlike professionals, do not require a 'licence to practise'. Managerial careers are forged in an organizational context. The fundamental difference between classic professional and managerial occupations that is being emphasized here, therefore, is that professional knowledge and expertise are regulated by an external standard, whereas managerial expertise is directly evaluated by the employing organization.

The long period of training required of doctors means that the domestic career also has to be planned, and many women doctors choose medical specialties that enable them to continue in professional practice (we will be examining these processes in even greater depth in Chapter 9). Thus conventional assumptions about domestic work (that is, that it will be organized by the woman) tend to be reproduced. The profession is rigidly structured, which makes it very difficult to alter working patterns once a medical specialism is chosen, but does enable women to plan ahead for their family lives by selecting specialisms that have more controllable hours, or are more likely to facilitate part-time work. Thus, whilst such structuring enables women to better manage the work–family interface, at the individual level, these kinds of biographies reproduce a relatively conventional gender division of labour that feeds through to the occupational level.

In contrast, bankers find it difficult to make family–friendly working arrangements, have fewer children, and are more likely to have a less stereotyped gender division of labour. The organizational structure is such that those seeking a managerial career are locked into traditional, inflexible working practices. Working part-time or taking extended leave to care for children is not a viable option if a woman seeks to move upwards through the organizational hierarchy. With little scope to choose or negotiate working practices, bankers who have continued to juggle work and family life have, out of necessity, had to negotiate changes in their domestic circumstances. Family life is forcibly adapted to the obstinate intractability of organizational work practices. A banker describes her domestic division of labour:

We work as a team. [She leaves the house at 7.30 to take their son to nursery, and gets into work by about 8.50. Her husband picks up son at night, so she can work later, and make up time. Husband makes the tea, she feeds, bathes and gets son ready for bed.] We have to have quite a strict structure. [They would like another child but] The thought of trying to work with two children fills me with cold horror . . . the logistics of trying to do it are very very hard . . . and it physically wears you out.   (2/30 Britain, banker)[5]

A Norwegian banker had planned her anticipated family life with her husband, who has gradually assumed a greater share of the childcare responsibilities. When the children were born, she stayed at home for the first six months and then her husband was home for the second six months:

My husband began to stay at home one day a week when the last child was born . . . it was getting too much to send them out every day . . . When I was starting at business college I knew I wanted to 'go the distance' and we discussed how to do this . . . if he was going to work hard at his career than it would have been too much . . . he was happy with where he was . . . that's the reason he was the one to take the day off.   (3/33, three children)

At the individual level, therefore, these biographies are more likely to generate non-stereotypical gender relations at the interpersonal level—although men continue to dominate within the organizational structure of banking. More detailed analysis of the first coding round served to confirm our arguments as to the significance of the 'occupational effect'. For the respondents with children, a composite childcare code listed every possible childcare arrangement—in-house nannies, childminders, kindergartens or nurseries, relatives and husband or partner (many women, of course, had used more than one kind of childcare). We also included extended care by mothers such as a child-rearing employment break and/or a switch to part-time work. We found very little evidence of variation in the kinds of childcare arrangements used by doctors and bankers—with one exception. Fifty-four per cent of bankers reported that husbands or partners had helped with childcare, as compared to only 26 per cent of doctors. This finding supports our argument that the circumstances of bankers are such as to 'force' a relatively less stereotyped gender division of domestic labour.

It is possible, however, that this argument for the significance of the occupational effect on child-rearing strategies will be distorted by the fact that bankers will have had rather different occupational trajectories from doctors. Doctors will be unlikely to have experienced any occupational change (indeed, only six—8 per cent—of the doctors interviewed reported this), but many of the bankers will have done so. Forty-six per cent of the bankers interviewed had changed their occupation. Thus, many of the bankers will not have been employed in banking around the time that they had their children, thus undermining our case for the significance of the occupational effect. However, more detailed analysis revealed that, of the bankers who had had their children whilst pursuing a career in banking, fully 71 per cent cited their partners as a childcare 'resource'—thus confirming our original hypothesis.

Occupational demands, therefore, impact on family and domestic relations and thus the way in which men and women 'do gender' in a practical sense. It is from these kinds of beginnings, we would suggest, that wider normative changes in attitudes to gender relations develop. Very simply, as Chafetz and Hagan (1996: 200) have argued: 'when a large number of people begin to behave in a way that differs from past behaviours of that population . . . many will gradually begin to perceive and evaluate their world in ways that differ from characteristic definitions of the past'. Chafetz and Hagan argue that, with the growth of married women's employment, increasingly, women will attempt to 'satisfice'—that is, to achieve success in employment and family life without maximizing either set of goals. They suggest that today women (but not men) face conflicting demands between success in the public sphere of paid employment, on the one hand, and successful familial and domestic relationships, on the other. There are a number of problems with this argument. It may be suggested that, increasingly, *men* are placing a higher priority on family and domestic life. It may also be pointed out that to achieve more than one goal at the required level is best described as 'maximizing', rather than 'satisficing'. Nevertheless, there can be little doubt that the demands of employment and family *are* often in conflict, and that many women (and some men) will consciously make sacrifices in one sphere or both.

In developing the categories of the holistic coding, therefore, the notion of 'satisficing' was used as a starting point from which to develop a classification of employment and family-life management amongst the women we interviewed. The largest single category we identified had indeed 'satisficed'—that is, there had been a conscious scaling-down of employment and/or family goals in order to achieve their combination.

In some ways I feel I've had the best of both worlds, and in some ways I've had the worst of both worlds 'cos I haven't been a real mummy-mummy . . . I can't go and help at school . . . and then you lose out at work because you're not there every day . . . It's a compromise, and it suits me . . . I think perhaps I could have had a more dynamic career, if that is what I'd wanted.   (2/07 Britain, consultant anaesthetist (part-time), three children)

However, other women, whilst realizing both goals to some extent, had definitely given priority to their domestic lives:

I always wanted a family and from home, I knew what was involved (her parents are doctors, her husband a surgeon). I took my husband's job into account when I was deciding on my specialism, when I decided to marry him I knew that his job would come first . . . I knew I would support him . . . in this sense, I am the 'second sex'.   (1/05 Czech Republic, radiologist, two children)

Others, rather than 'satisficing', had refused to compromise and had sought to maximize their goals in respect of both employment careers and family lives. For example, a Czech banker (1/21) divorced her husband 'because he did not know whether he wanted a competent woman or a hen' and now lives with her new partner and her daughter—but does not intend to marry. Looking back on her career, she 'knows that some personal qualities make life difficult for me, but I take no notice. It is important for me to be myself and I am not interested in male ways of making a career'. Nevertheless, she is in charge of a department of 150 people and has developed a pricing system that has been adopted nationally.

   We have coded such women as 'maximizers', separately from the 'careerists'—that is, women who consciously put their employment careers before their families. We identified two categories of 'careerist': by choice, and of necessity. In the former category, women have indicated their deliberate decision to give priority to their employment careers, often by deciding not to marry or have children:

At 36 years old, with a very intensive professional life . . . If I were to have children, I think that I should have had them earlier. To be perfectly honest, the institution I work for is not very conducive to having children . . . the decision not to have children is really a very important one, I'm giving it a lot of thought. It's the sort of decision that I might well regret as time goes on, but, to be quite honest, the kind of pressure I'm under at work means that I wouldn't be in a position to give a child the right kind of upbringing. (5/10 France, medecin conseil, cohabiting)

'Careerists by necessity', however, are women who have felt constrained to give priority to their employment careers—as a consequence of circumstances such as divorce or other personal and/or economic crises such as the collapse of state socialism in Eastern Europe:

. . . in 1993 my husband died. So I found myself alone with my child, and the elderly parents. And I had to think hard about how to earn money in order to maintain, to some extent, the welfare level we had before the death of my husband . . . I had to leave the work I liked (teaching) and take a money-making job, a job with a very strict time schedule requiring everyday presence at work and overtime work in the evenings.   (4/25 Russian, banker, 1 child)

As can be seen from Table 7.1, all 'careerists by necessity' were bankers (it is simply not possible to decide that a career in medicine is the answer to pressing financial difficulties!). Table 7.1 reflects the occupational variations that we had already identified in our first round of non-interpretative coding. In total, 61 per cent of the doctors had satisficed or put their family lives first, as against 41 per cent of the bankers. An interesting outcome of our exercise in classification, however, is that the proportion of 'maximizers' and 'careerists by choice' did not vary as between the two occupations—a point to which we will shortly return.

TABLE 7.1. *Occupational variations in types of employment and family-life management (%)*

Employment/family management	Doctors	Bankers
Domestic life first	24	15
Satisficer	37	26
Maximizer	17	15
Careerist (by choice)	16	19
Careerist (by necessity)	—	15
Unclear/undecided	5	9
N^a	*75*	*78*

^a Includes all five countries.

Occupational differences were also reflected in the reasons given by respondents for changes in their work-life biographies, which were also identified in our second round of coding (Table 7.2). Changes in work-life biographies reflected 'epiphanies', or turning-points—that is, moments when a decision had been taken to change career direction in one way or another. For example, a British banker took maternity leave (whilst still on a clerical grade), and in her absence other staff were upgraded (she was not):

I was absolutely incensed, and I think that's what did it . . . it took me to 25 to really wake up and say well this isn't acceptable, I won't have it . . . that's the time that I decided I've got to wake up, and that in this organization if you make things happen, they're only going to happen if you do it. Nobody's going to come along and help you. I think that was the rude awakening for me, a bit late in the day.   (2/37)

A Russian woman banker had grown up on a collective farm and married (at 17) an actor who came with a concert brigade to their village. They moved to Moscow:

I had to find a job. At first I worked for some years in the job I'd trained for at technical school—as a shop assistant. But one day something happened that changed all my life. I was working in a department store at that time and when I was serving a customer, she told me something that seemed awfully humiliating to me. She said, 'If you had an education, you would not be standing here at the counter.' It was then that I decided to get (a) higher education at all costs.   (4/30)

Occupational turning-points were not a specific topic identified in either the interview guide or the recording document, but the issue nevertheless emerged very clearly in over three-quarters of the interviews.

TABLE 7.2. *Occupational variations in changes in work-life biographies (%)*

Change in work-life biography	Doctors	Bankers
Family life course change	43	15
External or organizational shock/change	4	35
Personal life (crisis) change	26	14
Self-development change	3	17
No change	25	19
N	*75*	*78*

Doctors were far more likely to have altered their work-life biographies as a response to changes over the family life cycle—for example, taking up part-time work, or a less demanding job, when children are young (e.g. deciding not to specialize but to take up general practice). A Czech doctor (married, two children) had to decide whether to continue with private work or not:[6]

I was more and more busy, I wasn't happy about it at all . . . my children were just coming up to the age of puberty and I felt they needed me more than ever . . . I was working for a pharmaceutical company . . . suddenly I decided that I was only going to do the most important, most fundamental things to do with my job, so that my family wouldn't lose out.　(1/13)

Bankers, however, are more likely to have changed career direction in response to *external* 'shocks'—such as organizational restructuring, or economic crises such as those that accompanied the collapse of state socialism in Eastern Europe. Personal life crises have been classified separately, and would include, for example, reactions to the break-up of a relationship, or the death of a close relative. A French banker with two grown-up daughters describes the situation she faced:

I don't have a husband . . . I was separated a long time ago, when the children were young and I brought them up by myself . . . and then my husband died (four years after the separation) . . . and there you are . . . *I had to make a choice*, to make a professional life or (another) marital life . . . it wasn't the marital life I chose . . . I can stay (at work) until six or seven o'clock . . . I don't have a husband to say that the dinner isn't ready or who's invited his friends round.　(5/30)

The distribution by occupation of the categories developed in the second round of coding, therefore, tended to confirm the explanations relating to the occupational impact on work–family careers that we had developed as a consequence of our initial analyses. Hakim's argument that women's labour-market behaviour may be explained as corresponding to the choices made by different types of women, therefore, would seem to be contradicted by this evidence, which has emphasized the significance of structural (occupational) constraints in the shaping of women's employment and family lives. Hakim identifies her categories of women on the basis of US longitudinal survey evidence reported in 1987, which demonstrated an association between employment and family-life preferences expressed as teenagers and adult work-life combinations. These categories are then mapped onto British data gathered in 1980.[7] However, our evidence suggests that any explanation based upon individual choice or preferences must be supplemented by an account of the structural factors shaping these choices. Nevertheless, it may still be argued that self-selection is important in explaining our results, in that the kinds of women who train for medicine are very different people from the kinds of women who become bank managers. However, an examination of the backgrounds of the women interviewed suggested a remarkable similarity of social origins and early experiences as between women in the two occupations (Table 7.3).

TABLE 7.3. *Personal characteristics of respondents, selected items (%)*

	Doctors	Bankers
Family background		
Father's occupation higher professional/		
managerial	46	43
Childhood experiences:		
Mother did not work when respondent		
was pre-school age	48	46
Only child	18	21
Encouraged by parents to do well	67	63
Encouraged by school to do well	31	29
Present circumstances:		
Lives with partner, dependent children	53	45
Partner's occupation higher professional/		
managerial	80	62
N	*75*	*78*

Note: All figures relate to the first round of coding.

Given the academically competitive nature of entry into medical school, we had expected to find that the doctors were more likely than the bankers to have been targeted—that is, particularly encouraged—both by their parents and in respect of their schooling. These items, therefore, were specified in the topic guide and recording document. However, as Table 7.3 demonstrates, this proved not to be the case, and the level of both school and parental encouragement reported by doctors and bankers proved to be comparable. Table 7.3 also suggests that the social backgrounds of the two groups of women were broadly similar. Our evidence does not suggest, therefore, that there were marked differences between the two groups of women *before* their entry into their employment careers. Doctors have been more likely to go into domestic partnerships with other professionals (frequently other doctors) than have bankers, but this aspect of their personal lives relates to adult decision-making, rather than their early socialization.

Our data, therefore, do not lend much support to the self-selection hypothesis as an explanation of occupational differences. It would seem that the occupational context has had an important impact on employment/family career choices. We would not argue, however, that individual characteristics have no impact whatsoever on the way in which women manage their lives. In Table 7.1, we have already shown that two of the categories of women we identified—maximizers, and careerists by choice—did not vary in their level of representation as between the two occupations—that is, an occupational effect was not discernible. What, therefore, had shaped the experiences of these women? We were particularly interested in the maximizers, as these were likely to be the women whose personal lives and experiences were most likely to give rise to change. When we examined our evidence relating to earlier childhood experiences, clear differences emerged between the maximizers and the women who had been coded into the other employment and family-life categories (Table 7.4).

Table 7.4 cross-tabulates our first and second rounds of coding. Questions relating to school and parental encouragement had been included in the interview guide, and had therefore been coded in the first round. As described above, the holistic coding was undertaken in the second round of coding, independently of the first round. As we have seen in Table 7.3, the majority of the women interviewed had been encouraged by their parents to do well, and a substantial minor-

TABLE 7.4. *Employment and family-life management categories compared with experiences of encouragement in childhood (%)*

Encouragement in childhood	Domestic	Satisficer	Maximizer	Career first
Encouraged by parents to do well	58	61	88	63
Encouraged by school to do well	25	26	39	30
N	*28*	*47*	*26*	*26*

Note: We have not given details for 'careerists by necessity' (who were all bankers), or the 'undecided' category here.

ity had been encouraged at school as well. However, Table 7.4 suggests that maximizers were much more likely to have experienced parental encouragement than the other women interviewed (this difference is significant at the 99 per cent level), and were also somewhat more likely to have been encouraged at school as well.

In both occupations, therefore, the maximizers stand out as individuals, and these differences would seem to be related to differences in their childhood experiences. There would also seem to be differences between the maximizers and the other women in their perceptions of, and the way in which they had pursued, their employment careers. Sixty-nine per cent of maximizers were aware of, and opposed to, gender discrimination in employment, as compared to 40 per cent of interviewees overall. Thirty-five per cent of maximizers reported having personally experienced discrimination (not necessarily to their ultimate disadvantage), as compared to 21 per cent of all interviewees. Not unexpectedly, maximizers reported themselves as having been proactive in overcoming gendered obstacles in their employment and family lives, and 50 per cent reported having overcome such difficulties, as compared to only 17 per cent of all interviewees.

Maximizers shared a dynamic approach to both their employment and their family lives. It would seem reasonable to assume that, whatever these women had chosen to do, and wherever they had chosen to do it, they would have effectively made the most of their opportunities and achievements. One British example, a consultant gastroenterologist (married to another hospital doctor, two small children, childcare shared in accordance with an agreement made before marriage), may be used to illustrate our argument:

[She went to the local comprehensive, where she was one of the brightest; her parents encouraged her to do medicine, which she decided on at A level. She wanted to specialize (women 'were encouraged to be GPs at medical school') but didn't choose surgery because] I thought it was going to be hard enough, and I wasn't going to make it that hard. [Nevertheless, the consultants tried to put her off] chats in the corridor about what my husband was doing, lots of advice to go and do part time schemes, and all the rest of it . . . [so she decided to] play the game their way. . . . I am a feminist by definition, but a non-confrontational one . . . if you get to where you want to go, you can change things, but there's no point arguing with them all the way . . . and getting exhausted, and never making it past SHO . . . I'm quite ambitious in what I want to do as a consultant . . . I want to do some committee work, and actually have some influence on how the hospital works, and perhaps other things like the Royal Colleges.   (2/08)

We appreciate that we are developing a complex argument on the basis of a relatively small number of cases, but the extent of the contrasts between the kinds of women in the different employment and family-life management categories is nevertheless very striking. The fact that these differences hold constant across countries that are themselves very different, from Western capitalist economies to ex-state socialist, would increase our confidence in the reliability of these findings.

DISCUSSION

In this book, one of our aims has been to demonstrate the utility of a theoretical approach that recognizes that gender, and gender relations, are both shaped by gendered structures that reflect stereotypical or conventional binary classifications, whilst at the same time being an outcome of the manner in which women (and men) actively interpret and develop their *own* biographies. Putting the matter simply, our approach recognizes the significance of both structure and action without necessarily privileging either—although, in particular explanatory instances, an argument from structure might be more appropriate than an argument from action.

We would also argue that our evidence provides a useful critique of Hakim's explanation of the structuring of women's employment. As we have seen, she argues that this can be explained by the fact that there are psychologically different categories of women, the committed, who give priority to their employment careers, and the uncommitted, who give priority to their family lives, as well as the drifters or adaptives. Our evidence reveals that the actual situation is infinitely more complex than this. All of the women interviewed within the project might be described as committed, in that they had made extensive investments in their training and careers. However, as we have demonstrated, there were in fact very considerable differences between them in the way in which they had managed the employment–family interface. Some of these differences may be explained by systematic variations in the kinds of constraint and opportunity offered by banking and medicine—and we would suggest that these systematic differences might be extended to relate to professional and managerial occupations more generally.[8] *Within* each occupation, however, there were differences between the women interviewed that cut across occupational differences—in short, although we would wish to argue for an occupational effect, we would not wish to be seen as 'occupational determinists'.

As we have seen, Hakim's work offers no explanation of why women should fall into the three categories she describes (or indeed, any other category) in the first place, or why they might switch from one category to another. Given Hakim's endorsement of psycho-biological accounts of patriarchy, it might be suggested that the women in question are characterized by variations in their levels of testosterone—that maximizers, for example, possessed demonstrably more of this hormone than other women.[9] However, we would not be content with such an explanation.

We would not wish to argue that there are no psychological differences between women—obviously there are, as our analysis of the maximizers suggests. It would seem that the psychological attributes of the maximizers reflected childhood experiences and, in particular, parental encouragement. This finding is, of course, based on very small numbers, but it does suggest that the heterogeneity of women's approaches to employment and family life (which we have never denied) is not a reflection of innate characteristics (as would seem to be implied in Hakim's reliance on psycho-biological explanations), but is deeply rooted in early patterns of socialization.[10] As sociologists, our focus has been on how the *social* structure affects individuals—without in any way seeing individuals as entirely 'determined' by structure. Hakim (1991: 114) has argued that 'theory and research on women's employment seems particularly prone to an over-socialized view of women, or with structural factors so weighted that choice flies out of the window'. However, we have been able to demonstrate, across a range of differentially 'gendered' contexts, *how* these contexts are reflected in the choices that shape individual lives. These choices have incorporated change, as well as continuity (see Table 7.3). Although Hakim's discussion accepts the possibility of change, she does not offer any explanation of it—in particular in relation to the women she describes as committed or uncommitted to paid employment. We would suggest that much of the explanation will in fact reside in the choices that are available to different women. Thus, although it would be mistaken to see women as 'structural dopes' (any more than men are), it is equally misleading to see their behaviour as being entirely determined by the fact that they are female, or even a particular kind of female, as Hakim argues.

Sociologists have always emphasized that human action has to be explained and understood in relation to norms and values (what Weber would describe as substantive rationality) as well as individual self-maximization (or formal rationality). The assumption that women should take the major responsibility for care and nurturing, particularly of children, is a very powerful normative assumption (although, as Pfau-Effinger has argued in Chapter 4, ideals of motherhood have been subject to considerable variation historically). Women were the major carers of children before industrialism, and before the development of the institutions and structures of labour-market regulation that placed women as a whole in a position of considerable disadvantage in the labour force. Even if all normative assumptions relating to motherhood were to disappear overnight, the occupational structure would still be likely to retain the imprint of the arrangements required for pregnancy, lactation, and the care of very young children. Although gender relations may be changed and transformed, they will not disappear, and gender differences will continue to be reflected in the labour market. Thus we would agree with Hakim that some level of occupational segregation by sex is likely to be a persisting feature of the labour market, and that the phenomenon cannot simply be understood as a consequence of patriarchal exclusionary processes (see Crompton 1997).

However, we would suggest that, if the arguments of those who have attributed occupational segregation largely to the processes of patriarchal exclusion should be modified, then Hakim's alternative explanation is not acceptable either. Hakim (1998: 236) gives a functionalist account of occupational segregation (or sex differentiation in the labour market), as providing 'clearly differentiated groups of occupations for primary [men] and secondary [women] earners'. She rejects the patriarchy thesis relating to occupational segregation—which would include a wide range of arguments, including the historical undervaluation of 'women's' work and the lower pay of female-dominated occupations, men's role in excluding women from better jobs in order to ensure masculine dominance, and women's position as 'disadvantaged workers' on account of their caring responsibilities. In Chapter 1, use of 'patriarchy' as an organizing concept through which to explain the totality of gender relations was criticized. However, this does not mean that the concept has no explanatory value, nor that the effects of past patriarchal practices are not apparent today (or have disappeared altogether). Patriarchal practices are still significant in occupational structuring—as our discussion of internal segregation by sex within the medical profession (Chapter 9) will demonstrate.

More generally, although functionalist explanations should not be rejected out of hand, we need to continue to be aware of one of the standard critiques of the functionalist approach—that is, the rhetorical question: 'Functional for whom?' Thus a particular arrangement might be 'functional' in that it achieves a particular end, but at some cost to (some of) the parties involved. As Folbre (1994: 10) has noted, the male-breadwinner model was never fair, but at least it was partly functional in that it underwrote social reproduction. However, it was also unstable in that it systematically denied opportunities to women as individuals, and thus came into direct conflict with egalitarian ideals. It also depended on labour-market conditions that no longer hold—the widespread institution of a breadwinner wage for adult males, together with the formal restrictions on women's choices. As male-breadwinner arrangements crumble, alternative arrangements for the combination of employment and caring are beginning to emerge (these possibilities are discussed at greater length in Chapter 10). Hakim's arguments focus on the British case, which is characterized by the rapid growth of non-standard (particularly part-time) employment (and, some would say, the proliferation of 'junk jobs'). In fact, cross-national evidence—some of which is reviewed in this book (Chapters 2, 4, and 5)—demonstrates the existence of a range of possibilities. Rather than attempting to argue, therefore, that the British case represents a 'functional adaptation' to the labour-market changes under way, we suggest it would be more useful to explore a range of possibilities that depend not just on role reversal between men and women, or the perpetuation of 'disadvantaged' employment, but the development of a gender division of labour that is both fair and achieves social reproduction.

In conclusion: certainly, women can and do make choices—although in aggregate, their relative lack of power and resources relative to men means that both today and in the past they have been less able to do so than the opposite sex. Women—and men—can choose but are also constrained, a fact that lies at the root of sociological explanations of human behaviour.

NOTES

1. Comparative cross-national research drawing upon interviews is more usually carried out using a structured questionnaire—as in, for example, the ISSP surveys also used in the project. However, finance was not available to carry out the extensive piloting required for such an exercise, and, resources were only available to carry out only a small number of interviews. In any case, it may be argued that a structured questionnaire was not the most suitable instrument for the exploration of a number of topics central to the Gender Relations project—most notably the question of gender identity, which is explored in the next chapter. There were some problems, however, in arranging cross-national collaboration. Feminist research, and research methods, do not have widespread acceptance in Eastern Europe. There is some variability in these interviews, which has restricted the range of the coding exercise.
2. Biographical analysis is a laborious process. See Connell's (1995: 89 ff.) discussion of his analysis of life histories.
3. See Hakim (1991: 106), and Ginn *et al.* (1996: 168).
4. It may also be noted that Hakim's characterization of the choices open to women fails to take account of the increasing numbers of women living in families but without men—i.e. lone parents. However, Hakim would seem to assume that all women who are not in work have access to a male supporter. For example, in adjusting the data on levels of work commitment in order to incorporate non-working women (who were not actually asked the question), she states that: 'by definition non-working women are choosing *not* to work given even a moderate income supplied by their husband' (Hakim 1996: 105). However, the data in question give no evidence of marital or partnership status.
5. The system of interview numbering, which is described in the Appendix, indicates country and occupation.
6. Many doctors in Eastern Europe were paid extra either by their patients (through the system of gift-giving) or by laboratories and pharmaceutical companies for running trials—as in the West.
7. See Martin and Roberts (1984). It may be noted that this survey, although path-breaking and important in its time, would not have been able to gather data on the cohort of young women coming to maturity in the 1970s, a period from which women's educational attainments and levels of further qualification rose quite sharply (Crompton and Sanderson 1986).
8. It may be noted that Hakim (1997: 245) suggests that a comparison between these two occupational categories might be a fruitful area for further research.
9. For example, Hakim states (1996: 205–6) that: 'Women who change over to being men are amazed to discover they go out into the world charged with aggressive energy when they start taking the testosterone tablets, wanting to fuck everyone and fight everything.'
10. An Australian study came to very similar conclusions as to the importance of parental encouragement in the case of women who hoped to 'maximize' both domestic and employment careers. See Poole and Langan-Fox (1997).

McDowell's research on successful women in Merchant Banking also emphasized the importance of social background and parental encouragement (1997: 115).

8

Gender, Occupational Feminization, and Reflexivity: A Cross-National Perspective

NICKY LE FEUVRE

INTRODUCTION

This chapter analyses some of the conceptual questions relating both to gender and occupational feminization. It demonstrates how different conceptions of 'gender' can be related to different predictions as to the likely outcomes of occupational feminization. A social-constructivist perspective on gender is adopted. By stressing the processes of gender *differentiation* rather than difference, it will be argued that one important outcome of the social construction of gender associated with the male-breadwinner model has been the denial of autonomy to women and the association of dependency with femininity. However, the entry of women into higher-level occupations suggests that this is changing. The work of Dubet (1994) is used to develop a model that indicates possible causal pathways between gendered logics of action, social experience of gender, and outcomes of occupational feminization. This model is illustrated using biographical acounts of professional women gathered, as part of the Gender Relations project, in Britain and France.

Comparative cross-national analysis of the feminization of professional occupations is confronted with a double challenge. First, the need to develop a sufficiently dynamic and subtle framework for grasping the considerable complexities and ongoing transformations of gender and the gender order (Connell 1987) in advanced capitalist, reflexively modern, societies. Secondly, adapting the conceptual tools developed in the post-war period for the sociological analysis of the professions in the face of significant changes to their internal

The author wishes to thank Rosemary Crompton for her stimulating comments on a previous draft of this chapter and for her unfailing commitment and support throughout the Gender Relations project.

characteristics—in part as a consequence of their feminization (Burrage and Torstendahl 1990; Hassenteufel 1997).

Failure to address these two dimensions simultaneously may lead to a truncated vision of the theoretical and empirical complexities that surround the numerically significant influx of women into sectors of the labour market that have traditionally been constructed as a male preserve. It is necessary to recognize that both gender and professions are socially constructed entities with their own specific historical dynamics. There has been considerable attention paid to the mechanisms through which women have been (and, to a certain extent, still are) excluded from the most prestigious professional occupations (or at least from the most prestigious strata of such professions), while less attention has been paid to their widespread inclusion during the 1990s. The conceptual frameworks developed to analyse this inclusion have been inspired by those used to analyse and explain women's previous exclusion. Thus, much recent research, including my own (Witz 1992; Le Feuvre and Walters 1993; Crompton 1995; Crompton and Le Feuvre 1996, 1997; Davies 1996) has tended to stress the internal (re)stratification by sex that has accompanied the feminization of professional occupations and to read this as proof of the French adage 'plus ça change, plus c'est la même chose'.

Thus a number of discussions of professional feminization would seem to suggest that, although women as a social group are no longer excluded *en masse* from the higher levels of the occupational hierarchy, the gender regime under which they are admitted to these positions shows little sign of change. It will be argued that, although this approach might describe the professional situation of many women,[1] it is increasingly unstable as an *analytical* tool.

ABOUT GENDER

As the quantity of academic research on the situation of women in contemporary Western societies increases, there is evidence of the development of diverse (and often contradictory) uses of the term 'gender' in current sociological literature. The most obvious development concerns the increasing tendency to use 'gender' as an analogy, a metaphor (or a straightforward euphemism) for 'sex'. I would argue that this tendency serves to blur the conceptual cutting edge of 'gender' and to reinforce the 'gender as an attribute' perspective that has already received widespread criticism in other circles (Connell 1987; Acker 1992).

Thus, as many authors have already argued, 'gender' does not tell us very much about the characteristics of individuals, but is useful for grasping a system of social relations that produces the sexual duality of the human race as a *socially significant division*. As a number of contemporary French sociologists have argued (Bourdieu 1990, 1998; Delphy 1991; Mathieu 1992), what is usually referred to as the 'gender system' should not be seen as something that is based on a pre-existing natural division between male and female, rather each society constructs the norms, behaviour, and attitudes of members of each of these groups along fairly arbitrary but nevertheless coherent and consistent lines, which may or may not vary over time. [2]

As I see it, gender does not have much to do with difference; it is wholly tied up in a social process of *differentiation*. For gender to become meaningful from a sociological perspective, differentiation has to be seen not only as a process that creates sexual duality as something that has a socially significant outcome (as opposed to the physical traits associated with other forms of natural difference—like that of having light or dark hair, for example), but also as a process that creates a hierarchical framework for the manifestation and interpretation of the differences it has produced. It is about the relationship between the two categories and not about one or other of the categories themselves, which have no intrinsic meaning outside the relationship that defines them.[3]

The gender (differentiation) process operates simultaneously on several levels. Thus, for example, the four-dimension framework proposed by Joan Acker (1992) for analysis of gendered organiza-tions could equally be used to describe and analyse the differentia-tion process that operates at the societal level. Acker (1992: 252–4) argues that the gender process involves:

- the production of gender divisions (i.e. of an objective hierarchy between the sexes);
- the creation of symbols, images, and forms of consciousness that explicate, justify, and, more rarely, oppose gender divisions;
- interactions between individuals in the multiplicity of forms that enact dominance and subordination and create alliances and exclusions;

- internal mental work of individuals as they consciously construct their understandings of the . . . gendered structure of work
and opportunity and the demands for gender-appropriate
behaviours and attitudes. Such internal work helps to reproduce
divisions and images even as it ensures individual survival.

It therefore follows that: 'The daily construction, *and sometimes
deconstruction*, of gender occurs within material and ideological constraints that set the limits of possibility. For example, the boundaries
of sex segregation, themselves continually constructed and reconstructed, limit the actions of particular women and men at particular
times' (Acker 1992: 251; emphasis added).

However, as Delphy (1991) and Mathieu (1992) have argued, for
the majority of authors (including many feminist researchers), 'sex
is presumed to come, chronologically, and so therefore, logically,
before gender' (Delphy 1991: 93). Once the idea that gender is *based
on* a pre-existing, natural binary division between the sexes is introduced, it becomes theoretically impossible to adopt a truly sociological perspective on gender—that is, to analyse the social reasons for
its existence and the logical possibility of its demise.

According to Delphy (1991), the inability of a whole range of theoretical paradigms to extract their conception of gender from the evidence of human sexual duality represents a serious threat to the
quality of research and serves to weaken the theoretical grounds for
political mobilization in favour of equality. Her criticisms are valid
for research carried out in what could be called a 'new essentialist'
perspective, where the differentiated biological functions of males
and females in the human reproductive process are taken to require
at least a minimum level of sexual division of labour in all the other
social spheres and, therefore, to produce starkly different personal-
ity traits in all men and all women. This perspective suggests that the
major risk of any successful equal opportunities programme would
be to make women like men and to deprive societies of the altruistic
feminine qualities that carry the potential to make the world a better
place. Delphy's analysis also holds for what she calls a 'cognitivist'
perspective on gender, which attributes the existence of gender to a
(pre-social) characteristic of all human societies—the necessity to
operate solely on the basis of binary distinctions and oppositions (or
differances, as Derrida suggests). According to contemporary fol-
lowers of Lévi-Strauss (1967) in the French structuralist tradition,

this necessarily binary vision of the world exists because the visual and cognitive impact on even the most primitive forms of social organization of the most fundamental, primary binary division of all—the biological distinction between male and female human beings—has served as a cognitive template for all forms of human thought (Héritier 1996). However, as Delphy rightly points out, this perspective fails to account for the fact that gender is not simply about difference. It is essentially a question of hierarchy.

Following this line of argument, I will develop the idea that gender (the differentiation/ hierarchy process) produces the natural binary divide we call sex (or rather 'the sexes'). Once gender is seen in terms of the production of a relationship between the binary sexual categories of humanity, thus turning natural difference into a socially significant division, a number of logical conclusions can be drawn. The first and most obvious of these is, from a sociological perspective, the need to recognize that 'sex' is as much a socially constructed phenomenon as 'gender': without the structural relationship between the sexes ('gender'), the natural differences between males and females (biological sex) would have no inherent meaning for us as social scientists.[4] This first step implies a radical break with any form of essentialist-inspired analysis of women's (and men's) position in society. Secondly, this perspective enables us to think more constructively about the complexities of the relationships that exist between gender and other forms of social differentiation that affect individuals and groups on both a material and symbolic level.

Thirdly, and perhaps most importantly, this vision of gender implies that the very existence of a binary biological difference between the sexes does not imply, *in itself*, any particular form of social organization. Were the differentiation process of gender as we know it to cease tomorrow (or were the differentiation process to operate along different lines), approximately half of the human population would nevertheless continue to have wombs, along with the capacity to fall pregnant during a certain period of their adult lives, while the rest of humanity would continue not to have these attributes. One can reasonably expect that these composites of humanity would also continue to do what is biologically necessary to produce human offspring. Without gender, humanity would not cease to exist. We must, therefore, recognize, at least as a hypothetical stance, that, since gender is not built on the foundations of natural difference, its capacity for transformation is relatively unlimited. To take this a step further, the perspective of gender's eventual demise should figure, at least as a conceptually coherent possibility, in any analysis of its mechanisms of production–reproduction–transformation.[5] This does not mean that all human beings would be produced according to a single (masculine) model. As Delphy comments: 'From a gender perspective, this fear [that women would come to resemble men] is totally incomprehensible; if women were to gain equality with men, men would no longer be as they are today; why should women come to resemble what men would have ceased to be?' (Delphy 1991: 99).

However, the force and strength of the masculinity/femininity divide (which can be seen to possess the qualities of what Bourdieu (1984) has called an 'allant de soi'—something so deeply entrenched in our mental vision of the world that it cannot even begin to be questioned as what it is—that is, an arbitrary social construction) is such that, even as astute (feminist) sociologists, we are caught in its trap. What are we really talking about when we refer to 'masculinity' and 'femininity', and their relation to occupational feminization? Are these inherent characteristics of biological males and females or does their binary opposition refer to two distinct (though interrelated) positions within the specific form of division of labour, which, for twentieth-century capitalist countries could be termed the 'male-breadwinner' model. If 'masculinity' is a sophisticated and more or less subtle way of referring to 'being a man' (maleness—having male genitals), then the first position would seem to hold. If, on the other hand, the definition of 'masculinity' incorporates a position in the division of labour where the individual has access to sufficient resources to maintain his or her own labour power (and possibly that of others), where he or she has the ability to obtain and retain a supply of domestic and emotional services, where his or her relation to the most significant others is mediated through employment rather than the marriage contract, and so on, what does this actually tell us about the *women* who are now entering the most prestigious professions in relatively large numbers?

ABOUT OCCUPATIONAL FEMINIZATION

The ambiguities surrounding the conceptualization of gender become particularly apparent when it comes to analysing the influx of women into the most prestigious positions on the occupational hierarchy. In previous work I have identified a number of theoretical perspectives on occupational feminization (Le Feuvre 1998), which can be related to particular theoretical visions of gender. Conceptual and theoretical ambiguities arise because the term 'feminization' is used both to describe the empirical increase in the proportion of women within a given occupation, as well as to infer changes in the characteristics of the professional group in question and/or to analyse the potential effects of occupational feminization on the gender process. Broadly speaking, different perspectives on feminization can be summarized as follows:

1. Feminization = gender reproduction: the potentially transformative effects of the increase in the number of women gaining access to the most prestigious positions in the occupational hierarchy are erased by the simultaneous redefinition of the prestige and earnings-related characteristics of these occupations. The influx of women is either taken as the cause or as the result of the downgrading of the occupation (Reskin and Roos 1990) and serves to maintain women in the least advantageous positions on the labour market, reinforcing their dependency on a male breadwinner or on the state (Walby 1990). The main conceptual tool of this perspective would be a fairly universal notion of patriarchy, which serves to restrict the effects of occupational feminization, both on the professions and on the gender process.[6]

2. Feminization = feminitude: the influx of women into the male bastions of power and prestige offers the opportunity for the diffusion of feminine values (altruism, sensitivity, empathy, etc.) within the public sphere of employment and (potentially) politics. In sufficient numbers, women transform the (inherently masculine) value systems of high status occupations, notably making them more receptive to the needs and requirements of women professionals/clients/patients, and less sensitive to the traditional criteria of success (income, peer-group recognition, etc.) (Menkel-Meadow 1989). In this perspective, feminization is also seen as a causal factor in the transformation of the objective organizational principles of professional groups, notably as far as work-time norms are concerned. However, the underlying conceptualisation of gender here would seem to suggest the continuation of a binary (masculinity/femininity) divide even after widespread occupational feminization.

3. Feminization = virilitude or surrogate maleness: the proportion of women gaining access to the most prestigious positions in the
occupational hierarchy remains too restricted for a major transformation of occupational values. However, the few exceptions that
confirm the rule serve to illustrate that the inherent feminine qualities associated with gender socialization may be singularly absent
from the behaviour of women when they reach positions of power.
On the one hand, this is taken to indicate the inherent masculinity of
high-status professions, which is in turn used to explain the difficulty
women experience in gaining access to the upper echelons of such
occupations (Aubert, 1986; Davies 1996; Halford and Savage 1995).
The theoretical framework of this perspective would be a postmod-
ern-inspired analysis of the gendering of professions and organizations. Whilst recognizing the empirical possibility for women to act
as surrogate men under certain organizational or personal circumstances, this framework nevertheless suggests that these women have
little power to transform the underlying masculine logic of professional practice. On the other hand, however, the virilitude perspective may also be adopted to suggest that occupational feminization
may potentially lead to a redefinition of the male = masculinity/
female = femininity gender-process equation and thus to some (limited) form of transformation of the gender process (see Le Feuvre
1998).

4. Feminization = gender transformation: this perspective develops the traditional equality-agenda analysis, which is based on the
idea of equal numbers or equal representation. Increasing numbers
of women moving into higher-level occupations are not simply taken
as one example of the factors that are making relations between the
sexes more equal. Rather, they are taken as an indication of the
transformations of the differentiation process that reveal substantial
changes in the nature of gender as a set of life-chance determining
social relations. In this case, empirical examples (however limited in
number) of women gaining access to positions of professional power
and prestige serve to illustrate the weakening link between biological
sex and life chances under advanced modernity (Giddens 1992: 199).
Although this perspective shares with others the idea that occupational feminization has transformative potential, the outcomes of
this process of change are envisaged rather differently than in the
perspectives discussed previously. This approach requires what
could be called a 'constructivist' conception of gender, which, in line

with the points made above, stresses the fact that the socially defined qualities or characteristics associated with males and females depend entirely on the existence of a systematic differentiation/hierarchy process, which itself depends on women's exclusion from autonomy.

In practice, much research on occupational feminization has tended to use various combinations of these different (and often contradictory) theoretical perspectives and implicit conceptualizations of gender (see Le Feuvre 1998). However, when taken separately, each perspective gives rise to varying expectations as to the degree of change to be expected as a consequence of occupational feminization. The nature of these expectations in relation to both gender and professions are summarized in Figure 8.1.

Theoretical perspective	Gender reproduction	Virilitude	Feminitude	Gender transformation
Potential gender change	−	+	−	+
Potential occupational change	−	−	+	+

FIGURE 8.1. The potential consequences of occupational feminization on occupations and gender

The social-constructivist perspective on gender, as articulated in this chapter, is careful to distinguish between the differentiation *process* (gender) and the specific *differences* (the effects or outcomes of gender, as measured by so-called sex differences produced at a particular moment in time in a specific societal context). To give what are not purely gratuitous examples, there is nothing about the way that gender functions as a process that makes it necessary for rationality and autonomy to be permanent composite characteristics of masculinity, and for altruism and dependency to be permanent composite characteristics of femininity (Davies 1996). Indeed, at any point in time, there may be any number of potential human qualities that are not explicitly mobilized in and through the gender differentiation process (for example, having a sense of humour). From a social-constructionist perspective, gender is as open to transformation and change as it is to reproduction.

The development of the male-breadwinner model, as discussed in this and previous chapters of this book, was accompanied by the erosion of any capacity for women's autonomy—or rather, their structured dependence on men. This was reflected in their labour-force disadvantage, which itself became an element of a particular social construction of femininity. Thus: 'The quest for female emancipation from patriarchally determined subordination encompasses more than the striving for equality and rights. It can be defined best as the *quest for autonomy*. Autonomy means women defining themselves and the values by which they will live, and beginning to think of institutional arrangements that will order their environment in line with their needs' (Learner 1979: 162; emphasis added). This vision of autonomy is also central to the description of advanced modernity proposed by Giddens (1992: 185): 'Autonomy means the capacity of individuals to be self-reflective and self-determining. . . . Clearly autonomy in this sense could not be developed while political rights and obligations were closely tied to tradition and fixed prerogatives of property. Once these dissolved, however, a movement towards autonomy became both possible and seen to be necessary.'

It is, nevertheless, important to note that the ideal type of the male-breadwinner model was rarely institutionalized in a totally pure form in any national context. Indeed, in reaction to the gender blind typology of welfare states presented by Esping-Andersen (1990), several authors have attempted to characterize various welfare-state regimes along a continuum representing various degrees of the male-breadwinner model (see, for example, Hantrais 1990; Lewis 1992; O'Reilly and Fagan 1998). Recent research in this field has been sensitive both to the differences between various societies at particular moments in time, notably the historical transition from agrarian to capitalist production (see Pfau-Effinger, Chapter 4 in this volume) and to the emergence of more contemporary pressures for change within a given historically defined gender system (Hirdman 1988).

The societal and historical relativity or variability of the institutionalization of the male-breadwinner model, therefore, should imply caution when it comes to making sweeping statements about the changes taking place for women in advanced capitalist societies. Nevertheless, the experience of the women who are now working in significant numbers within the élite professions in all European societies provides insights into the ways in which women can and, indeed, in some circumstances, are contesting and deconstructing the very material, symbolic, interactive, and identity foundations of the mid-twentieth-century gender (differentiation) process in a quest for autonomy. Furthermore, I would argue that the forms of resistance to the gender process that can be observed on the part of a proportion of women professionals have relatively little to do with masculinity and femininity as such; they are more to do with a direct attack on gender as I have defined it above—that is, a questioning of the legitimacy of the binary differentiation process itself—rather than with contesting the results or outcomes of this process.

   The stress placed in the following sections of this chapter on women's agency in resisting the gender process should not be seen as a denial of the fact that, despite the removal of most of the formal barriers to women's investment in the public sphere on a par with men, the foundations of gender (differentiation) have, at least at the societal level, shown more signs of adaptation than of demise. The *idéel* (Godelier 1984) notions of femininity and masculinity that were an integral part of the gender-differentiation process under early capitalism in most European societies, along with the subordination of women and the internal mental work (or identity) dimensions of gender, have combined to produce new objective (and thus subjective and ideological) forms of gender differentiation and hierarchy. In aggregate, most women have not yet attained equal access to the same degree of individual autonomy as most men—they are concentrated in the lowest-paid jobs, over-represented amongst part-time and other flexible employment contracts, and continue to bear the brunt of the unpaid domestic and caring responsibilities within society (Maruani 1995). However, it would be as equally misleading to suggest that the changes outlined in the Introduction to this volume have made no impact whatsoever on the specific forms of gender (differentiation) that directly affect the experiences and identities of at least certain groups of women, particularly those whose access to a considerable share of economic, social, and cultural capital (Bourdieu 1984) enables them to envisage life along somewhat different lines from those defined under the male-breadwinner period of the gender contract.

GENDER, AGENCY, AND REFLEXIVE MODERNITY

In this section we will draw on the work of Dubet in order to develop a theoretical framework for the analysis of gender and occupational feminization. The approach developed attempts to identify the mechanisms through which women (and some men) are changing the dominant twentieth-century male-breadwinner gender contract in Europe.

The sociology of experience outlined by Dubet (1994) draws on the work of Simmel (1986) and Weber (1971). Dubet develops a threefold analysis, based on the general principle that the loss of social unity constitutes the fundamental characteristic of advanced capitalist societies. Within increasingly diverse, heterogeneous social situations and societies, individuals are led to determine the meaning of their decisions and actions and to construct the overall coherence of their lives. Thus, there is 'heterogeneity in the social and cultural principles which organize individual actions' (Dubet 1994: 16): 'Social roles, social positions and cultural background no longer provide a stable basis for actions because individuals are not programmed in advance. Rather, they attempt to build unity from the diverse elements of their social experiences and from the wide range of potential orientations they have open to them. Thus, social identity is not about "being", but about working at who one is' (Dubet 1994: 16).

The second aspect of advanced modernity concerns the 'subjective distance that individuals place between themselves and the social system' (Dubet 1994: 17). According to Dubet, because of the 'heterogeneous diversity of the founding principles of social actions', each individual

feels like the author of his/her own experience—an author with only a relatively free rein, because the composite elements of the biographical construction do not depend on individual will alone. The plurality of social experiences creates a feeling of distance and detachment as individuals are unable to adhere totally to a range of social roles and values which are not necessarily internally coherent . . . Insofar as this critical distancing and individual reflexivity are a part of social experiences, they should be analysed from a sociological perspective as constitutive of a process which defines a degree of individual autonomy and creates the subject. (Dubet 1994: 17)

Thus, 'social experiences are subjective combinations of objective elements' (Dubet 1994: 136), which require recognition that the diverse and often contradictory elements that make up social experiences pre-exist the individual combinations that may be observed in given circumstances: 'these elements are imposed through culture and social relations, objective constraints or particular forms of domination or subordination' (ibid.: 135), but the individual experience of particular combinations of structural elements nevertheless carries the potential to transform the objective and subjective impact of structure on individual life chances. The 'sociology of experience' must, therefore, be particularly sensitive to the 'tensions' that characterize the relationship between the range of prescriptive (and potentially contradictory) social roles and constraints and the particular social experience combinations of individuals (ibid.: 178).

Dubet identifies (Figure 8.2) three distinct (but interrelated) levels of social experience and proposes three different types of causal explanation (underlined), related to the nature of the three major components of the social system (bold) and to each of the specific 'underlying logics of action' (italics). As far as the mechanisms of social integration are concerned, Dubet suggests that a 'causal or structural' explanatory framework based on the traditional sociological notion of socialization is the most adequate. He cautions us nevertheless about the risk of adopting a functionalist perspective on socialization, whereby 'the correlation between a model of social integration and elements of the socialization process becomes the cause of individual action and this cause is taken as a conscious objective' (1994: 140). In his model, agency or individual strategies are conceived within a 'system of interdependence' (Boudon 1979).

Although the use of the term 'strategy' in sociological literature is notoriously ambiguous, it is used here on the dual understanding that, first, 'strategies are not exclusively the preserve of dominant groups . . . Dominated groups, too, may devise strategies, perhaps in response to those of dominant groups that impinge on them' (Crow 1989: 4) and, secondly, that 'strategic analysis does not allow institutional analysis to be dispensed with' (ibid.: 20). In this vein, Dubet (1994: 145) argues, 'Optimum choice is often already determined by the objective distribution of resources, the nature of individual aspirations and social game rules. . . . Individual strategic actions and the relationship between social actors and the social system should be defined as a game (rules) situation rather than as a perfect market sit-

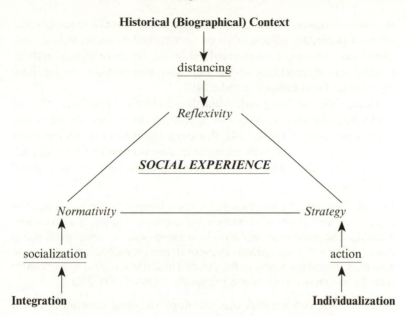

FIGURE 8.2. Components of social experience

uation.' This does not necessarily imply that the game rules are so defined as to foreclose any inventive ways of playing the game. However, it is important to note that the 'capacity to transform the rules of the game is less likely to result from a deliberate strategy of individuals than, in the majority of cases, from an unintended consequence of the game rules themselves' (ibid.: 146).

Finally, the 'historical (biographical) action system' refers to the auto-determination capacity that individuals acquire as a result of the tensions and contradictions that exist between the socialization (integration) and agency (individualization) dimensions of complex societies within a specific historical and/or societal context.

Individual action conceived as an ability or a desire to 'lead one's own life' implies both reference to a number of 'values' and the identification of barriers or obstacles to their accomplishment. The historical past, various forms of domination and the general social order may act as barriers to the 'self-realization' of an individual who possesses the ability to place him/herself above the society and to adopt a critical perspective on it. (Dubet 1994: 148)

As Dubet stresses, the development of critical distance requires some form of preceding adhesion to or acceptance of social values and, therefore, 'the people most involved in this reflexive/critical activity usually occupy positions where adhesion (acceptance) and (critical) distance go hand in hand' (ibid.: 149).

Thus, although 'Any individual faces identical problems, that of combining the diverse logics of social action within his/her social experience' (Dubet 1994: 254), this does not mean that all members of a given society at a given moment in time possess an identical ability to create unity and meaning from the diversity of their social experiences:

Individual or collective groups subjected to a form of domination tend to be deprived of their ability to unify their experience and to give it autonomous meaning. The investment they have to make in order to achieve this feat is much greater and more arduous than for dominant individuals and groups, who have immediate access to the cultural and social resources that enable them to become actors of their experiences.   (Dubet 1994: 256)

It therefore follows that the sociology of social experience is not just about agency; it proposes to analyse

representations, emotions, behaviour and the way social actors explain these phenomena. It is a sociology of subjectivity whose objects of study . . . are very likely to have subjectivities that are out of tune with prescriptive attitude and representation models. . . . The sociology of experience is particularly apt for [studying] behaviour which reveals some degree of discrepancy between 'objective' social expectations and individual 'subjectivities'. (Dubet 1994: 257)

Dubet's work has many parallels with the kinds of commentaries developed by Giddens (1991, 1992), Beck (1992), and Beck *et al.* (1995), which we have already discussed in relation to their account of changes in gender relations. Although Dubet makes no specific reference to gender in his work, his analytical perspective provides a useful framework for the analysis of gender and occupational feminization in so far as he stresses the plurality of theoretical or explanatory orientations that are required to grasp the complexity of any type of social relation under advanced capitalism. These arguments parallel those developed by Marshall (1994) in relation to feminist theory, as discussed in the Introduction to this volume.

In the final section of this chapter, I will illustrate the analytical potential of a theoretical perspective based on what could be called 'the social experience of gender and employment'. I attempt to show that, as far as the transformation of gender is concerned, the (social and sociological) consequences of the increase in the number of women entering the élite professions needs to be analysed in relation to the three dimensions of social experience—socialization (integration), individualization (agency), and reflexivity (distancing)—outlined by Dubet. This approach suggests that it is impossible to adopt *a priori* any single one of the competing explanatory models of occupational feminization discussed earlier. Neither is it possible to conclude unambiguously as to the consequences of occupational feminization for the gender-(differentiation) process.[7] The meaning attributed to the entry of women into the upper echelons of the occupational hierarchy needs to be situated in the wider social experience of gender and employment of the women concerned and cannot simply be read off from the statistical measurements of their presence/absence or indeed of their relative positions within the occupational hierarchies.

GENDER AND OCCUPATIONAL FEMINIZATION

This section draws on research and interviews carried out, in Britain and France, as part of the Gender Relations project.[8] It will be argued that women's entry into élite professions does not necessarily imply, *in itself*, any major transformation of the principles or foundations of the gender-differentiation process. However, the interview data from the British and French respondents suggest that there has been a significant shift in the ways in which the gender-differentiation process now operates in both these countries. Different nationally specific institutional gender arrangements and norms continue to shape women's attitudes and behaviour in relation to the employment–family interface in Britain and France. This would seem to be the case even under the revised gender contract characterized in both countries by the new social norm of (middle-class) women's increased access to academic credentials and to the upper echelons of the labour market. Nevertheless, within the two occupations studied here (banking and medicine) in both countries, we found examples of women whose social experiences had produced both a degree of distancing *vis-à-vis* the founding logic or principles of the gender contract (even in its advanced modernity revised form) and thus resistance to the gender-(differentiation) process. However, the mere increase in the presence of women within banking and medicine is not a sufficiently reliable empirical indicator of these phenomena, since many of the women interviewed within these professions were deeply entrenched in an integration logic in relation to the reproduction of the gender-(differentiation) process.

The causal relationship between occupational or career outcomes and women's overall experience of gender and employment is difficult to establish with any degree of precision. It would seem that, in some circumstances, women's distancing from the gender process may indeed lead them to the most prestigious strata of the occupational hierarchy and, thus, increased autonomy, but it also appears that the quest for autonomy may be facilitated by the social and cultural resources that a dominant position within the profession provides. It is thus important to stress that, in relation to their gender perspectives, the female professionals we interviewed do not fit neatly into distinct categories that can be distinguished with a limited number of variables. The nature of their objective and subjective relationship to the gender process is forged through a series of social experiences in all the spheres of society, in the face of what may be totally contradictory or totally coherent expectations and requirements made of them. The direction that the search for unity within the complexities of their experiences of socialization, education, training, employment, partnerships, domestic arrangements, and sexuality may take is itself related to the resources, constraints, and opportunities that their objective and subjective experience of these spheres provide.

Finally, although the different forms of what could be called women's 'resistance or integration to the gender process' can be shown to vary over time and between countries, in all cases these represent guiding principles in their lives that are expressed in a relatively stable and coherent manner on all of the four dimensions of the gender process outlined above—that is, on a material level (what they do, the objective resources they have access to), on a symbolic level (how they think about what they do in terms of masculinity and femininity), and in terms of their interaction with significant others (their degree of autonomy/dependence or subordination)) and on an identity level (how they think and feel about who they are in gender-differentiated or non-differentiated terms).

I suggest that the experiences of professional women in Britain and France are largely constructed through what could be called their 'social experience of gender and employment'. I use this term to refer to the degree to which women professionals identify with and act in accordance with or contest and transgress the logic and legitimacy of the gender-(differentiation) process and social order. It follows that the different dimensions of this experience refer simultaneously to the family, personal identity, and professional spheres. In turn, I would argue that this experience is constructed through the search for coherence and unity in the face of the increasing complexity of women's lives, where the contradictions between, on the one hand, the traditional (male-breadwinner) socially ascribed gender norms and expectations and, on the other hand, the growing individualization of their trajectories create the potential for dissonance and disorder. Within the moving sands of such experiences, the objective, cognitive, and subjective resources of individuals may combine in such a way as to favour an integration model of action (gender reproduction) or to produce discordant forms of action and reflexivity, which may potentially threaten the founding principles of the gender process.

The discussion of the biographical interviews that follows illustrates the manner in which the integration–individualization–historical (biographical) context dimensions of the experience of gender and employment combine to produce different consequences of occupational feminization, both in terms of the potential change to professional practice and in terms of the potential transformation of the gender order.[9] The recounting of the biographies demonstrates the processes through which gender is constructed, reproduced, and potentially contested through the social experiences of women working in élite professional occupations. These processes are summarized in Figure 8.3, which links social experience, logics of action, and possible outcomes of occupational feminization. The solid lines in the diagram indicate the causal links between biographies and occupational outcomes, thus normativity and dependency are linked with gender reproduction, and reflexivity and autonomy with (potential) gender and occupational transformation. A 'transgressional' strategy, in which a woman behaves 'like a man' (virilitude) in professional terms, is unlikely to be associated with professional or occupational transformation, but may serve to modify the symbolic foundations of the gender process, as suggested in Figure 8.1. The 'feminitude' perspective has not been incorporated into the model, given that, as argued in a previous section of this chapter, it has no bearing on the transformation of the gender process as such. [10] The arrows at either end of the solid lines indicate that the patterns of occupational feminization will also have some bearing on the logics of action developed by future generations of women entering the professions, since these will feed into the historical (biographical) context within which they live out their lives.

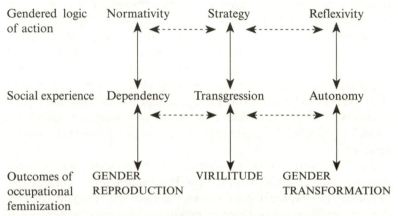

FIGURE 8.3. Social experience, logics of action, and outcomes of occupational feminization

We have already established that one of the consequences of the male-breadwinner model was the denial of autonomy to women as a socially and materially constructed group. Women's dependency on a bread-winning male (or on public services provided to cover for the unexpected and temporary loss or absence of such a person) is thus a constitutive element incorporated in this model of socialization within the gender (differentiation) process. Women's gaining of autonomy may, therefore, be taken as a decisive indicator of changes to the gender order. However, this access may take varying forms. On the one hand, women in exceptional historical or personal circumstances (major world wars, enforced celibacy, a crisis of welfare-state-services provision) may be denied the opportunity to construct their lives around the principle of dependency and the priority of domesticity. Alternatively, some women may actively choose to avoid emotional and family ties in order to pursue an upwardly mobile career trajectory. In either case, these women will adopt what has traditionally been termed a career-woman profile, based on the belief that, *for women* and women alone, occupational success is incompatible with any form of long-term emotional or family commitment. The financial and possible social autonomy gained under these circumstances is nevertheless experienced *within* the bounds of the gender (differentiation) process. Women who 'act like men' in the professional sphere have to pay the price associated with their transgression of the standard gender norms. Unlike their male counterparts, they are constrained to choose between professional and family life and, in choosing a professional career, they are simply transgressing the gender norms that associate femaleness with domesticity (an outcome of the gender process), rather than contesting the legitimacy of the binary divide in itself.

However, the ultimate form of autonomy lies in the ability to transcend the constraints of the gender (differentiation) process. Whilst the tensions between the integration and the individualization dimensions of social experiences may be resolved *within* the binary logic of the gender (differentiation) process—leading to a logic of action focused on normative dependency or on strategic transgression—the reflexivity or critical distance produced by the resolution of such tensions may lead to the development of autonomy that transcends (and therefore threatens) the logic and legitimacy of the differentiation process itself. Individual professional women cannot be neatly classified into a particular logic of action.[11] On the contrary, our biographical interview data suggest that elements or events in the historical (biographical) context of women's experiences can lead them to adopt a series of different logics of action over the course of their adult lives. These possibilities are indicated by the dotted lines in Figure 8.3.

Thus, for example, specific patterns of differentiated gender socialization mean that some women had started out on their employment biographies with an explicitly *normative* logic of action that had been overtaken by events in their historical (biographical) context. This was the case for this English banker (2/35, aged 40),[12] who joined the bank after leaving school at 17: 'There was a good social life. More like a continuation of your school days. I didn't see myself as a manager, I just saw myself working there.' She married at 19 and left the bank at 21 to have a baby. Her *normativity* and *dependency* were shaken when her husband left her and her daughter when she was 22:

'We got married too young, he wanted his freedom. It [divorce] wasn't a decision I made, it was forced on me.' After a period spent in waitress and bar work, she returned to the bank on a part-time basis: 'When I was part-time, I was more determined to work through the ranks and realize my potential, because you were treated like some sort of second class citizen.' Part-time hours were then changed: 'Suddenly the hours would be cut by half, or there was the possibility to work full-time. . . . I was a single parent, I needed the money, so I had to go back full-time.' She married again (a fellow bank employee) when her daughter was 6, but her increasing *autonomy* as a consequence of her comparatively greater employment success destabilized this relationship: 'he used to say "your precious job" . . . towards the end of it, it became a release for me to be at work really, because of the home life not being happy.' Her third and current relationship with a bank manager is increasingly gender *reflexive*: 'He ... has arranged for things like ironing services and dishwashers . . . He's a graduate, he was at university with women he still keeps in touch with and he's more open-minded . . . He's encouraged me to do my exams, he's encouraged me in my job . . . and been supportive at home.'

Another case, from France, also serves to illustrate the interweaving of historical (biographical) context and logics of action. A French banker (5/22, aged 42) escaped parental pressures in a gender conventional way by giving up her university course and marrying at 19. Her husband had career problems: 'I couldn't give up work, because he wasn't earning enough', but her academic ability meant that she was the first woman to gain entry to the bank through the competitive selection examination. Shortly after the birth of her son, the relationship broke down and career opportunities at the bank took a turn for the better. She then realized the advantages of being financially independent: 'I believe that I was very lucky to have a decent salary. I've always said that if I had been on a really low wage, I would never have been able to get divorced.' After divorce, she was 'forced' to throw herself into her job and looking after her son, but she continued to aspire to a more *normative* lifestyle. This was difficult for her to obtain because she was emotionally involved with a married man, who, after fifteen years, had still not fulfilled his promise to leave his wife. Her relatively successful career was thus more the result of her thwarted *normative* ambitions than of an explicit transgressive *strategy*: 'I have to admit that if I had had a husband and children at home, I would probably never have been able to set up the new department'. At the same time, however, she also felt very bitter about the blatant sexism and discrimination she faced at work and this anger transformed her vision and expectations of life. She gradually gained a degree of *autonomy* that not only fed into her professional life, but also transformed her attitude towards her personal relationships. She has recently become involved with a much younger man, who has different expectations about the domestic division of labour than her previous partners. She is proud of her professional success and feels that she can contest the normative assumptions about the gender hierarchy (female dependency) that she was tied into during the early stages of her adult life.

Another case, an English doctor (2/01, aged 39), also serves to illustrate the role of personal experience in reflexive development. She unexpectedly failed her second MB: 'One of those real traumas of actually failing, something that stayed with me for a long time' and gave up any idea of taking a specialty: 'I was not career minded . . . did what I thought was the easiest option—general practice—no more exams!' She went to work abroad, where encouragement from her medical colleagues brought back some of her lost confidence. Married to a local man, she returned to a research post in England with her husband to gain postgraduate qualifications, intending to return abroad later: 'I thought about children when I was doing research work because it would have been easy—regular hours and nice boss.' However, at this point her marriage broke up—'I would not blame my career at all for the break-up of my marriage'—and she continued to build a career in Britain, where she has recently obtained a consultant's post. Although she is a successful woman in a highly competitive specialty, she is not conscious of overt discrimination: 'but you could say to me "you're behaving like a man any-way—you've got total mobility and no dependants." I consider it a lot of personal sacrifice to have to keep moving around and not to have a family.' Although this respondent was 'forced' into a trans-gressional career *strategy* by the demands of her specialty and the break-up of her marriage, the degree of autonomy gained from her career means that her hopes for the future are nevertheless imbued with *reflexivity*: 'I hope things change here—we need to improve all the support agencies and benefits for women bringing up children. I don't think it's right that women should have to give up a family . . . People have to rethink fundamentally.'

Above we have described careers in medicine and banking in which the vicissitudes of biography and social experience had played their part in generating reflexivity. In other cases, however, self-consciously reflexive professional women had found their logic of action difficult or impossible to follow. Their particular vision and early experience of a largely non-differentiated gender process has met with opposition and resistance, which had served to limit the potential for change. A French banker (5/28, aged 38), was actively encouraged by her mother to be independent on the understanding that 'nowadays you can't be sure to spend your whole life with the same man' and received further confirmation of this attitude from the Business School she attended, which promoted the belief that professional success was as important for women as for men:

On the very first day, at the oral exam, they said things like 'So, you've decided to continue your education, we presume that it is not with a view to cooing, changing nappies or feeding babies. You are all here to have successful careers and to build up a good professional position.' . . . Whether you were a man or a woman, you were treated in exactly the same way. . . . So when you get out of there and have to face the world of work, it's completely different and it comes as a huge shock.

The first knock to her ambitions came when she was turned down for management status after three years on clerical grades. The second setback came when she decided that she wanted to change jobs (to branch management) in order to improve her promotion prospects, only to be told by the managing director (in 1993): 'Madame, as long as I am in charge of this company, there will never be a woman branch manager . . . there will never be any women in a position of power.' At this point, she thought about leaving the bank and looking for another job, but the economic climate was poor and her husband, who wanted children more than she did, persuaded her that this setback to her career provided the perfect opportunity to have a family. After the birth of two daughters (and further promotion) she again applied for a branch-manager position that she didn't get. In exasperation she went 80 per cent part-time and now considers herself to be more 'family centred' than before, but is increasingly angry about the way she has been treated at work and continues to adopt a *reflexive* attitude to bringing about change in both the professional and domestic spheres.

In other biographies, however, the interviewee had carried through her initial logic of action, which was confirmed and consolidated at various points in her life. A French doctor (5/02, aged 38) was the third child in a traditional Catholic family of five daughters. She thought about becoming a nun until she was 14, then decided to go into medicine because of what she saw as the caring aspect of the profession. She married (against parental advice) during her second year at medical school and had her first two children while she was still a student and a third after she had qualified. She adopted a *normative* logic of action by combining her medical training, childcare, and working to support her husband's studies and effectively took ten years to qualify as a GP: 'at certain times I really did have to sacrifice my own training.' After qualifying, she decided not to specialize—'I didn't want to sacrifice my children in the name of personal ambition'—and spent the next five years working on a very irregular basis as a locum, providing holiday cover for GPs in the country (she could take her children with her). Having set up in private practice three years ago, she continues to adhere to the male-breadwinner principle of female *dependency*: 'Men have a different conception of medicine, because they are men, they have families to support, whereas I'm a doctor because I enjoy the job. I say to myself that if I really get fed-up, I can put the key under the door, because I have my husband who has a good job and so we would survive'.

In a parallel fashion, others had consistently maintained a transgressional logic of action, as in the case of this English banker (2/27, aged 32). Her working-class parents were both made redundant when she was still in her teens, so she decided to leave school and take a secure job in the bank. She always intended to have a career: 'The first day in the bank, I went to see the manager, I told him I wanted to do the exams and I had his support. Other women who joined at the same time as me have said they did not have the support and were not encouraged. Personally, I take the view that if you show willing, you get the support.' In 1985 she got married: 'that didn't change anything as far as career paths were concerned.' The marriage was based on the understanding that they wouldn't have children: 'This was something we had discussed before we got married, that neither of us was interested in having kids.' However, the relationship didn't last long: 'I was still one of the rare females passing her exams at this point . . . up to 1987, everything was fine, but, basically, he [husband] changed . . . He decided he wanted a family and he wanted it and he was going to get it and he didn't care that it would affect my career.' This biography illustrates a so-far-consistent *strategy*, which is *transgressive* in so much as the respondent appreciates that she was somewhat unusual in having chosen to take a 'masculine' route through the organization, but continues to believe that, as a woman, she must be prepared to sacrifice relationships and family life in order to do this.

Not all biographies, however, result in coherence and unity and are more or less permanently torn by conflict. An English banker's (2/26, aged 36) father was a bank manager and her mother didn't have a job: 'very much the old school . . . always there dependable, a mother figure for us.' She married whilst in her first year at university (with the consent of her parents). Her husband also came from a traditional background and she describes him as 'not a new man'. She always expected to have responsibility for home and children, and took a career break to have her two children, returning to work full-time before she had intended to because an excellent opportunity came up. Her parents care for the two children: 'My parents were very keen for me to be a high achiever . . . and pushed and encouraged me and developed a high achievement motive in me . . . You could say it's now gone full circle in that now I'm a career woman, with a family of my own, my Mum is now not as keen on the fact . . . She thinks I've got my priorities wrong.' This respondent is acutely conscious, therefore, of the conflict between normativity and pressures towards individualism, which she describes in gendered terms: 'It's not easy, but I think a lot of it is pressure we've brought to bear on ourselves, as women wanting to be men . . . I can't blame anybody for it. I've come to it myself and it's what I wanted to do, so I've got it.' The illness of her youngest child, together with the guilt and pressure she experiences and expresses so eloquently, make it probable that her logic of action will remain predominately *normative* and her social experience *dependent*: 'I would never expect him [husband] to make sacrifices for my career. . . . When you look to your future, it will be his pension that will be the thing that we're looking to preserve. Mine's extra, mine's always been the luxury.'

Others find themselves in conflict over a 'failure' to realize a normative logic of action, despite a career profile that might initially appear as 'transgressional' or even autonomous. A French banker (5/23, aged 32) was always considered 'the genius' of her family and was academically more successful than any of her four brothers and sisters and most of her peers. Her early socialization was gender differentiated, and her parents had little understanding of the higher education system. After having contemplated a career in medicine, she was encouraged by one of her teachers to take the entrance exams for the Business School. She was ambitious and joined the bank at branch level with management status and continued to progress rapidly through the bank hierarchy, particularly when she accepted a post at the Head Office. A relationship ended (at her instigation): 'effectively from 1988 onwards, I was really determined to build up my professional success and so I think that I probably considered the personal and sentimental side of things as coming second to that.' Nevertheless, her logic of action at this point would seem to be largely *reflexive* in that: 'I know that if I ever have children myself one day, and I hope that I do . . . a successful professional career that goes hand in hand with success in personal relationships, that's really something to be proud of.' But this potentially reflexive logic is somewhat contradicted by the difficulties she has experienced in finding a partner and the value she attaches to the *normative* principles of the male-breadwinner model:

The reason why things didn't really work out with the person I was living with before is because he didn't have the same social standing or education as myself . . . it's very important for me that the man should be the main breadwinner . . . it really is up to the man to keep the family together and to earn their success and of course there is a financial element to that . . . I'm really looking for someone with that kind of situation and that makes it quite difficult.

These biographies illustrate the way in which gendered logics of action are shaped and in some cases transformed by the social experience of both gender and employment. Individual cases have, of course, been chosen to illustrate particular arguments, but it is important to emphasize that, potentially, *every* interview might have been mapped onto the framework described in Figure 8.3. The parallels that may be drawn between the experiences of French and British women would lend support to the arguments developed by Giddens and Beck as to the increased capacity of women reflexively to construct their 'own' biographies in 'advanced modernity'.

Nevertheless, even with the small number of interviews available, the effects of cross-national variations in both occupational structuring and discourses of feminism were still apparent. Historically, although informal exclusionary practices are widespread, French (married) women have not been *formally* excluded from the banking hierarchy in the same manner as British women. In the British case, both formal and informal exclusionary practices in banking were directly challenged by an Equal Opportunities Commission action in the 1980s (Crompton 1989). As a consequence, self-conscious equal-opportunity strategies have been widely adopted in the finance sector in Britain since the 1980s, and many of the women interviewed were conscious of the bank as a 'good employer' in this respect.[13] No such policies have been adopted by French banks, and, because of the explicit and direct discrimination they experienced within their employment, French women bankers were more likely to complain of continuing discrimination.

In medicine, national occupational differences were again important. Timetable flexibility during medical studies and the lack of geographical mobility required for specialist training combined to make a normative logic of action more tenable for female doctors in France than in Britain. A number of French medical respondents argued that, as women, with particular 'feminine qualities', they were in a position to transform medical practice from within; this 'feminitude' perspective on occupational feminization was never expressed in the British interviews. This difference, it may be suggested, may be linked to the different feminist discourses available within each national context. It would be interesting to examine the extent to which the so-called French feminist stress on difference (see e.g. Irigary 1989, 1997) has shaped the ways in which professional women interpret the family–employment interface within the medical profession in each country.

CONCLUSIONS

In conclusion, I would argue that a rigorous definition of the gender process in terms of differentiation rather than difference provides a more dynamic perspective on occupational feminization than has been the case in much recent research on this theme. A conception of women's quest for autonomy as the vital step in the transformation of the mid-twentieth-century gender process sheds new light on the factors that enable us to provide an insightful sociological analysis as to the meaning and consequences of the recent wave of professional feminization. This is particularly useful at a time when the researchers working on the major changes effecting professional status and practice are increasingly insisting on the importance of recent changes to the relative autonomy of the professions as a whole within the advanced capitalist labour market (Hassenteufel 1997). A radical break with the conceptual frameworks that create a static and rarefied vision of masculinity and femininity opens up new avenues for grasping the duality and simultaneity of the massive influx of women into the higher levels of the occupational hierarchy and their equally massive over-representation at the very bottom of this hierarchy.

I have no definitive answers as to the long-term effects of occupational feminization on the gender process, but I am fairly certain that the foundations of the male-breadwinner model will be shaken (although perhaps not destroyed) by the opportunities that access to professional occupations represents for women. It is nevertheless the case that the rapid numerical increase of women professionals remains an unsatisfactory indicator of real or potential changes in the nature of the dominant gender identity and experiences of women professionals under advanced capitalism. Rather than seeing women as a homogeneous category, future research needs to pay greater attention to the influence of the specific combinations of identity, beliefs, and behaviour of female (and male) individuals in the professional and the domestic spheres, as essential factors both in their relationship to the traditional model of the male-breadwinner model and in the degree to which the gender (differentiation) process at the basis of this model is likely to be transformed over time.

NOTES

1. As the data presented in Chapter 9 indicate, women doctors, like women in many other élite sectors of the labour market, tend to be concentrated in the lower, least-prestigious, and least-well-paid sectors of the medical profession (see Riska and Weger 1993; Allen 1994; Borrel 1995; Ruelland 1995).
2. As much of the anthropological research from Margaret Mead (1966) onwards has shown, although there is no evidence of a society that does not construct the sexual duality of the human race as a socially significant division, the emotions, attitudes, behaviour, and beliefs expected of 'men' and of 'women' nevertheless show considerable diversity over time and place. In much the same vein, the *relative* importance of this differentiation according to sex with regard to other organizing principles of human societies (age, occupation, colour of skin, etc.) may also vary significantly between societies and/or at different periods of their existence.

3. This definition of gender requires certain linguistic precautions. Since the relational character of gender is at the heart of this definition, the use of terms such as 'gender relations' becomes somewhat misleading, since this expression seems to rest on an (often implicit) 'attribute' definition of gender.
4. Indeed, much recent research in the field of human genetics has questioned the biological reality of the neat binary XX vs. XY division between the sexes (see Peyre *et al.* 1991).
5. Within the institutional context of contemporary academia, it is perfectly understandable that the struggle for recognition of the scientific legitimacy of 'gender' as an object of enquiry and research should have led to the invisibility of (or the refusal to explicitly acknowledge) this point. This is all the more surprising given that the theoretical perspective of a demise of capitalism (inherent in Marxism) has never been used to limit or restrict the quantity (or quality) of research on class.
6. For a critical assessment of patriarchy as a conceptual tool, see Pollert (1996) and Crompton (1998*b*).
7. The potential effects of feminization on the professions are discussed more fully in Chapter 9 of this volume.
8. Interviews were carried out by Rosemary Crompton, Fiona Harris, Nicky Le Feuvre, and Florence Benoit.
9. Although there is some overlap here with the analysis of women's biographical trajectories in banking and medicine presented by Crompton and Harris in Chapters 6 and 7 of this volume (see also Crompton and Harris 1998*b*), I am less interested in explaining the occupational and family formation trajectories of professional women in different occupational and societal contexts than in exploring the consequences of the feminization of élite occupations as far as the reproduction/transformation of the gender process is concerned.
10. As an explanatory framework, it is, however, discussed critically in Chapter 9 of this volume.
11. I must stress at this point that I am in no way suggesting that these observations imply the existence of 'qualitatively different types' of women, whose individual 'preferences' determine their social experience of gender and employment (cf. Hakim 1996; Crompton and Harris 1998*a*).
12. The system of interview numbering, which is described in the Appendix, indicates country and occupation.
13. Although it should be stressed that this was not the case for all the British bank respondents.

9

The Restructuring of Gender Relations within the Medical Profession

ROSEMARY CROMPTON, NICKY LE FEUVRE, AND GUNN ELISABETH BIRKELUND

INTRODUCTION

In all European countries, women are increasingly qualifying for, and practising, professional occupations. Medicine, law, accountancy, pharmacy, and a host of other occupations requiring degree- and postgraduate-level training and qualifications have all seen an increase in their female complement. In this chapter we will argue that this ongoing restructuring within the higher levels of the occupational hierarchy has a number of implications for our thinking about gender, as well as for the long-established 'sociology of the professions' itself. We will be developing these arguments through an analysis of the medical profession in Britain, France, and Norway. In all of these countries the medical profession is in a process of feminization, and women now make up more than a half of students in training for medicine.

In the next section, we will review and discuss theoretical issues relating to both the sociology of the professions and the concept of gender. In particular, we will raise the question of whether the entry of women into the professions means that we should revise or abandon our existing frameworks of analysis. In the sections that follow, our three-country comparative analysis will demonstrate that, despite the entry of women, the medical profession still remains male dominated as a consequence of both masculine exclusionary practices, as well as the choices of career and specialty made by women doctors as a consequence of their 'working through' their employment and family biographies.

THE SOCIOLOGY OF THE PROFESSIONS, GENDER, AND MEDICINE

The sociological and historical analysis of the professions has a long pedigree, whose evolution can be seen as reflecting both the creation of a body of theory and research relating to these privileged occupations, as well as trends and developments within sociology itself (Crompton 1990). In the 1940s, Parsons's (1939) influential discussion highlighted a number of issues that set in motion a series of debates.[1] First, he made a distinction between 'professionals' and 'bureaucrats' in terms of the different bases of their authority. Whereas bureaucratic authority, he argued, derived from the position within the *organization* held by the office-holder, professional authority rested upon the knowledge and expertise acquired by the *individual* as a consequence of long years of professional training. Parsons viewed professions as having an important regulatory function in modern capitalist societies. Whereas market-oriented managers were compelled by a combination of self-interest and organizational pressures to maximize profits, professionals, he argued, were motivated more by altruistic ideals of service and the maintenance of professional standards. The emergence of the professions, therefore, was seen as a counter to the more negative effects of the development of capitalism (see also Perkin 1989). In relation to the medical profession in particular, Parsons explained the social organization of medical practice—the maintaining of social distance, the doctor's status as an 'expert'—in terms of the functional requirements set by a given level of science and technology within medicine. Thus professions were functional for social cohesion, and the characteristics of medical practice were functionally determined. In the sociology of the professions that developed from the 1960s, therefore, efforts were made to discover essential professional 'traits' (Johnson 1972), not only in the spirit of sociological enquiry, but also as a model for others to follow.

Parsons's normative functionalist analysis of the professions was extensively criticized throughout the 1970s and 1980s. Rather than being altruistic occupations oriented towards and motivated by the requirements of the wider society, professions were increasingly described as occupations that had been uniquely successful in gaining and monopolizing a privileged position largely for their own advantage. The 'actual' value of the professional's expertise was held up to close (and often hostile) scrutiny, his or her disinterestedness and altruism questioned. The professions' claims to privilege and special treatment were, in the prevailing spirit of the times, thoroughly debunked (Esland and Salaman 1980).

An emphasis upon the negative aspects of professional exclusion, therefore, was a large part of the radical critique of professionalism that was developed in sociology from the 1970s. This opened up the path for analyses of the gendered nature of professional practice. Women had been excluded from most professions at their emergence. In addition, many semi-professional occupations in which women predominated, such as nursing and midwifery, were systematically subordinated to male-dominated professions such as medicine (Leeson and Gray 1978; Witz 1992). Much professional employment demanded a two-person career: that is, the professional's capacity to work depended upon unpaid input from a partner—usually wives (Finch 1983; Crompton 1986). It is not too difficult, therefore, to see the history of professional development as an important element in securing the masculine dominance of the modern occupational structure associated with the male-breadwinner model, in which women were, initially, systematically denied access to occupations which would have enabled them to live independently (Hartmann 1976; Walby 1986).

Discussions of gender and the professions, therefore, have tended to focus on male exclusionary practices, as well as the continuing subordination of women within professions such as medicine (Crompton 1990; Riska and Wegar 1993). Nevertheless, over the last half of the twentieth century, the formal restrictions on women's rights to train for and practise professional occupations have been removed, and other forms of discrimination have been made illegal (for example, the informal gender quota that was in operation in many British medical schools until the 1980s (see Elston 1993)). As a consequence, women have entered the professions in ever-greater numbers (Crompton and Sanderson 1990).

However, from the end of the 1980s the sociology of the professions has had less of a focus on exclusion and discriminatory practices within these occupations (although these have by no means disappeared). Attempts to identify a universal definition of 'profession' have been abandoned, and there has been a shift towards the analysis of the processes of professional emergence and restructuring, in which many different routes (and thus professional types) can be identified (Abbott 1988). Earlier critiques of essentialism had argued that, in any case, 'professionalism' was a 'folk' rather than a socio-logical concept, and a symbolic interactionist strand within the sociology of the professions had emphasized the significance of pro-fessionalism not only in creating and developing a professional iden-tity, but also in socializing and regulating the professionals themselves (Dingwall 1976).

From this perspective, professionalism is seen as a discipline that regulates the *individual* (rather than just the occupation) through a professional code of conduct. Professionalism is viewed in these analyses as a mode of individual control, one of the 'softwares of control', which is drawn upon as part of a battery of techniques for regulating the labour process in advanced capitalism. Writing of the medical profession, for example, Foucault emphasizes the 'notion of competence, that is . . . a set of possibilities that characterise the very person of the doctor: knowledge, experience, and . . . "recognised probity" . . . The medical act is worth what he who has performed it is worth' (Foucault, quoted in Osborne 1993: 348).

It may be noted that, in this extract, the doctor is described as 'he', suggesting that masculinity is amongst the qualities constituting the occupation. In a similar vein, it has recently been argued (Davies 1996) that professions are 'masculine' not only because of the numer-ical predominance of the male sex, but also because that 'profession' itself is deeply 'gendered'. In a parallel with Bologh's analysis of bureaucracy, Davies (1996: 669) argues that 'profession . . . cele-brates and sustains a masculinist vision'. Bologh (1990) argued that, in a public world comprised of 'hostile strangers', bureaucracy regu-lates aggression and competition amongst men and provides a nec-essary stability. The detached, unemotional (and masculine) bureaucratic leader controls by maintaining distance (Davies 1996: 666). On this reading, bureaucracy is seen as embodying a rejection and denial of 'feminine' qualities such as understanding, connected-ness, empathy, and so on (see also Craib 1987).[2]

Davies argues that professional knowledge is gained by dint of 'lengthy and heroic individual effort', creates specialisms, and sus-tains expertise. Like bureaucracy, it is rational, impersonal, and impartial. Masculine professional autonomy is sustained by the preparatory and follow-up work of others—nurses, cleaners, secre-taries, etc.—who are usually women. Gender, therefore, is constitutive of professional relations both in the sense of embodying masculine profession itself, as well as the feminized groups it subordinates. However, Davies suggests that, as more women enter the professions, there is the possibility of 'transformation from within'. Feminization might lead to a 'challenge to professional hegemony' and a 'questioning of masculinity and masculine identity' (1996: 673). As professions feminize, and humanize, so the 'masculinist' aspect of their constitution might be eroded.[3] An important strand of Davies's argument, therefore, has parallels with neo-essentialist arguments relating to the 'feminitude' outcome of occupational feminization, as discussed in Chapter 8.

In her analysis of the professions, Davies (1996) develops a relational approach in which gender is seen as socially constructed. The qualities that women represent are constructed as those of the 'devalued Other' thus Davies (1996: 663–4) also views gender as having a binary form. Although we would be in sympathy with Davies's emphasis upon the socially constructed and non-fixed nature of gender, we have some difficulties with the binary elements of her approach. The definition of 'feminine' as 'not masculine' (and vice versa) makes the possibility of the transformation of the relationships between the sexes problematic—the 'devalued Other', by definition, cannot be superseded but will be reproduced anew. At the level of the individual, it may be argued that an awareness of diversity is required in order to be able to contemplate the possibility of transformation in gender identities and relationships. As argued at some length in the Introduction and in Chapter 8, we would be more in sympathy with an approach that emphasizes the socially constructed nature of gender and the diversity of both masculinities and femininities, but assumes neither its complete separation, nor the automatic inferiority of the feminine.

An emphasis upon the diversity of gendered biographical possibilities does not, however, necessarily mean a collapse into deconstructionist relativism. Dualist categories, such as public/private, individual/society, and family/economy, have been used in the development of theories of modernity, and have been widely criticized. However, they can, nevertheless, be historically reanalysed in order to demonstrate their *de facto* interpenetration.[4] That is, it is possible to operate simultaneously within binary, as well as more discursive, frameworks of feminist analysis. We would, therefore, endorse an approach that sees women as 'gendered subjects who actively interpret, *within historically available modes of interpretation* their identities' (Marshall 1994: 159; emphasis added) rather than as being confined to the qualities available to the 'devalued Other'.

Furthermore, it may be suggested that the definition of 'profession' as 'masculine' negatively labels characteristics that may be neither masculine nor feminine, but, rather, necessary to the practice of the occupations in question. We would question whether expertise, impartiality, and impersonality are specifically *masculine* characteristics. Indeed, as professionals have argued, they may be required for the successful pursuit of the occupation. A degree of impartiality is required if professionals are to be able to operate in what are often emotion-laden work environments. Expertise is very necessary if an individual is to be allowed to prescribe poisonous substances, and/or assault other human beings in a way that would be a criminal offence outside a medical context. In short, without collapsing into a Parsonian essentialism relating to necessary professional traits, it may nevertheless be recognized that these are necessary features of the occupation in question. It is important not to replace a Parsonian essentialism relating to the particular characteristics of a profession as an occupation with a femininist essentialism relating to the gender characteristics of particular occupations.

These arguments do not mean, however, that we consider that women within the medical profession have a non-gendered set of professional choices available to them, nor would we argue that there are no differences at all in the way in which male and female doctors approach their profession. Women doctors behave as women as well as doctors; this means that they are subject to both exclusionary pressures within the profession, as well as gendered expectations in respect of their family lives. We will address these questions through a comparative analysis of the medical profession in Britain, France, and Norway. Amongst other things, this evidence will demonstrate that the development of intra-professional segregation of medicine by specialty and sex suggests that any transformation of the medical profession from within is likely to be slow, and, indeed, that men's domination of the profession is likely to persist.

THE MEDICAL PROFESSION IN BRITAIN, FRANCE, AND NORWAY

Britain has one of the lowest proportions of doctors per head of population amongst the developed countries—15.6 per 10,000 inhabitants in 1994. In contrast, in the same year, France had 28.5, and Norway 27.1, doctors per 10,000 people (OECD 1997). The explanation of this difference between Britain and the other two countries is no simple matter. Despite spiralling costs, the organization of health care in Britain is reckoned to be relatively cost efficient (Moran and Wood 1993: 7), and general practitioners (GPs) play an important role in controlling access to expensive hospital services and specialist treatment. As we shall see, patient demand for specialist consultation in France is high, and not subject to the same controls as in Britain. Both the greater wealth and geographical area of Norway may account for the extent of doctor provision in that country. Doctors may be employed or self-employed, work in private or public medicine, in hospitals or in the community. In fact, the complexities of medical provision mean that there is often considerable overlap between these categories as far as individual doctors are concerned.

In all three countries, doctors may specialize, or be generalists or GPs (*omnipracticiens* in France, *almenpraktikers* in Norway).[5] However, the nature of the 'specialist' and 'generalist' categories varies between the three countries. In Britain, where separate figures are presented for hospital doctors and GPs (and there is hardly any overlap at all between the two categories), 33 per cent of medical staff in hospitals, and 20 per cent of all doctors, are, specialist consultants, the élite of the medical profession.[6] In Norway, aggregate national figures are presented for all doctors, and 56 per cent of all gainfully employed doctors under 70 years of age are specialists. Similarly, nearly half (49 per cent) of doctors in France are specialists. These figures suggest that the proportion of specialists is lower in England, and, in any case, although there will be broad parity between the most senior hospital doctors in all three countries, the category of 'specialist' is not necessarily comparable.

In Britain and Norway, patients are registered with a doctor's practice, which is the first port of call for non-emergencies. GPs in Britain are self-employed, *almenpraktikere* in Norway may have their own practices or may be salaried doctors working in municipal health centres. In both countries, the doctor's practice acts as a gate-keeper (through a process of referral) for access to specialists— although, as we shall see, in Norway there are some important exceptions to this rule.[7] In Britain, patients do not pay directly for visits to the doctor,[8] or for hospital treatment. In Norway, patients above a certain level of income pay a small fee for consultation, which varies by the type of treatment. In France, access to non-emergency medical care is more patient driven. As noted above, a high proportion (60 per cent) of specialists are located in private practices (*cabinets*), where they may be accessed directly by the patient (as are GPs in Britain). Patients pay doctors and specialists for consultations, and are subsequently reimbursed through the social-security system. These differences are reflected in the employ-ment of doctors, and, whereas 62 per cent of doctors in Britain, and 61 per cent of doctors in Norway, work in hospitals, 69 per cent of doctors in France are self-employed private practitioners.

Medical Training

In all three countries access to medical training is academically com-petitive. However, there is open access to the first year of medical study in France, after which a *numerus clausus* (introduced in 1971) operates. Before medical reforms in 1984, medical graduates could either (*a*) go into private practice as a generalist; (*b*) enter the *con-cours d'internat* to undertake hospital-based training as a specialist; (*c*) study for a *Certificat d'Études Specialisées* (*CES*) taking three years. Within the context of the European harmonization of medical training, the *CES* route to specialization has disappeared. There was a tendency for women doctors to become specialists using the *CES* route.

Post-1984 in France, all doctors undertake a period of hospital-based training after graduation. This can be a two-year period of hos-pital-based training to become a generalist, or, for those who have been successful in the *concours d'internat*, a four-year period, leading to examinations for a *Diplôme d'Études Specialisées* (*DES*), for which there is now a *numerus clausus*. Once a specialist, doctors may remain primarily within hospitals, working their way up the hierarchy as *Assistant des hôpitaux* or *Chef de clinique* on to the most prestigious academic teaching and research positions as *Maître de conférences/*

Praticien hospitalier or, ultimately, *Professeur universitaire/Praticien hospitalier*. Alternatively they may set up in independent (private) practice. Many specialists in private practice will nevertheless maintain some contact with a local hospital or private clinic, on a sessional basis, as *Attaché des hôpitaux* or *vacataires*. Specialists may also work in salaried posts in public health, in advisory positions to the social-security administration, or as *médecins du travail*.

In Britain, five years of medical school are followed by a post-registration year. GP training involves a further year of hospital-based training and a year as a practice trainee. Hospital medicine has involved working up the hierarchy of the chosen specialty from SHO to Registrar, Senior Registrar.[9] This may often involve considerable geographical mobility, on a six-monthly basis (as noted in Chapter 8, geographical mobility is not required to the same extent in the training of specialists in France). Having passed the relevant professional examinations, specialists usually become consultants. The long years (sometimes over ten) of specialist training, with no guarantee of eventual success, have been subject to widespread criticism, and, following the 1993 Calman report, schemes are being implemented to regularize specialist training.

In Norway six years medical school are followed by one and a half years as *turnustjeneste* (house officer), which is often accompanied by geographical mobility. During the *turnustjeneste* the candidates spend one year in a hospital, and six months as an assistant to a doctor within the public health system—often in a remote rural area. After this a doctor may practise independently. Specialist training is acquired via further hospital work, together with passing the relevant examinations. Specialists may work in hospitals (*overleger*), or may set up in private practice (*privatpraktiserende spesialister*), particularly as dermatologists, opthalmologists, and gynaecologists.

FEMINIZATION

In all three countries, the profession is feminizing, and women now comprise over 50 per cent of medical students. In 1993, 29 per cent of doctors in England, and, in 1995, 33 per cent of doctors in France and 27 per cent of doctors in Norway, were women.[10] However, in all three countries, women are not evenly distributed within the medical profession, and there is extensive internal segregation by sex.

As we have noted, in Britain, the status of medical specialists within the profession is high, as is their remuneration. Women doctors are under-represented amongst specialists, and comprise 18 per cent of hospital consultants in England. Similarly (by coincidence), women are 18 per cent of *overleger*—the highest level of specialist— in Norway. In some specialties, notably surgery, women are a very small minority indeed (4 per cent in Britain; 3 per cent in Norway). In contrast, in both England and Norway, women doctors have moved fairly rapidly into General Practice/*Almenpraksis*, where they are represented in their due proportion (29 per cent in Britain, 28 per cent in Norway). In France, women are, relatively speaking, slightly *over*-represented amongst specialists at 33 per cent, and are 32 per cent of generalists. Nevertheless, women hospital doctors make up only 6 per cent of university professors, and 15 per cent of other hospital-based teaching posts, but are 45 per cent of hospital assistants (Vilain 1995: 31).

The explanation of these cross-national differences relates not only to the fact that, as we have seen, it has historically been 'easier' to become a specialist in France, but also to the organization of medical provision and the implications of this for the working arrangements of doctors themselves. In France, specialists in private practice are available for direct access by patients, and many women specialists will work from their own *cabinets* and will have some control over their own hours of working. However, in England and to a lesser extent in Norway (where some specialists, including medical gynaecologists, may be independent practitioners), specialists are largely hospital based and access is controlled by referral from the GP, *almenpraktikere*, or municipal doctor. In the hospital setting, the hours worked by doctors are a function of both medical hierarchies, as well as the nature of the specialty. Some specialties, such as surgery and obstetrics, demand long and/or irregular working hours, whereas the hours worked by other specialties, such as dermatology or anaesthetics, tend to be more regular. In Britain, junior doctors (specialists in training) have by tradition worked very long hours, with long periods 'on call' (that is, available for emergencies).

In community or general medicine, however, doctors are more able to regulate their hours of working, and/or work part-time. This is certainly an important factor explaining why there are relatively more women in general practice in Britain and Norway, and, as we have seen, women specialists in France are rather more likely to work from their own *cabinets* than in hospitals. In all three countries, women doctors are also likely to work shorter hours than male doctors. In England, just under a quarter of women GPs were either job sharing or part-time in 1992, whereas 92 per cent of male GPs work full-time. The rate of part-time working amongst women doctors would seem to be even higher in France, where 51 per cent of women *omnipracticiens*, and 66 per cent of specialists, work full-time, as compared to 93 per cent of male doctors (Vilain 1995). It should be noted, however, that doctors' full-time hours are long, and 'part-time' work for doctors in Britain, for example, is defined as thirty-seven hours a week. In Norway, female doctors work on average forty-seven hours a week, as compared to the average fifty-five-hour week of male doctors (Hofoss and Gjerberg 1994). Women doctors may work fewer hours than male doctors, therefore, but their hours are still relatively long as compared with women in other occupations.

FEMINIZATION AND THE NATURE OF MEDICAL SPECIALIZATION IN BRITAIN, FRANCE, AND NORWAY

In all three countries, therefore, women are going into the medical profession in ever greater numbers. However, as we have seen, the profession is internally segregated by sex, and this is particularly apparent in respect of the medical specialties taken up by men and women. We have stressed that the category of medical 'specialists' in the three countries is not directly comparable. There are a greater proportion of specialists in France as compared to the other two countries, and 60 per cent are found in private practice, who may be accessed directly by the patient without referral from a generalist gatekeeper.[11] This fragmentation of specialists has resulted in greater numbers and subsequent status dilution of specialists in France. In Norway, a limited number of specialists (7 per cent of all doctors) operate as *sole* private practitioners, although a substantial minority will also do private practice in medical gynaecology, paediatrics, and dermatology. However, in Britain, specialists are hospital based, although some consultants operate private practices in parallel with NHS work. Only a very small minority of doctors are employed entirely in the private sector. In Norway, 41 per cent of doctors in hospitals are specialists (*overleger*), indicating that the category is rather broader than that of consultants in Britain. The fact that women are only 18 per cent of *overleger* suggests that, relatively speaking, women doctors in Norway are even less well represented amongst specialists than in Britain. In contrast, women make up 47 per cent of young hospital doctors in Norway.

As we shall see, these differences of specialism are intimately bound up with the internal gender stratification of the profession. As is demonstrated in Table 9.1, there is a clear tendency for women specialists in all three countries to be concentrated in certain fields. As might have been expected, the detailed classification of medical specialties is not cross-nationally comparable. However, in Table 9.1, we have selected those groupings that appear to be the most nearly comparable, although we have also included some exceptions that 'prove the rule'.

The pattern of intra-professional segregation by sex shows continuities in all three countries. For example, relative to their representation amongst specialists, in all three countries women are over-represented amongst dermatologists, paediatricians, and psychiatrists, and under-represented amongst surgeons, cardiologists, and gastroenterologists. That is, in all three countries women tend to be over-represented amongst 'caring' specialties, as well as amongst specialties in which working hours are unlikely to be too demanding, such as dermatology. However, the *differences* in the feminization of specialties as between the three countries also reflect gender segregation within the profession.

Obstetrics and gynaecology are an interesting example here. In both England and France, women are slightly under-represented in the surgical specialty of obstetrics and gynaecology. However, the lower status, non-surgical, specialism of medical gynaecology in France is 86 per cent women, but is not to be found in England. In France, *gynécologie médicale* includes family planning, preventative medicine such as cervical smears, etc., as well as gynaecological complaints. In France these services have been organized as a separate specialty, whereas in Britain they are available through the GP.[12] This cross-national difference in the organization of medical services has, therefore, led to the creation of a virtual 'woman-only' niche in medicine in France. Similarly, in Norway, and somewhat against the trend given that the under-representation of women amongst specialists is somewhat greater than in the other two countries, women

TABLE 9.1. *The feminization of a selection of medical specialties in England (1994), France (1994), and Norway (1995)*

Discipline	England		France		Norway	
	Total no.	% women	Total no.	% women	Total no.	% women
All specialists of which:	24,691	21.2	83,339	33.5	7,142	17.7
Medical specialists						
Anaesthetics	3,368	25.0	7,887	38.0	390	13.8
Cardiology	466	6.9	4,707	12.3	154	3.9
Nephrology	197	6.6	651	22.3	58	8.6
Gastroenterology	360	6.7	2,652	14.0	117	2.6
Gynécologie médicale	—		1,963	85.8	—	
Dermatology	356	32.3	3,100	58.9	100	25.0
Radiology	1,646	31.3	4,527	22.4	298	24.8
Rheumatology	388	20.1	2,411	25.7	92	17.4
Paediatrics	1,447	36.5	5,334	52.7	310	21.9
Surgical specialists						
General surgery	1,414	3.2	3,898	3.3	809	3.0
Obstetrics and gynaecology	1,306	20.6	4,519	32.2	397	28.7
Otolaryngology	588	6.1	2,730	11.4	220	5.0
Other specialists						
Psychiatry	3,319	34.3	11,015	38.5	680	26.8
Santé publique et médecine du travail/ Samfunnsmedisin og Arbeidsmedisin	n.a.	n.a.	3,076	65.9	416	14.4

Source: Health and Personal Social Services Statistics for England, 1995; Ministère du Travail et des Affaires Sociales, SESI 1996; Taraldset (1998).

doctors would seem to be over-represented amongst obstetricians and gynaecologists. However, in Norway, this specialist category includes *non-surgical* medical gynaecologists. These non-surgical specialists practise independently, as in France, and many of these independent practitioners are women. Yet again, therefore, the apparent over-representation of women in a particular medical specialty proves to be an artefact of cross-national variations in the organization of medical services, as well as in the definition of medical specialties.

Women are, relatively, over-represented in radiology in England and Norway, yet under-represented in France. Again, these variations in levels of feminization may be explained by differences in the organization of medical services. In Britain and Norway, radiology is a salaried, hospital-based specialty offering regular hours. In France, radiological services are also available through independent specialists (*cabinets*). The hours are still regular, but the capital investment required to set up in private practice has had the effect of deterring women. Finally, we may point to the category *médicine du travail/Arbeidmedisin*, as well as *santé publique/Samfunnsmedisin*, neither of which has an exact British equivalent. In France, women are over-represented in both specialities, whereas Norwegian female doctors are over-represented in *Arbeidsmedisin* (25.9 per cent), but not in *Samfunnsmedisin* (10.3 per cent). These specialities are salaried positions, which offer regular working hours. Indeed, in France, 63 per cent of doctors in non-hospital-based salaried practice are women (Vilain 1995: 27).

In all three countries, therefore, although the entry of women into the prestigious and highly paid medical profession might seem to be evidence of a decline in vertical occupational segregation, intra-professional segregation within medicine reflects the broad contours of occupational segregation by sex. This is the case even in Norway, which, as we have demonstrated in Chapter 6, is one of the more liberal countries concerning attitudes to women's equality and changing roles, and might have been expected to have a greater representation of women within the higher levels of the medical profession. However, our figures suggest that women are even less well represented in the different medical specialties in Norway than they are in the other two countries.[13]

WOMEN'S MEDICAL CAREERS

As more women enter this previously male-dominated profession, it is apparent that many of them are deciding on their specialties, and shaping their careers, with a view to working part-time, or flexibly, and thus being able to combine professional employment with family life. Indeed, during biographical interviews carried out, as part of the Gender Relations project, with forty-five women doctors (fifteen in each country), many made this absolutely explicit:[14]

I decided to be a GP before finals, once I'd seen the lot of the specialties, and you realized how many hours were involved . . . realistically we were going to have kids and I didn't want to have either a massive career break or just not be there at all for them.   (2/05 Britain, GP (part-time), 2 children, one expected)[15]

I decided after I was married and doing house jobs that I didn't want to stay in the rat-race that was hospital medicine . . . 'cos my husband was doing that.   (2/02 Britain, GP Principal (part-time), three children)

I would have liked to have done paediatrics, but during the course of my training I chose another option—I got married and I decided to have children, because I didn't want to wait too long . . . to have children when I was too old.   (5/02 France, généraliste, three children)

When it came to choosing a specialty, I chose something that was typically feminine, that was compatible with family life, which didn't involve . . . we always consult by appointment, we have very few emergencies, no weekend cover . . . that's something I really didn't want to get involved in.   (5/03 France, dermatologist (part-time), three children)

I chose to specialize because I really couldn't see myself setting up in practice as an *omnipracticien*, not as a woman . . . I thought that for a man that would be fine, but for a woman . . . having to be on-call day and night . . . At the time I didn't have any family responsibilities, but in anticipation of those to come I thought it would be better to specialize.   (5/05 France, salaried radiologist (part-time), 1 child)

I knew all the time that I wanted children and family. When I specialized, I chose as I did because of my age and the family. If I had been twelve years younger I would probably have made a different choice. Not surgery, but something similar. This has got a lot to do with shift work and the 'pointed elbows' which one finds within certain specialties.   (3/08 Norway, psychiatrist (full-time), 3 children)

I decided to go for dermatology because this was a field one might enter without being totally eaten up with regard to the family. Dermatology is possible to combine with a family life. I did some investigations in this before I chose a specialty.   (3/10 Norway, dermatologist (full-time), 2 children)

The fact that many women doctors make such choices in relation to their actual or anticipated domestic responsibilities means that the increasing entry of women into medicine is likely to have less of an impact on the masculine dominance of the profession than their numerical representation might suggest. Working flexibly and part-time, fitting in a medical career around the demands of family life, does not leave much space for the 'challenge to professional hegemony' that Davies (1996: 673) has suggested might take place. Other research on highly educated women has revealed a similar reluctance amongst them to pursue a career 'at any cost' (Ferrand *et al.* 1996). Although the medical profession might seem to be feminizing with some rapidity, therefore, internal resegregation by sex means that masculine domination of the profession persists, and it is likely that any change will be very gradual.

At the same time, it is important to remember that there is continuing evidence of widespread masculine exclusionary practices within medicine. Direct masculine exclusionary practices in the most prestigious surgical specialties are both widespread and well documented in Britain (Allen 1994: 76), and were graphically described by many of our interviewees: 'The surgeons . . . when I left, the younger one he said to me "oh we're getting a proper houseman next time" and I said "What do you mean a man" and he said "yes" and he used to introduce me: "here's our local Sunday school teacher", he used to make a lot of sexist comments to me, and never made me feel I was very good.' Although there has been no such systematic research on this issue in France, our interview data would seem to suggest that women's experiences are very similar in this respect. As one of our interviewees in France (herself a plastic/hand surgeon) said: 'the stereotypes about surgeons are perfectly correct, they really are an awful bunch. I think that it's to do with the abnormal power we have over the human body . . . the surgeons end up believing that they have, or that they should have, the same sort of control over everything around them.' In short, in surgery in particular, the medical profession would seem to exemplify the aggressive and negative 'masculine' stereotyped characteristics of profession that are emphasized by Davies (1996).

Male-dominated specialties within medicine are also those which are the highest paid. In Britain, opportunities for private practice are clustered in the male-dominated specialties: for example, surgery and general medicine, rather than female specialties such as psychiatry or geriatrics. The system of merit awards (now distinction awards) is administered within the profession itself—that is, doctors make awards to other doctors.[15] These awards (which are made to consultants) enhance salaries by an average of 18 per cent, but some awards can add 95 per cent to a salary (Moran and Wood 1993). They tend to be concentrated in the male-dominated specialties. For example, with reference to the specialties described in Table 9.1, over 50 per cent of cardiologists, and 48 per cent of general surgeons (both 'male' specialties), have merit awards. However, only 30 per cent of anaesthetists, 27 per cent of radiologists, and 29 per cent of psychiatrists have merit awards—all specialties in which women are relatively over-represented. A similar pattern is found in France. Psychiatrists earn an average 313,000 francs per annum, whereas surgeons earn 748,000 francs (CERC 1991). There are also significant sex differences in income *within* each specialty. Thus whereas male *omnipracticiens* earn 327,100 francs, women earn 170,700 francs per annum (these differences also reflect variations in working time between the sexes). The data for Norway do not give details of income by specialty, but, as we have seen, women are over-represented amongst the lower-paid junior hospital doctors and municipal doctors, and under-represented amongst the better-paid specialists and *overleger*.

Many women doctors may make family-oriented career decisions, therefore, but within a pattern of constraints of which they are well aware. We have argued in Chapters 6 and 7 that women doctors are, in fact, more likely to have relatively traditional work-life biographies as compared with other professional (managerial) women. They are more likely to take major responsibility for the domestic division of labour, and to work flexibly in order to accommodate childcare (Crompton and Harris 1998*b*).

DISCUSSION AND CONCLUSION

From the nineteenth century onwards, professions such as medicine and law consolidated their position as élite occupations restricted largely to men. The struggles of first-wave feminism included campaigns for women's access to professional training as well as other institutions of higher education (Witz 1992: ch. 3). As Marshall (1994: 148) has argued: 'As a political movement, feminism continues to use egalitarian rhetoric as the basis of most of its political demands . . . feminism is wedded to the modern by virtue of its rootedness in the space opened up by the rights discourse and by the ideals of the bourgeois public.' In part as a result of these struggles, at the end of the twentieth century the feminization of these occupations is but one manifestation of ongoing changes in gender relations and the gender division of labour.

In this chapter, we have critically debated suggestions that the entry of women into the medical profession might radically transform this occupation, along the lines that the more caring qualities of women will be reflected in 'feminized' medicine ('feminitude'). We have queried whether particular occupational characteristics of professions can be unambiguously labelled as 'masculine' or 'feminine', and have warned of the dangers of substituting a gender essentialism for a Parsonian essentialism in respect of these occupations.

Nevertheless, the fact that women are, increasingly, entering previously male-dominated occupations such as medicine does represent an important social change. In this chapter, we have carried out an in-depth analysis of the entry of women into medicine in three rather different countries—Britain, France and Norway. We found that, despite the entry of women, the medical profession remains male dominated. In part, this is because, despite the pace of change both in the regulation of the profession and in attitudes to women, men still continue to exclude women from the best-paid and most prestigious medical specialties. However, it is also because women doctors have often decided to train for and enter medical specialties that are compatible with family life in that they offer regular and/or controllable working hours. Women doctors also work fewer hours than male doctors, and part-time work is widely available within the medical profession.

Thus many women doctors are 'practitioners' rather than 'careerists' (Crompton and Sanderson 1986). In relation to discussions within the sociology of the professions, this gender-based division of labour within medicine has been used as evidence of occupational downgrading. For example: 'a dual labour market for physicians has developed: one (*i.e. male*) which displays the features of the traditional privileged social position of physicians and another

(*i.e. female*) in which physicians show both the features of deprofes-
sionalization . . . and of proletarianization' (Riska 1993: 143).
However, whether the relatively lower status of the medical specialties taken up by women is a consequence of their entry into these specialties is a moot point. Psychology and geriatrics, for example, have
always had a relatively low status within medicine as compared to
surgery, even when men were numerically completely dominant
within the profession. The latter specialty is seen within the medical
profession as somewhat heroic, as demanding total commitment and
very long hours, and this is reflected in the deference given to the
specialty by medical peers (as well as in popular representations of
medicine such as television soap operas). Nevertheless, as empirical
research has demonstrated, women do choose specialties such as
anaesthetics, radiology, pathology, or psychiatry (in Britain) not
because they are low status, but because they are seen as compatible
with family life (Tait and Platt 1995).

The gender coding of the sexual division of labour has, historically, given women the major responsibility for caring, both within
the family and in occupations which provide caring outside the family. The occupational demands that are made by the various medical
specialties are well known within the profession. Medical training is
long and arduous, and it is not surprising, therefore, that women
who are planning to have children at some time in the future, and
who assume that they will take the major responsibility for caring
within the family, should 'choose' medical careers, and medical specialties, that are compatible with this. However, in a parallel with our
critique of essentialist thinking in respect of gender in this and the
previous chapter, we would argue that the work of caring *as such* is
not 'masculine' or 'feminine'. Men may care, as well as women. As a
British respondent (a consultant psychiatrist) commented: 'In this
department . . . the men seem to be a bit more sensitive than men in
surgery—in psychiatry—it's probably easier to seek out more supportive men here just by nature of the job they do. Most people we
look after are old and vulnerable—(you) can't do that if you're a
complete bastard I suppose' (2/13).

Indeed, current discussions of male and female roles suggest that
many men would be favourably disposed towards a loosening of the
gender codings attached to work (that is, employment), and caring.
It is apparent that many specialties within the medical profession are
not compatible with even a modest participation in family life, and

the respondents (all consultants) in a recent British study attributed personal problems such as divorce and infertility to the stress of medical training. As the authors of the study concluded: 'Perhaps it is time to stop demanding superhuman efforts and cater (i.e., in terms of work/family combination) for the motivated professional person of either sex' (Tait and Platt 1995: 375). In this chapter we have carried out an in-depth empirical investigation of one of the perspectives on occupational feminization—feminitude—described in Chapter 8. Besides being critical of the gender essentialism inherent in this perspective, we would also suggest that the channelling of women into particular occupational slots (either by choice or by constraint) within medicine means that the male dominance of the profession—and thus many of its masculine characteristics—are likely to persist for some time. Nevertheless, changes in gender relations, and the parallel pressures coming from within the profession itself (such as those noted above), mean that the existing gender regime within the medical profession is becoming increasingly untenable. Change within the medical profession is and has been slow, but, with the entry of women, it is possible that medical feminization might eventually be accompanied by moves towards a wider decoding of the sexual division of labour both in the profession and in the lifestyles of the doctors themselves.

NOTES

1. The concept of 'profession' has itself been contested, and it has been argued to be an Anglo–American, rather than a European concept (and therefore unsuitable for cross-national research). This distinction relates mainly to the manner in which professions have been organized, in that Anglo–American professions have been held to possess a greater capacity for self-regulation than European professions. This claim may, in fact, be contested (Moran and Wood 1993). However, this distinction relates to the organization of the occupation rather than the capacity for autonomous decision making based upon the possession of a recognized body of expertise, a characteristic that is common to all definitions of a profession, and a crucial element of the definition we employ here, as well as in Chapters 6 and 7 of this book, and one that is contained within Parsons's original definition.
2. Similar arguments, deriving from the work of Gilligan, have been developed in rspect of the legal profession, into which women are entering in ever greater numbers. (See Menkel-Meadow 1989; see also Fuggelli 1989/90).
3. These arguments have many parallels with those developed by second-wave feminists from the 1970s, in which 'caring' female health professionals, such as nurses, were seen as controlled by 'technicist' male health professionals

(doctors), to the detriment of female patients in particular. (See, e.g., Leeson and Gray 1978; Davies and Rosser 1986). They are discussed in Wegar (1993).

4. For example, the coming of industrialism has often been characterized as resting upon a 'separation of home and work'. However, (i) women continued to contribute to the market economy, often through home-based work such as outwork or taking in lodgers, etc., and (ii) women's work in the domestic sphere was essential to sustain labour in the market (see Glucksmann 1995).

5. In all three countries, specialist qualifications have been introduced for general practice. In Britain, a GP principal is considered to be the equivalent of a hospital consultant.

6. In Norway *overleger* have reached the top of their profession, although the fact that *overleger* make up 41 per cent of doctors in Norwegian hospitals suggests that the category reaches further down the medical hierarchy than does that of consultant in Britain.

7. In Norway there is also the possibility of direct access to gynaecologists and paediatricians in the larger cities. In addition, there has been an expansion of private medicine from the mid-1980s, which was arrested by a considerable increase in the level of doctor's salaries in 1996. *Overleger* (specialists) in public hospitals were granted a wage increase of 28.5 per cent, and *tutnuslege* (junior doctors) an increase of 34.9 per cent.

8. The introduction of fund holding during the 1990s (17 per cent of all practices, 25 per cent of doctors in 1992) has not changed the basic structure of access for patients, although concerns have been expressed that the patients of fundholding GPs might be given privileged access. There is a minority but expanding private sector, but nevertheless acute/more complicated treatment is overwhelmingly NHS based.

9. Following the Calman reforms, these two grades have been merged.

10. In Norway, female doctors celebrated 100 years of women's medicine by publishing *Kvinnemedisin: 100 år med kvinnelige leger*, edited by Berit Schei, Grete Botten, and Johanne Sundby.

11. As the previous paragraph makes clear, specialists are available for direct (private) consultation in Britain, but fees would not be refunded or paid by the NHS. As such consultations are extremely expensive, this is a minority élite practice.

12. In France, specialist training in *gynécologie médicale* ceased in 1986, thus the category will gradually decline. This specialist service is considered to be too expensive.

13. A Norwegian study by Dag Album (1991) shows that experienced doctors and nurses at hospitals have clear opinions about what types of medical specialities (as well as types of diseases) are prestigeous, and what types are not. The main finding was that those specialities that were given high prestige were also the specialities where women were usually not found, whereas those specialities with a high ratio of women had lower prestige. Exeptions were gynecology and paediatrics, which had fairly high prestige, and these specialities also have a fairly high female percentage. See also Gjerberg and Hofoss 1998.

14. These interviews were carried out as part of an ESRC-funded project. Rosemary Crompton, Fiona Harris, Nicky Le Feuvre, Florence Benoit, Gunn Birkelund, and Merete Helle carried out the interviews.

15. The system of interview numbering, which is described in the Appendix, indicates country and occupation.
16. The system of merit awards is about to be reformed, in particular via the participation of non-doctors in making awards. This follows a high-profile case in which a consultant in retirement was struck off for malpractice, but continued to receive an inflated pension as a consequence of the extensive merit awards he had received during his career.

10

Discussion and Conclusions

ROSEMARY CROMPTON

This book has examined one of the major changes in the organization of work in the second half of the twentieth century: the division of labour between men and women. In many of the chapters in this book we have used the male-breadwinner model as an ideal type from which to begin to analyse these changes. In this final chapter, I will draw together some of the themes we have been exploring previously. First, there is the question of national variations in the way in which the male-breadwinner model has evolved and been modified. A major sub-theme structuring our discussion here will be the question of equality—both between women and men, and within society as a whole. In this book, from Chapter 6 onwards, we have seen that different national patterns of gender arrangements are cross-cut by systematic similarities, in which occupational differences play a major role. This raises the important question of the significance—or otherwise—of individual choice in shaping the gender division of labour, and the nature of gender relations, amongst particular individuals and their families. Finally, there is the question of how individual choices are reflected in the transformation of institutions and gender norms, and vice versa.

THE MALE-BREADWINNER MODEL OF THE GENDER DIVISION OF LABOUR

The gender coding of particular kinds of work has been ubiquitous, although there has not been consistency in the allocation of particular tasks. The male-breadwinner model is an ideal-typical description of a form of the gender division of labour that emerged alongside the process of industrialization in many societies. Caring work and market work were gender coded, and only the latter was regarded as 'work'. Beck has described this as the 'feudal' model of the gender division of labour, in that, whereas a man's life chances might be seen as being largely determined by the market, women were from birth largely fated for an adult lifetime of domestic labour.

However, as we have seen in Chapters 2 and 4, we should be careful of making the assumption that the breadwinner model has been either an inevitable or a universal stage of societal development. In making use of this ideal type, therefore, our assumptions must be tempered by a recognition of national differences, as well as class differences, within predominantly male-breadwinner national regimes; as has frequently been pointed out, sole breadwinning is often not a viable option for the poorest in society.

Nevertheless, in Europe, North America, and Australasia, the gender coding of caring and market work, corresponding to the breadwinner model, has been incorporated into many of the major institutions of industrial society, including welfare states, education systems, and systems of labour market and occupational regulation. It has been reflected in a range of other practices, including retail opening hours and the length of the school day. In the labour market, women have been historically subject to direct and indirect exclusionary practices, including their exclusion from professional and skilled craft occupations, the blocking or absence of promotion opportunities, the marriage bar (not, of course, ever applied to men), as well as sexual harassment and other forms of discrimination. Thus the labour market has been characterized by systematic occupational segregation, in which women have been concentrated in sex-typed and poorly paid occupations.

Given the cumulative disadvantage suffered by women in the labour market, as well as in other aspects of the civil sphere such as the right to hold property, take out mortgages, open bank accounts, and so on, the most rational strategy for the vast majority of women has been to ensure that they had access to a breadwinner of suitable quality. In order to attract and retain a breadwinner, women were often constrained to behave in a manner that reproduced the normative conditions of their exclusion and subordination—showing suitable deference to the male sex and abstaining from open competition with men, together with hostility and resentment towards those women who transgressed gender norms. These might be prostitutes, unwed mothers, or simply other women who 'got above themselves'. Conformity to gender norms might not be *experienced* as 'constraint', but the outcome—that is, the reproduction of gender practices that subordinate women—is the same in any case.

Thus the superior material and political power of men has historically been accompanied by a set of normative prescriptions that justify and reproduce it. These have included not only the preferred styles of behaviour indicated above, but also ideas about what is right and proper in respect of social reproduction—that women should care, whereas men should work. However, as we have indicated, the male-breadwinner model itself was unstable and lead to considerable tensions. Its institutionalization structured, along gender lines, the conflict between altruism (non-productive) and market rationality (productive). The gender division of work served to reinforce a misleading emphasis upon the separation of the economic and the social, which persists until this day. Besides these distortions of perception, the model also had inherent practical flaws, in that breadwinners might be in short supply or at times unavailable, and in some cases personally inadequate, leading to poverty and destitution for many women and families.

From the eighteenth century onwards, therefore, feminists have been arguing that the rights of some individuals (men) have been bought in the absence of rights for others. First-wave feminism sought to establish women's rights as individuals, but second-wave feminism (which might be approximately dated as having been influential from the 1960s) has systematically challenged both the norms as well as the institutions that have reproduced women's labour-market subordination. The breadwinner model depended on formal restrictions on women's choices, and the widespread institution of a breadwinner wage for adult males. In part as a consequence of pressure from feminists, these conditions no longer hold.

Nevertheless, as Folbre (1994: 10) has noted, although the male-breadwinner model was never fair, at least it was partly functional, in that it underwrote social reproduction. As more women go into paid employment (to paraphrase Folbre), who cares for the kids? Or, to put the same question in a rather different fashion, the breadwinner model may be on the wane, but what is taking its place?

GENDER SYSTEMS

In this book we have explored these topics via a gender-systems approach. Although the precise labels used by different authors in describing gender systems vary, gender-systems approaches share two important characteristics. First, they recognize the complexity of the structuring of gender relations and the multiplicity of their origins; thus economic determinism is avoided. Secondly, gender essentialism is rejected, and gender relations are viewed as socially *constructed*. Both cultural and interpersonal factors are seen as playing a part in the structuring of gender relations—although there is no attempt to erect a cultural determinism in the place of the economic determinism of approaches such as human-capital theory. As gender systems and gender relations are socially constructed and therefore variable, then, although patriarchy might be used to describe particular kinds of gender relations, the concept is not employed to describe their totality. In addition to the authors represented in this book, the gender-systems label would include Connell (1987), Hirdman (1988), Leira (1992), Duncan (1995), O'Reilly and Fagan (1998), Rubery *et al.* (1998).

Within the gender-systems approach, the division of labour is seen as a major element of any 'gender order' or 'gender regime' (Connell 1987). As we have emphasized, even in capitalist industrial societies, the division of labour is never merely an economic, but also a *cultural* phenomenon—as the gender coding of particular tasks attests. Thus, the major dimension structuring the gender division of labour has been the gender coding of caring and market work, which reaches its extreme form in the breadwinner model. In Chapter 4 Pfau-Effinger has explored national variations in gender arrangements or divisions of labour, and trajectories between different types. For example, Scandinavian welfare states such as Denmark and Sweden may be described as having moved from a 'male-breadwinner/female-carer' model, towards a 'dual-earner/state-carer' model.

In Figure 10.1, the male-breadwinner/female-carer model has been taken as a base (or ideal type) from which to explore a range of possible earning (that is, breadwinning) and caring alternatives. The point of the exercise is not to provide a matrix, or static taxonomy, within which nation states may be precisely located. Rather, the aim is to develop a flexible framework through which change may be conceptualized. It will also be used to suggest that variations in earner/carer gender arrangements may be linked with systematic variations in both gender equality, as well as in more general material inequalities. Thus Figure 10.1 ranges gender arrangements along a continuum reflecting the possibility of transformation in gender

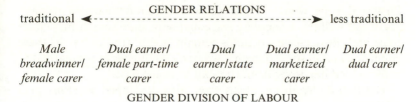

GENDER RELATIONS
traditional ◄- -► less traditional

| *Male breadwinner/ female carer* | *Dual earner/ female part-time carer* | *Dual earner/state carer* | *Dual earner/ marketized carer* | *Dual earner/ dual carer* |

GENDER DIVISION OF LABOUR

FIGURE 10.1. Beyond the breadwinner model

relations. If we first examine the poles of this continuum, it may be suggested that the male-breadwinner/female-carer model is most likely to reproduce the normative conditions of female subordination (or traditional gender cultures). At the other pole, by definition (given that the gender coding of care and market work is integral to a powerful normative conception of gender), the dual-earner/dual-carer model is most likely to generate less traditional gender relations.

The dual-earner/female-part-time-carer arrangement has emerged strongly in some countries, particularly Britain. However, a range of evidence relating to the division of domestic labour, control of money within households, and attitudes to gender roles more generally indicates that women's part-time working has not been associated with any substantial change in gender relations (Vogler and Pahl 1993; Gershuny *et al.* 1994). The same empirical evidence suggests that women's full-time work makes more of a difference. Dual-earner/female-part-time-carer arrangements, therefore, represent a modification of the breadwinner model, rather than its transformation. Chapter 6 has shown that material and situational factors do indeed have an important impact upon the domestic division of labour, but it has also suggested the possibly even greater significance of *normative* factors in shaping the division of labour at the level of the household.

Facilitating women's full-time employment by substitute care has been associated with a complex set of outcomes as far as gender relations are concerned. When women work full-time, care may be organized by the state, or within the marketized female domestic economy. The ex-state-socialist countries instituted a dual-earner/state-carer model, which supposedly constituted the conditions for women's 'liberation'. However, this economistic model of liberation paid little attention to the prevailing gender culture, which remained, and still is, very traditional, as we have seen in Chapter 6. Thus in

Eastern Europe, women remained the carers, and the major organizers of self-welfare. Following the collapse of state socialism, gender
roles and gender-role attitudes remain highly traditional in these
countries, and in some quarters women's employment is regarded as
a discredited hangover from the state-socialist past.

The Scandinavian countries have also developed versions of a
dual-earner/state-carer model, as well as encouraging the dual-
earner/dual-carer model, as Ellingsæter has argued in Chapter 3.[1]
However, these have been developed in a context much influenced by
second-wave feminism—that is, sustained efforts to transform gender cultures have accompanied structural changes in the gender
order. The concept of the woman-friendly state, which might redress
patriarchal inequalities and oppressions, has been developed in this
context. Although there is not complete equality between the sexes,
these policies have been followed by a narrowing of the wage gap in
the Scandinavian countries, and attitudes to gender roles have
moved a considerable distance away from those associated with the
male-breadwinner model. Thus, in contrast to Eastern Europe, the
male-breadwinner/state-carer model in Scandinavia has been associated with greater gender equality. This contrast between two versions of the dual-earner/state-carer model in Scandinavia and
Eastern Europe serves to underline our previous point concerning
the importance of gender cultures, and the role of feminism in shaping these cultures. Chapters 3, 4, and 5 all highlight the importance
of feminist political involvement in changing gender systems.

In many countries, however, the state plays little part in providing
substitute care, and the increase in women's paid work has been
followed by the development of dual-earner/marketized female-
domestic-economy gender arrangements, as discussed by Yeandle in
Chapter 5. The USA and Britain might be cited as examples here.
What are the consequences for gender equality of this model? The
evidence suggests that some women in dual-earner/marketized-carer
arrangements may do very well—for example, recent evidence suggests a relatively rapid increase in the proportion of women moving
into higher-level jobs in the USA and UK (Crompton 1998*a*). Thus,
in respect of access to employment, gender inequality *per se* would
seem to be in decline.

Women's full-time work in combination with substitute care,
therefore, is more likely to result in less traditional gender relations
and greater gender equality—with the important proviso that this

economistic association is by no means automatic. As Chapter 6 has demonstrated, the example of the Czech Republic (and Eastern Europe more generally) shows that gender cultures have to change, as well as the gender division of labour in employment. This fact—that gender systems and arrangements *are* multidimensional—means that the 'continuum' in Figure 10.1 is not in fact such, although the heuristic value of the figure may still be defended.

Dual-earner/dual-carer models are, by definition, associated with less traditional gender relations. The full implementation of such a model would be likely to be associated with a radical restructuring of paid employment itself—indeed, 'full-time' work as we know it might be superseded. As O'Reilly and Fagan (1998: 23) have suggested, 'good' part-time work might be an element in a renegotiation of gender arrangements that would resolve existing tensions between earning and caring work (in Chapters 3 and 4 Ellingsæter and Pfau-Effinger describe moves towards this solution in Norway and the Netherlands).

SOCIETAL INEQUALITY

To turn to the question of inequality more generally, rather than gender equality in particular. The development of the full-blown male-breadwinner model has, historically, often been associated with the reduction of material inequalities between households. Trade unions have used breadwinning as a lever to increase wages, and the removal of women has reduced labour supply and further contributed to raising wage levels (Humphries 1984). However, the entry of women into paid employment may be associated with an increase in levels of inequality between households, in particular where there is a widening gap between dual-earner and no-earner households. This situation was actually encouraged by state benefit rules in the UK, when women's earnings were counted against state benefits.

The relation of dual-earner/substitute-care gender arrangements to patterns of equality varies depending on whether substitute care is provided largely by the state or by the market. State-socialist dual-earner/state-carer models were associated with greater material equality, even if gender equality was not necessarily part of the picture. The state provision of care (and welfare services more generally) has been associated in the Scandinavian countries with the development of high-quality jobs; thus the expansion of caring employment has run in parallel with increasing equality. However, dual earning in combination with a marketized domestic economy has led to the expansion of 'junk jobs' and thus an increase in inequality (between men as a whole and women as a whole). Dual-earner/dual-carer gender arrangements should logically result in an increase in societal equality, in that the labour-market regulation and restructuring required to secure this outcome will result in properly regulated caring jobs, as well as non-marginal part-time employment.

Different types of earning/caring gender arrangements, therefore, are associated with different levels of inequality. Greater equality as between the sexes does not necessarily lead to greater equality overall—indeed, the dual-earning/marketized-care economy is particularly likely to be associated with rising levels of inequality.

Thus the dual-earner/dual-carer gender arrangement is most likely to be associated with both gender equality and equality more generally. However, this arrangement is unlikely to emerge in the absence of some kind of regulation. Although markets might sometimes serve to undermine ascriptive inequalities, the major impact of a lack of regulation (or deregulation) of markets is to increase inequality. As has been widely acknowledged, the neo-liberal turn to the market in politics and economic policy, which has taken place over the last two decades of the twentieth century, has resulted in a considerable widening of economic and social inequalities.

In respect of gender, these arguments are supported in Ellingsæter's analysis of the Norwegian case in Chapter 3. Her comparison between public- and private-sector employment in Norway demonstrates that the public sector is more woman friendly, and family friendly, than the private sector. Competitive private-sector-employment cultures mitigate against the full taking-up of the generous statutory family leave available, and working reduced hours, and/or taking up parental leave, has a negative impact on promotion. This is not found in the case of public-sector employment. Ellingsæter argues that this is because the public sector in Norway is still characterized by less of an emphasis on cost-benefit criteria, includes a high proportion of well-educated and well-organized women, and has developed a culture favourable to more flexible employment models, which do not put the workers involved at a disadvantage.

Our discussion so far has tended to have a primary focus on the effect of structural factors and their impact on gender relations, especially the particular form of the gender division of labour—although the key role played by gender cultures has also emerged. As previously stated, however, gender-systems approaches are not structurally determinist. In Chapters 7, 8, and 9 we have explored the significance of the individual's employment biographies, and their importance in transforming gender relations. These arguments parallel the social theories that have recently been developed by Giddens (1991) and Beck (1992), who have argued that, in 'reflexive modernity', individual women (and men) are increasingly cut loose from tradition (including traditional gender norms) to develop their 'own' biographies.

EMPLOYMENT AND CARING

National differences reveal themselves in aggregate-level statistics, but a wide variety of practices will be found within any particular national set of characteristic gender arrangements. The different categories that we have discussed above at the national level are also manifest at the level of the household, and it is, of course, the case that every one of these categories will be represented (to some extent) within particular nation states.

The research reported in this book has demonstrated that these variations in household arrangements are systematically related to occupational differences. The occupations studied in the Gender Relations project—medicine and banking—were selected with a view to contrasting 'professional' with 'managerial' women. Although we were, therefore, expecting to find differences between these occupational groups, they were rather greater, and rather different, from those that we had anticipated.

Our findings have been extensively discussed in Chapters 6 and 7 but may be briefly summarized here: in all countries we found that the doctors were more likely to have a relatively more conventional domestic division of labour, in which the woman assumed the major responsibility for housework and childcare, than the bankers. This point may be summarized with a simple statistic. Of those women interviewed who had had children (111 out of the 152 women interviewed), 54 per cent of the bankers, but only 23 per cent of the doctors, reported that their husbands/partners had helped with childcare. Other forms of childcare included nannies and child-minders, kindergartens, and relatives—as well as taking a child-rearing break in employment or working part-time. There was little variation in the extent to which these forms of childcare had been used as between the two occupational groups—in contrast to the rel-ative involvement of partners, which, as we have seen, was twice as likely amongst bankers' partners as amongst doctors'. Another dif-ference between the two groups was in the number of children. Doctors were (statistically significantly) more likely to have had two or more children than bankers.

We have explained the differences between doctors and bankers with reference to the relative opportunities for lifecourse planning offered by the two occupations, which are related to their character-istic career trajectories. Women who go into medicine make a career decision at a relatively early stage, and will decide, during or shortly after their period of training, which branch of medicine they wish to practise in. The relative advantages—and disadvantages—of the possibilities offered by different branches of medicine of combining employment with family life are well known within the profession. Thus women doctors tend to cluster in medical specialties that facil-itate the combination of medical practice and family life—notably in not making too excessive time demands, and enabling working hours to be controlled. These trends are found cross-nationally, notwith-standing the national variations in gender systems identified above.[2] Our interviews showed that the forward planning reflected in these doctor's medical careers was to a considerable extent reflected in their family lives as well. Many had assumed that they would take the major responsibility for domestic life and childcare, and this assump-tion served to reproduce a relatively conventional set of gender roles.

In contrast, women bank managers had had less opportunity for work–family career planning. Rather, they had been successful in their careers because they had responded to *organizational* demands, and had taken advantage of opportunities when they became avail-able. In all of the five countries in which we carried out our research, the banking industry has been in turmoil. Career paths have been transformed away from the stable masculine bureaucratic hierar-chies that once prevailed (see Crompton and Jones 1984). As a num-ber of other studies have demonstrated, the pressures and insecurities that have often accompanied recent developments in organizational and managerial practices are not particularly compatible with family life (Halford *et al.* 1997; Hochschild 1997). Under these kinds of pressures, many of those women bank managers who had had children had been 'forced' to involve their partners in childcare.

The fact that different occupations offer different possibilities for work–family combinations is hardly a startling new finding (consider the widespread feminization of the teaching profession). It is, however, of some interest that these associations persist, despite considerable cross-national variations in gender systems, suggesting that, although national differences are very important, nevertheless there remain substantial underlying continuities in gender relations that are reflected in the allocation and taking-up of caring responsibilities.[3]

That women doctors across a range of countries seem to have 'chosen' a relatively conventional set of gender arrangements leads us inevitably to raise another question. Might it not be the fact that doctors and bankers are just very different kinds of people? Thus the differences we have documented reflect not the different patterns of choice and constraint available in the two occupations, but, rather, the personal choices of the women who have taken them up?

An argument along these lines has been developed in Hakim's (1996) contentious account, which explains patterns of occupational segregation by sex in terms of, first, the innate differences between men and women, and, second, the fact that there are different types of women making different choices. This either/or debate, we have argued in Chapter 7, is not very productive. It is true that doctors have been able to take work/family life more into account in developing their careers, but it would be difficult to argue that women doctors have chosen to go into medicine because they were family oriented, or that a medical career was particularly compatible with family life. Working hours in medicine are uniformly long—'part-time' doctors in the UK, for example, work thirty-seven hours a week. The Norwegian example is a case in point here. Although Norwegian women doctors' average hours are lower than those of male doctors, nevertheless women doctors in Norway work on average forty-seven hours a week, a figure that is ten hours more than the national average.

Medicine has historically been regarded as a masculine profession, and the women who first went into medicine were regarded as gender pioneers. However, it is amongst the members of this profession that we find the more frequent adoption of employment–family combinations that are likely to result in the reproduction of relatively stereotypical gender-role relationships. We have explained this pattern via our finding that many women intending to be doctors engage, as individuals, in career planning that incorporates stereotypical gender-role tracks and thus their reproduction. This is the case even amongst those women doctors (of which there were a substantial minority) who had adopted a transgressive gender-role strategy in behaving as surrogate men, as discussed by Le Feuvre in Chapter 8. Women who transgress gender norms by striving for occupational or professional success are at the same time reinforcing them if they work with the assumption that women—but not men—who seek this kind of success must forgo domestic partners and/or families. However, as discussed in Chapter 9, within the medical profession itself there is increasing concern at gender segregation within it, and, as more women enter the profession, it is likely that the internal organization of the profession will itself be transformed. This will not be because of the importation of a feminine ethos, as some have argued, but rather because of the necessity to recognize the caring responsibilities of workers within the medical profession.

In contrast to the doctors, because of the turbulence of the finance sector, bankers who have achieved management positions have found it less straightforward to follow through conventional gender rules, particularly in a normative fashion, in relation to their family/ employment workload. In some cases, as is argued in Chapter 8, the relative failure of such gender rules may generate biographical reflexivity—that is, the assertion of individual autonomy and a questioning or rejection of conventional gender norms. Such reflexivity is more likely to be associated with less traditional gender relations at both the interpersonal and occupational level.[4]

It is important to remember, however, that *all* of the women interviewed during the course of the Gender Relations project had achieved a measure of autonomy via their access to relatively well-paid jobs. Conversely, women (and men) who are at a relative disadvantage in relation to employment are, *de facto*, less autonomous than more successful women (and men). However, as Millar has argued in Chapter 2, some welfare systems offer women a degree of autonomy as mothers (rather than employees), serving to remind us that autonomy and dependency are to a considerable extent constructs of welfare regimes and legal regulation. That is, autonomy should not be seen as simply an outcome of individual choice, even if discourses relating to autonomy are becoming increasingly pervasive. A parallel argument may be made in respect of reflexivity; some are born reflexive, some achieve reflexivity, and some have reflexivity thrust upon them.[5] As the biographies discussed in Chapter 8 demonstrate, many women who begin their work-life biographies in pursuit of a normative gender strategy find themselves in essence forced into reflexivity—although this does not mean that the changes in the way that such women 'do gender' is any less real. Of course, for some women, reflexivity might reflect more of a lifestyle choice, as the discussion of the maximizers in Chapter 7 suggests.

CONCLUSION

We have assumed a position of theoretical pluralism as far as both the nature of sociological explanations, as well as our understandings of gender, are concerned. Thus human behaviour has been analysed as reflecting both social structure and individual action. As Folbre (1994: 4) has argued, we need to develop an approach that 'emphasises choice *and* constraint, co-operation *and* conflict, individual *and* group dynamics'.

Following from this theoretical plurality, we have to recognize that the erosion of the male-breadwinner model might be followed by a number of possible alternatives—there is not likely to be 'one best way' of organizing the gender division of labour that meets every possible set of circumstances. Nevertheless, we can identify the combination(s) most likely to result in both gender and societal equality, and thus, arguably, the least long-term threat to the social fabric. Our discussion suggests that the most stable solution overall might be some version of a dual-earner/dual-carer model, backed up by some kind of state or collective provision.

This solution/conclusion might seem utopian, as likely to be followed by economic inefficiency (if not total collapse) and in any case requiring a radical restructuring of paid employment incompatible with either economic rationality or even gender norms themselves. Of course these arguments will be made, but before we reject these conclusions out of hand we should perhaps consider the alternatives. First, as a number of high-profile cases have demonstrated, the market on its own is an unreliable provider of care for the most vulnerable.[6] Secondly, for women there is another solution to the problem of combining childcare with paid work under present conditions: this is to make sure it never happens, by having no children. As we have seen in Chapter 1, European fertility is now below replacement level (note that fertility levels are actually lowest in those countries, such as Italy, with the historically most traditional family structures (see Yeandle, Chapter 5)). Unless the gender coding of employment and caring can be deconstructed, and some kind of alternative arrangement of employment and caring beyond the male-breadwinner model found, social reproduction itself might be compromised.

NOTES

1. There is considerable variation amongst the Scandinavian countries in the extent to which this model has been followed. Denmark and Finland are the closest exemplars. Sweden has provided extensive caring leave—i.e. time for care as well as substitute care—as has Norway, which has historically low levels of state childcare, although there have been substantial increases recently.
2. The medical specialties facilitating the control of time use are not identical cross-nationally, as we have seen in Chapter 9.
3. This should not be taken as a retreat into essentialism. To recognize the ubiquitousness of gender-role allocation does not mean that this cannot be changed.
4. We are not suggesting that the extent of reflexivity is occupationally specific, but, rather, that the circumstances of some occupations might make it more likely.
5. This tongue-in cheek statement has also a serious intent. It serves to reinforce the point that, despite the identification of individual pathways to reflexivity, as well as sets of circumstances that might be more likely to generate gender reflexivity in individuals, there still remains considerable variation in outcome.
6. Parents mistreat their children, and families neglect their elderly relatives. Altruism is not unknown in the world of paid work. Nevertheless, as noted earlier, one negative by-product of the gender coding of care and paid work has been the association of the latter with maximization, competition, etc., as well as the assumption of the inherent superiority of these features.

APPENDIX: INTERVIEW GUIDE

Listed below are the topics which should be covered during the interview. The interview need not necessarily be confined to these topics.

1. DEMOGRAPHICS

Personal

Age
Secondary education
University/professional qualifications
Mother:
    main occupation
    worked when respondent was pre-school/at school?
    full-time/part-time?
Father: main occupation
Siblings: main occupation(s)
Members of present household, and relationship to respondent.
Relationship(s)/marriage(s):
    duration
    age/main occupation of partner
    full-time/part-time?
Children:
    number/age
    childcare

Employment

Employment history. For each job leading to and including main occupation:
    duration
    employer
    job title
    full-time/part-time

Geographical mobility

With family of origin
When adult

2. TOPIC LIST

(*a*) Childhood and early socialization: was the respondent particularly encouraged by one parent or the other? Was there any other key individual—school teacher, relative—who had a significant influence upon the development of her aspirations and occupational choices? What is her recollection of male–female relationships in her household of origin? Conventional division of labour? Male dominant? Female dominant?

(*b*) Childhood and career/occupational decision making: was the respondent oriented towards a particular career from an early (school) age? If so, why? If not, what contingent factors contributed to her eventual destination? Did the respondent take anticipated marriage and child-rearing into account in making her career decisions?

(*c*) Education, qualification, and entry into employment: were these processes (i) linear or (ii) intermittent and many-stranded? Has the sex of the respondent ever been an overt or covert issue in the course of education and career development? Were there identifiable constraints or barriers which were gender related?

(*d*) Employment career: is the respondent happy (or not) with developments so far? Are there any barriers perceived to present or future progress? What would the respondent eventually like to achieve (in terms of employment)?

(*e*) Occupational change: have there been any significant changes in the respondent's occupation whilst they have been qualifying/working in it? Do they think there are likely to be any important changes in the future?

(*f*) Domestic and family life: (actual or anticipated) was the nature of the domestic division of labour anticipated prior to entering a relationship? What is the nature (actual, anticipated) of the respondent's domestic division of labour? Childcare arrangements (actual, anticipated). Impact of domestic sphere (marriage, children, other responsibilities) on employment career (actual, anticipated). Any impact (actual, anticipated) of domestic arrangements on partner's employment career? If the respondent had a daughter, would she recommend that she followed the same career as her own? Has the respondent achieved/what would she like to achieve in respect of domestic and family life?

(*g*) Have there been any changes in attitudes to women and gender relations (since the ending of state socialism)? Are things better, or worse?

Fill in life line.

Interview Numbering and Identification

Interviews were numbered by country and occupation as follows:

1 = Czech Republic
2 = Britain
3 = Norway
4 = Russia
5 = France

01–20 = doctors
21–40 = bankers

Thus, for example:

1/13 = Czech doctor
2/22 = British banker

This convention has been followed throughout the book.

REFERENCES

ABBOTT, A. (1988), *The System of Professions* (Chicago: University of Chicago Press).

ACKER, J. (1989), 'The Problem with Patriarchy', *Sociology*, 23: 235–40.

—— (1992), 'Gendering Organizational Theory', in A. J. Mills and P. Tancred (eds.), *Gendering Organizational Analysis* (London: Sage).

ADKINS, L. (1995), *Gendered Work: Sexuality, Family and the Labour Market* (Buckingham: Open University Press).

ALBUM, D. (1991), 'Sykdommer og medisinske spesialiteters prestisje', *Tidsskrift for den norske legeforening*, 111: 2127–33.

ALLEN, I. (1994), *Doctors and their Careers: A New Generation* (London: PSI).

ANTTONEN, ANNELI (1990), 'The Feminization of the Scandinavian Welfare State', in Leila Simonen (ed.), *Finnish Debates on Women's Studies*, University of Tampere, Tampere.

ARCHER, MARGARET S. (1996*a*), *Culture and Agency: The Place of Culture in Social Theory* (rev. edn., Cambridge: Cambridge University Press).

—— (1996*b*), 'Social Integration and System Integration: Developing the Distinction', *Sociology*, 30/4: 679–99.

AUBERT, NICOLE (1986), 'Pouvoir et féminité dans l'organisation: Réalité et imaginaire', in N. Aubert, E. Enriquez, and V. de Gaujelac (eds.), *Le Sexe du pouvoir: Femmes, hommes et pouvoirs dans les organisations* (Paris: Desclée de Brouwer).

BAILYN, L. (1993), *Breaking the Mold* (New York: Free Press).

BANKS, O. (1981), *Faces of Feminism* (Oxford: Martin Robertson).

BARRETT, M. (1987), 'The Concept of "Difference"', *Feminist Review*, 26: 35–47.

—— and PHILLIPS, A. (1992), *Destabilizing Theory* (Cambridge: Polity).

BARTH, E., and MASTEKAASA, A. (1993), 'Lønnsforskjeller mellom kvinner og menn: Hvilken betydning har utdanningsnivået?', *Søkelys på arbeidsmarkedet*, 10: 77–82.

—— and YIN, H. (1996), *Lønnsforskjeller og lønnssystem i staten* (Oslo: Institute for Social Research).

BAUMEISTER, H., BOLLINGER, D., CORNETZ, W., and PFAU-EFFINGER, B. (1990), *Atypische Beschäftigung—die typische Beschäftigung der Zukunft?* (Bremen: University of Bremen).

BEATSON, M. (1995), 'Progress towards a Flexible Labour Market', *Employment Gazette* (Feb.), 55–66.

BECK, ULRICH (1986), *Risikogesellschaft: Auf dem Weg in eine andere Moderne* (Frankfurt/M.: Suhrkamp).

—— (1992), *Risk Society* (London: Sage).

—— and BECK-GERNSHEIM, E. (1995), *The Normal Chaos of Love* (Cambridge: Polity).

BEECHEY, V., and PERKINS, T. (1987), *A Matter of Hours* (Cambridge: Polity).

BENJAMIN, O., and SULLIVAN, O. (forthcoming), 'Relational Resources, Gender Consciousness and Possibilities of Change in Marital Relationships', *Sociological Review*.

BENSON, E. (1993), 'Employment Protection', in M. Gold (ed.), *The Social Dimension: Employment Policy in the European Community* (Basingstoke: Macmillan).

BETTIO, F., PRECHAL, S., BIMONTE, S., and GIORGIO, S. (forthcoming), *Care in Europe* (Siena: Università degli Studi di Siena, Dipartimento di Economia Politica).

BEVERIDGE, W. H. (1942), *Social Insurance and Allied Services*, Cmnd. 6404 (London: HMSO).

BIMBI, F. (1993), 'Gender, "Gift Relationship" and Welfare State Cultures in Italy', in J. Lewis (1993).

—— (1997), 'Lone Mothers in Italy: A Hidden and Embarrassing Issue in a Familialist Welfare State', in J. Lewis (ed.), *Lone Mothers in European Welfare Regimes* (London: Jessica Kingsley Publishers).

BLAU, P., and DUNCAN, O. D. (1967), *The American Occupational Structure* (New York: John Wiley).

BLOM, S., NOACK, T. and ØSTBY, L. (1993), *Giftemål og barn—bedre sent enn aldri?* (Oslo: Statistics Norway).

BLOOD, R., and WOLFE, D. (1960), *Husbands and Wives: The Dynamics of Married Living* (Glencoe, Ill.: Free Press).

BLOßFELD, H.-P., and HAKIM, C. (1997) (eds.), *Between Equalization and Marginalization: Women Working Part-Time in Europe and the United States of America* (Oxford: Oxford University Press).

—— GIANNELLI, G., and MAYER, K. U. (1993), 'Is there a New Service Proletariat? The Tertiary Sector and Social Inequality in Germany', in Esping Andersen (1993*b*).

BOLOGH, R. W. (1990), *Love or Greatness: Max Weber and Masculine Thinking* (London: Unwin Hyman).

BOLTANSKI, LUC, and THÉVENOT, LUC (1987), *Les Économies de la grandeur* (Paris: PUF).

—— —— (1991), *De la justification: Les Économies de la grandeur* (Paris: PUF).

BORN, CLAUDIA, KRÜGER, HELGA, and LORENZ-MEYER, DAGMAR (1996), *Der unentdeckte Wandel. Annäherung an das Verhältnis von Struktur und Norm im weiblichen Lebenslauf* (Berlin: Sigma).

BORREL, CHRISTINE (1995), 'Le Revenu des médecins libéraux et ses déterminants', *Solidarité Santé*, 1: 35–50.

BOUDON, RAYMOND (1979), *La Logique du social* (Paris: Hachette).

BOURDIEU, PIERRE (1984) *Questions de sociologie* (Paris: Éditions de Minuit).

—— (1990), 'La Domination masculine', *Actes de la Recherche en Sciences Sociales* (Sept.), 3–31.

—— (1998), *La Domination masculine* (Paris: Seuil).

BRADLEY, H. (1989), *Men's Work, Women's Work* (Cambridge: Polity).

BRADSHAW, J., DITCH, J., HOLMES, H., and WHITEFORD, P. (1993), *Support for Children: A Comparison of Arrangements in Fifteen Countries* (London: HMSO).

BRANDTH, B., and KVANDE, E. (1992) 'Fedres arbeidsvilkår og omsorgspermisjoner', *Søkelys på arbeidsmarkedet*, 9: 158–66.

—— and ØVERLI, B. (1998), *Omsorgspermisjon med kjærlig tvang: En kartlegging av fedrekvoten* (Trondheim: Allforsk).

BRUEGEL, I. (1996), 'Whose Myths are They Anyway?' *British Journal of Sociology*, 47/1: 175–7.

BUCHMANN, M. (1989), *The Script of Modern Life* (Chicago: University of Chicago Press).

BUCKLEY, M (1989), *Women and Ideology in the Soviet Union* (Hemel Hempstead: Harvester Wheatsheaf).

BURRAGE, M., and TORSTENDAHL, R. (1990), *Professions in Theory and History* (London: Sage).

BUSSEMAKER, JET (1994), 'Gender Regimes and Welfare State Regimes: Gender Relations and Social Politics in the Netherlands', paper presented at the conference 'Crossing Borders: International Dialogues on Gender, Social Politics and Citizenship', Stockholm.

CASTLES, F. G. (1993), *Families of Nations: Patterns of Public Policy in Western Democracies* (Aldershot: Dartmouth).

CERC (1991), *Le Revenu des médecins libéraux et ses déterminants* (CERC/SESI; Paris: Ministère de la Santé).

CHAFETZ, J. S., and HAGAN, J. (1996), 'The Gender Division of Labor and Family Change in Industrial Societies: A Theoretical Accounting', *Journal of Contemporary Family Studies*, 27/2: 187–219.

CHAMBERLAYNE, P. (1993), 'Women and the State: Changes in Roles and Rights in France, West Germany, Italy and Britain, 1970–1990', in Lewis (1993).

CHODOROW, N. (1989), *Psychoanalysis and Feminism* (New Haven: Yale University Press).

CMND. 849 (1988), (London: HMSO).

COCKBURN, C. (1983), *Brothers: Male Dominance and Technological Change* (London: Pluto Press).

—— (1991) *In the Way of Women* (Basingstoke: Macmillan).

CONNELL, R. W. (1987), *Gender and Power* (Cambridge: Polity).

—— (1995), *Masculinities* (Cambridge: Polity).

COUSINS, C. (1997), 'Non-Standard Working in Europe: A Comparison of Recent Trends in the UK, Sweden, Germany and Spain', paper presented at the 15th International Labour Process Conference, University of Edinburgh.

CRAIB, I. (1987), 'Masculinity and Male Dominance', *Sociological Review*, 721–43.

CROMPTON, ROSEMARY (1986), 'Women and the "Service Class"', in R. Crompton and M. Mann (eds.), *Gender and Stratification* (Cambridge: Polity).

—— (1989), 'Women in Banking; *Work, Employment and Society*,' Vol. 3, No. 2, 141–56

—— (1990), 'Professions in the Current Context', *Work, Employment and Society* (Special Issue), 147–66.

—— (1995), 'Trajectoires féminines dans la banque et la pharmacie: Comparaison France/Grande Bretagne', *Les Cahiers du MAGE*, 1: 63–74.

—— (1997), 'Women, Employment and Feminism in the Czech Republic', *Gender Work and Organization*, 4/3: 137–48.

—— (1998a), *Class and Stratification* (Cambridge: Polity; 1st edn., 1993).

—— (1998b), 'Women's Employment and State Policies', *Innovation*, 11/2: 129–46.

—— and HARRIS, FIONA (1996), 'Contrasting Attitudes to Gender and Family Relations in Europe', paper presented at the European Workshop 'Analysing European Gender Systems and Gender Inequality in Household/Family' of the European Science Foundation Network on 'Gender Inequality and European Regions', Barcelona.

—— —— (1997a), 'Women's Employment and Gender Attitudes: A Comparative Analysis of Britain, Norway and the Czech Republic', *Acta Sociologica*, 40:183–202.

—— —— (1997b) 'Attitudes, Women's Employment and the Changing Domestic Division of Labour: A Cross-National Analysis', paper presented at the Third Project Seminar, Dept. of Sociology, University of Bergen, Norway.

—— —— (1998a), 'Explaining Women's Employment Patterns: "Orientations to Work" Revisited', *British Journal of Sociology*, 49/1: 118–36.

—— —— (1998b), 'Gender Relations and Employment: The Impact of Occupation', *Work, Employment and Society*, 12/2: 297–315.

—— and JONES, G. (1984), *White-Collar Proletariat* (London: Macmillan).

—— and LE FEUVRE, NICKY (1996), 'Paid Employment and the Changing System of Gender Relations: A Cross-National Comparison', *Sociology*, 30/3: 427–45.

—— —— (1997) 'Choisir une carrière, faire carrière: Les Femmes dans la profession médicale en France et en Grande-Bretagne', *Les Cahiers du Gedisst*, 19: 49–75.

CROMPTON, ROSEMARY and SANDERSON, K. (1986), 'Credentials and Careers', *Sociology*, 20/1: 25–42.

—— —— (1990), *Gendered Jobs and Social Change* (London: Unwin Hyman).

—— GALLIE, D., and PURCELL, K. (1996) (eds.), *Changing Forms of Employment* (London: Routledge).

CROW, GRAHAM (1989), 'The Use of the Concept of "Strategy" in Recent Sociological Literature', *Sociology*, 23/1: 1–24.

DAHL, T. S. (1991), 'Likestilling og fødselsrett', in Haukaa (ed.), *Nye kvinner—nye menn* (Oslo: Ad Notam).

DAVIES, C. (1996) 'The Sociology of the Professions and the Profession of Gender', *Sociology*, 30/4: 661–78.

—— and ROSSER, J. (1986), 'Gendered Jobs in the Health Service', in D. Knights and H. Willmott (eds.), *Gender and the Labour Process* (Aldershot: Gower).

DAVIS, J. A., and JOWELL, ROGER (1989), 'Measuring National Differences', in R. Jowell, S. Witherspoon, and L. Brook (eds.), *British Social Attitudes: Special International Report* (Aldershot: Gower).

DELPHY, CHRISTINE (1991), 'Penser le genre: Quels problèmes?', in M. C. Hurtig, M. Kail, and H. Rouch (eds.), *Sexe et genre: De la hiérarchie entre les sexes* (Paris: Éditions du CNRS).

DENZIN, N. (1989), *Interpretative Biography* (Newbury Park, Calif.: Sage).

DEPARTMENT OF HEALTH (1997), *Children's Day Care Facilities at 31 March 1996: England* (Personal Social Services Local Authority Statistics A/F 96/6; London: Government Statistical Service).

DINGWALL, S. (1976), 'Accomplishing Profession', *Sociological Review*, 24: 331–49.

DUBET, F. (1994), *Sociologie de l'expérience* (Paris: Seuil).

DUNCAN, S. (1994), 'Theorizing Differences in Patriarchy', *Environment and Planning A*, 26: 1177–1194.

—— (1995), 'Theorizing European Gender Systems', *European Journal of Social Policy*, 5/4: 263–84.

DURKHEIM, E. (1964), *The Division of Labor in Society* (New York: Free Press).

EISENSTEIN, H. (1983), *Contemporary Feminist Thought* (Boston: G. K. Hall).

EISENSTEIN, Z. (1983), 'The State, the Patriarchal Family, and Working Mothers', in I. Diamond (ed.), *Families, Politics and Public Policy* (New York: Longman).

ELLINGSÆTER, A. L. (1990), *Fathers Working Long Hours: Trends, Causes and Consequences* (Oslo: Institute for Social Research).

—— (1995*a*), 'Kjønn, deltidsarbeid og fleksibilitet i arbeidsmarkedet', in D. Olberg (ed.), *Endringer i arbeidslivets organiserin* (Oslo: Fafo).

—— (1995*b*), 'Women's Right to Work, the Male Breadwinner Norm and the Impact of Unemployment: The Case of Norway', paper presented at the Second European Conference of Sociology, Budapest, Institute for Social Research, Oslo, Norway.

—— (1998*a*), 'Dual Breadwinner Societies: Provider Models in the Scandinavian Welfare States', *Acta Sociologica*, 41: 59–73.

—— (1998*b*), 'Labour Market Restructuring and Polarisation Processes: The Significance of Political-Institutional Factors', *Economic and Industrial Democracy*, 19: 579–603.

—— and HEDLUND, M.-A. (1998), *Care Resources, Employment and Gender Equality in Norway* (Oslo: Institute for Social Research).

—— and RØNSEN, M. (1996), 'The Dual Strategy: Motherhood and the Work Contract in Scandinavia', *European Journal of Population*, 12: 239–60.

—— and WIERS-JENSSEN, J. (1997), *Kvinner i et arbeidsmarked i endring* (Oslo: Institute for Social Research).

—— NOACK, T., and RØNSEN, M. (1997), 'Sosial ulikhet blant kvinner: Polarisering, utjevning eller status quo?', *Tidsskrift for samfunnsforskning*, 38: 33–69.

ELSTON, M. A. (1993), 'Women Doctors in a Changing Profession: The Case of Britain', in Riska and Wegar (1993).

EMPLOYMENT OBSERVATORY (1993), 44 (Winter 1993).

ENGELS, F. (1940), *The Origins of the Family, Private Property, and the State* (London: Lawrence & Wishart).

ESKILD, A. (1994), 'Kvinnene tar fødselen tilbake . . .', *Dagbladet*, 26 Nov.

ESLAND, G., and SALAMAN, G. (1980), *The Politics of Work and Occupations* (Milton Keynes: Open University Press).

ESPING-ANDERSEN, G. (1990), *The Three Worlds of Welfare Capitalism* (Cambridge: Polity).

—— (1993*a*), 'Mobility Regimes and Class Formation', in Esping Andersen (1993*b*).

—— (1993*b*) (ed.), *Changing Classes: Stratification and Mobility in Post-Industrial Societies* (London: Sage).

—— (1996), *Welfare States in Transition* (London: Sage).

—— ASSIMAKOPOULOU, Z., and VAN KERSBERGEN, K. (1993), 'Trends in Contemporary Class Structuration: A Six-Nation Comparison', in Esping Andersen (1993*b*).

EUROPEAN COMMISSION NETWORK ON CHILDCARE (1995), *A Review of Services for Young Children in the European Union* (European Commission V/D/5—Equal Opportunities for Women and Men Ref.LV/1334/96-EN).

EUROSTAT (1985, 1990, 1995), Labour Force Survey for the European Union.

EUROSTAT (1996), *Social Europe 1996* (Brussels).

FAIRBROTHER, P. (1991), 'In the State of Change: Flexibility in the Civil Service', in A. Pollert (ed.), *Farewell to Flexibility?* (Oxford: Blackwell).

FELDBERG, R. L., and GLENN, E. N. (1979), 'Male and Female: Job versus Gender Models in the Sociology of Work', *Social Problems*, 26/5: 524–38.

FERRAND, M., IMBERT, F., and MARRY, C. (1996), 'L'Excellence: Une affaire de famille', *MIRE Info*, 36 (Nov.), 100–3.

FINCH, J. (1989a), *Family Obligations and Social Change* (Cambridge: Polity).

—— (1989b), 'Kinship and Friendship', in R. Jowell, S. Witherspoon, and L. Brook (eds.), *British Social Attitudes: Special International Report* (Aldershot: Gower).

FINCH, J. (1983), *Married to the Job* (London: George Allen & Unwin).

FOLBRE, N. (1994), *Who Pays for the Kids? Gender and the Structures of Constraint* (London: Routledge).

FREVERT, U. (1989), *Women in German History: From Bourgeois Emancipation to Sexual Liberation* (New York: Berg).

FRIESE, M. (1996), 'Soziale Ungleichheit-Bildung-Geschlecht-Ethnizität: Modernisierungsfallen und ihre Überwindung', in P. Ahlheit *et al.* (eds.), *Von der Arbeitsgesellschaft zur Bildungsgesellschaft: Perspektiven von Arbeit und Bildung im Prozeß europäischen Wandels* (Bremen: University of Bremen).

GEISSLER, BIRGIT, and OECHSLE, MECHTHILD (1996), *Lebensplanung junger Frauen: Die widersprüchliche Modernisierung weiblicher Lebensläufe* (Weinheim: Deutscher Studien-Verlag).

GERSHUNY, J., GODWIN, M., and JONES, S. (1994), 'The Domestic Labour Revolution: A Process of Lagged Adaptation', in M. Anderson, F. Bechhofer, and J. Gershuny (eds.), *The Social and Political Economy of the Household* (Oxford: Oxford University Press).

GIDDENS, A. (1991), *Modernity and Self Identity* (Cambridge: Polity).

—— (1992), *The Transformation of Intimacy* (Cambridge: Polity).

GILLIGAN, C. (1982), *In a Different Voice* (Cambridge, Mass.: Harvard).

GINN, J., ARBER, S., BRANNEN, J., DALE, A., DEX, S., ELIAS, P., MOSS, P., PAHL, J., ROBERTS, C., and RUBERY, J. (1996), 'Feminist Fallacies: A Reply to Hakim on Women's Employment', *British Journal of Sociology*, 7/1: 167–74.

GJERBERG, E., and HOFOSS, D. (1998) ' "Dette er ikke noe for småjenter": Legers forståelse av kjønnsforskjeller i spesialitetsvalg', *Tidsskrift for samfunnsforskning*, 39: 3–27.

GLENDINNING, C., and MCLAUGHLIN, E. (1993), *Paying for Care: Lessons from Europe* (London: HMSO).

GLUCKSMANN, M. (1995), 'Why "Work"? Gender and the "Total Social Organization of Labour" ', *Gender Work and Organization*, 2/2: 63–75.

GODELIER, MAURICE (1984), *L'Idéel et le matériel* (Paris: Fayard).

GOLDTHORPE, J. H. (1980), *Social Mobility and Class Structure in Modern Britain* (Oxford: Oxford University Press; 2nd edn., 1987).

GORNICK, J. C., MEYERS, M. K., and ROSS, K. E. (1997), 'Supporting the Employment of Mothers: Policy Variation across Fourteen Welfare States', *Journal of European Social Policy*, 7/1: 45–70.

GOTTSCHALL, KARIN (1995), 'Geschlechterverhältnis und Arbeitsmarktsegregation', in R. Becker-Schmidt and G. A. Knapp (eds.), *Das Geschlechterverhältnis als Gegenstand der Sozialwissenschaften* (Frankfurt: Campus).

GREGSON, M., and LOWE, N. (1994), *Servicing the Middle Classes* (London: Routledge).

GUMBEL, A (1997), 'Baby? I'd Rather Have a Mobile', *Independent on Sunday*, 2 Mar., p. 16.

HAGEN, K. (1991), 'Welfare State Employees: Where Did They Come From?', in J. E. Kolberg (ed.), *The Welfare State as Employer* (New York: M. E. Sharpe).

HAKIM, C. (1991), 'Grateful Slaves and Self-Made Women: Fact and Fantasy in Women's Work Orientations', *European Sociological Review*, 7/2: 101–21.

—— (1992), 'Explaining Trends in Occupational Segregation: The Measurement, Causes, and Consequences of the Sexual Division of Labour', *European Sociological Review*, 8/2: 127–52.

—— (1995), 'Five Feminist Myths about Women's Employment', *British Journal of Sociology*, 46/3: 429–55.

—— (1996), *Key Issues in Women's Work* (London: Athlone Press).

—— (1997), 'A Sociological Perspective on Part-Time Work', in Bloßfeld and Hakim (1997).

—— (1998), *Social Change and Innovation in the Labour Market* (Oxford: Oxford University Press).

HALFORD, SUSAN, and SAVAGE, MIKE (1995), 'Restructuring Organizations, Changing People', *Work, Employment and Society*, 9/1: 97–122.

—— —— and WITZ, A. (1997), *Gender, Careers and Organizations* (London: Macmillan).

HALL, R. (1993), 'Family Structures', in D. Noin and R. Woods (eds.), *The Changing Population of Europe* (Oxford: Blackwell).

HANSEN, M. N. (1995), 'Kjønnssegregering i det norske arbeidsmarkedet', *Tidsskrift for samfunnsforskning*, 36: 147–77.

HANTRAIS, L (1990), *Managing Professional and Family Life: A Comparative Study of British and French Mothers* (Aldershot: Dartmouth).

—— (1993), 'Women Work and Welfare in France', in Lewis (1993).

—— (1995), *Social Policy in the European Union* (Basingstoke: Macmillan).

HARTMANN, H. (1976), 'Capitalism, Patriarchy and Job Segregation by Sex', in M. Blaxall and B. Reagan (eds.), *Women and the Workplace* (Chicago: Chicago University Press).

HASKEY, J (1998) *Population Trends* (Aldershot: Avebury).

HASSENTEUFEL, PATRICK (1997), *Les Médecins face à l'état: Une comparaison internationale* (Paris: Presses de la Fondation de Sciences Politiques).

HEILIGERS, P. (1992), 'Gender and Changing Perspectives of Labour and Care', paper presented at the First European Conference of Sociology, Vienna.

HEITLINGER, A. (1979), *Women and State Socialism* (London: Macmillan).

HÉRITIER, FRANÇOISE (1996), *Masculin/féminin: La Pensée de la différence* (Paris: Odile Jacob).

HERNES, H. (1987), *Welfare State and Woman Power* (Oslo: Norwegian University Press).

—— (1988), 'The Welfare State Citizenship of Scandinavian Women', in K. Jones and A. Jonasdottir (eds.), *The Political Interests of Gender* (Newbury Park, Calif.: Sage).

HERZLICH, C., *et al.* (1993), *Cinquante ans d'exercice de la médecine en France: Carrières et pratiques des médecins français 1930–1980* (Paris: Inserm/Doin Éditeurs).

HINRICHS, K., *et al.* (1991), 'From Standardization to Flexibility: Changes in the Political Economy of Working Time', in K. Hinrichs *et al.* (eds.), *Working Time in Transition* (Philadelphia, Pa.: Temple University Press).

HIRDMAN, Y. (1988), 'Genussystemet—reflexioner kring kvinnors sociala underordning', *Kvinnovetenskapligtidskrift*, 3: 49–63.

—— (1990), 'Demokrati och makt i Sverige', *Statens offentliga utredningar*, 44 (Stockholm).

HOBSON, B. (1994), 'Solo Mothers, Social Policy Regimes and the Logics of Gender', in Sainsbury (1994).

HOCHSCHILD, A. (1990), *The Second Shift* (London: Piatkus).

—— (1997), *The Time Bind* (New York: Metropolitan Books).

HOEL, M. (1995), 'Yrkestilpasning og yrkesutvikling' (University of Oslo, doctoral thesis).

HOFOSS, D., and GJERBERG, E. (1994), 'Legers arbeidstid', *Tidsskrift for den Norske Legeforening*, 26/114: 3959–63

HÖLLINGER, F. (1991), 'Frauenerwerbstätigkeit und Wandel der Geschlechtsrollen im internationalen Vergleich', *Kölner Zeitschrift für Soziologie und Sozialpsychologie*, 43/4: 753–71.

HONEGGER, C., and HEINTZ, B. (1981) (eds.), *Listen der Ohnmacht: Zur Sozialgeschichte weiblicher Widerstandsformen* (Frankfurt/Main: Europäische Verlagsanstalt).

HÖRNING, K. H, GERHARDT, A., and MICHAILOW, M. (1995), *Time Pioneers* (Cambridge: Polity).

HORRELL, S. (1994), 'Household Time Allocation and Women's Labour Force Participation', in M. Anderson, F. Bechhofer, and J. Gershuny (eds.), *The Social and Political Economy of the Household* (Oxford: Oxford University Press).

HUMPHRIES, J. (1984), 'Protective Legislation, the Capitalist State, and Working Class Men', in R. Pahl (ed.), *Divisions of Labour* (Oxford: Blackwell).

INSTITUT FÜR DEMOSKOPIE ALLENSBACH (1996) (ed.) 'Muttersein und Teilzeitarbeiten. Für jede zweite Frau wäre das Ideal', *Allensbacher Berichte*, 5.

IRIGARY, LUCE (1989), *Le Temps de la différence* (Paris: Hachette).

—— (1997), *Être deux* (Paris: Grasset).

JENSON, J. (1986), 'Gender and Reproduction', *Studies in Political Economy*, 20: 9–46.

—— HAGEN, E., and REDDY, C. (1988) (eds.), *Feminization of the Labour Force* (Cambridge: Polity).

JOHNSON, T. J. (1972), *Professions and Power* (London: Macmillan).

JOWELL, R., BROOK, L., and DOWDS, L. (1993), *International Social Attitudes* (Aldershot: Dartmouth).

KAUFMANN, F. X. (1989*a*), *Zukunft der Familie. Stabilität, Stabilitätsrisiken und Wandel familialer Lebensformen sowie ihre gesellschaftlichen und politischen Bedingungen, Gutachten zu Händen des Bundeskanzleramtes* (Bonn: Bundeskanzleramt).

KAUFMANN, F.-X. (1989*b*), 'Christentum und Wohlfahrtsstaat', in F.-X. Kaufmann (ed.), *Religion und Modernität* (Tübingen: Mohr).

KIERNAN, K., and WICKS, M. (1990), *Family Change and Future Policy* (London: Family Policy Studies Centre).

KITTERØD, H. R., and ROALSØ, K.-M. (1996), 'Arbeidstid og arbeidstidsønsker blant foreldre', *Samfunnsspeilet*, 10: 12–23.

KJELDSTAD, R., and LYNGSTAD, J. (1993), *Arbeid, lønn og likestilling* (Oslo: Scandinavian University Press).

KNIJN, TRUDIJ (1994), 'Fish without Bikes: Revision of the Dutch Welfare State and its Consequences for the (In)dependence of Single Mothers', *Social Politics*, 1: 83–105.

—— and KREMER, M. (1997), 'Gender and the Caring Dimension of Welfare States: Towards Inclusive Citizenship', *Social Politics*, 4/3: 238–361.

KOHN, M. L. (1987), 'Cross-National Research as an Analytical Strategy', *American Sociological Review*, 52: 713–31.

KORPPI-TOMMOLA, A. (1991), 'Education—the Road to Work and Equality', in M. Manninen and P. Setälä (eds.), *The Lady with the Bow* (Helsinki: Otava).

KOVEN, SEITH, and MICHEL, SONYA (1990), 'Womenly Duties: Maternalist Politics and the Origins of Welfare States in France, Germany, Great senschaften (Frankfurt/Main: Campus), 195–219.

Britain and the United States, 1880–1920', *American Historical Review*, 95 (Autumn), 1076–108.

KRÜGER, H. (1995), 'Dominanzen im Geschlechterverhältnis: Zur Institutionalisierung von Lebensläufen', in R. Becker-Schmidt and G. A. Knapp (eds.), *Das Geschlechterverhältnis als Gegenstand der Sozialwissenschaften* (Frankfurt/Main: Campus), 195–219.

—— and BORN, CLAUDIA (1990), 'Probleme der Integration von beruflicher und familialer Sozialisation in der Biographie von Frauen', in E.-H. Hoff (ed.), *Die doppelte Sozialisation Erwachsener: Zum Verhältnis von beruflichem und privatem Lebensstrang* (Munich: DJI).

KUHNLE, S. (1996), 'European Integration and the National State', paper to the Peder Sæther Symposium on 'Challenges to Labor: Integration, Employment and Bargaining in Scandinavia and the United States', Center for Western European Studies, University of California, Berkeley.

KUMAR, K. (1995), *From Post-Industrial to Post-Modern Society* (Oxford: Blackwell).

KÜNZLER, JAN (1995), 'Geschlechtsspezifische Arbeitsteilung: Die Beteiligung von Männern im Haushalt im internationalen Vergleich', *Zeitschrift für Frauenforschung*, 13: 115–32.

LAND, H. (1994), 'The Demise of the Male Breadwinner', in S. Baldwin and J. Falkingham (eds.), *Social Security and Social Change* (London: Harvester Wheatsheaf).

LANE, C. (1993), 'Gender and the Labour Market in Europe: Britain, Germany and France Compared', *Sociological Review*, 41/2: 274–301.

LAPIDUS, G. (1978), *Women in Soviet Society* (Berkeley and Los Angeles: University of Calfornia Press).

LAYDER, D. (1994), *Understanding Social Theory* (London: Sage).

LE FEUVRE, NICKY (1998), 'The Feminization of Professional Groups in a Comparative Perspective: Some Theoretical Considerations', in V. Oligati, L. Orzack, and M. Saks (eds.), *Professions, Identity and Order in Comparative Perspective* (Onati: International Institute for the Sociology of Law).

—— and WALTERS, PATRICIA (1993), 'Égales en droit? La Féminisation des professions juridiques et France et en Grande-Bretagne', *Sociétés contemporaines*, 16: 41–62.

LEARNER, GAIL (1979), *The Majority Finding the Past: Placing Women in History* (Oxford: Oxford University Press).

LEESON, J., and GRAY, J. (1978), *Women and Medicine* (London: Tavistock).

LEIBFRIED, STEFAN (1992), 'Towards a European a Welfare State? On Integrating Poverty Regimes in the European Community', in S. Ferge and J. Kolberg (eds.), *Social Policy in a Changing Europe* (Boulder, Colo.: Westview Press).

—— and Ostner, I. (1991), 'The Particularism of West German Welfare Capitalism: The Case of Women's Social Security', in M. Adler, C. Bell, J. Clasen, and A. Sinfield (eds.), *The Sociology of Social Security* (Edinburgh: Edinburgh University Press).

—— and Tennstedt, Friedrich (1985), 'Einleitung', in S. Leibfried and F. Tennstedt (eds.), *Politik der Armut und Spaltung des Sozialstaats: Einleitung* (Frankfurt/Main: Suhrkamp).

Leira, A. (1992), *Welfare States and Working Mothers* (Cambridge: Cambridge University Press).

—— (1993), 'The "Woman-Friendly" Welfare State? The Case of Norway and Sweden', in Lewis (1993).

—— (1994), 'Combining Work and Family: Working Mothers in Scandinavia and in the European Community', in P. Brown and R. Crompton (eds.), *A New Europe? Economic Restructuring and Social Exclusion* (London: UCL Press).

—— (1996), 'Fra statsfeminisme til statsfamilisme? Om mor, far, stat og marked i 1990-åra', in B. Brandth and K. Moxnes (eds.), *Familie for tiden: Stabilitet og forandring* (Oslo: TANO Aschehoug).

Leiulfsrud, H., and Woodward, A. (1989), 'Cross-Class Encounters of a Close Kind: Class Awareness and Politics in Swedish Families', *Acta Sociologica*, 32: 75–93.

Lévi-Strauss, Claude (1967), *Les Structures élémentaires de la parenté* (2nd edn., Paris: Mouton).

Lewis, J. (1980), *The Politics of Motherhood: Maternity and Child Welfare in England 1900–1939* (London: Croom Helm).

—— (1992), 'Gender and the Development of Welfare Regimes', *Journal of European Social Policy*, 2/3: 159–73.

—— (1993) (ed.), *Women and Social Policies in Europe: Work, Family and the State* (Aldershot: Edward Elgar).

—— (1997), 'Gender and Welfare Regimes: Further Thoughts', *Social Politics*, 4/2: 160–77.

—— with Hobson, B. (1997), 'Introduction', in J. Lewis (ed.), *Lone Mothers in European Welfare Regimes* (London: Jessica Kingsley Publishers).

Ligestillingsrådet (1998), *Lige nu*, no. 6 (Copenhagen).

Likestillingsrådet (1996), *Likt og ulikt*, 20 (Nov.).

Lipovetsky, Gilles (1997), *La troisième femme: Permanence et révolution du féminin* (Paris: Gallimard).

Longva, E. (1997), 'Kjønnsforskjeller i lønn og opprykk blant ansatte i Statoil', in M. Hoel (ed.), *Fra stat til marked* (Oslo: Institute for Social Research).

McDowell, L. (1997) *Cultures of Capital* (London: Sage).

McLaughlin, E., and Glendinning, C. (1994), 'Paying for Care in Europe: Is there a Feminist Approach', in L. Hantrais and S. Mangen (eds.),

Family Policy and the Welfare of Women (Cross-National Research Papers, University of Loughborough).

MARSHALL, B. (1994), *Engendering Modernity* (Cambridge: Polity).

MARTIN, J. R. (1994), 'Methodological Essentialism, False Difference and Other Dangerous Traps', *Signs*, 19/3: 630–57.

MARTIN, J., and ROBERTS, C. (1984), *Women and Employment: A Lifetime Perspective* (London: HMSO).

MARUANI, MARGARET (1995), La Traversée des turbulences: L'Emploi féminin dans l'Europe des années quatre-vingt-dix', in M.de Manassein (ed.), *De l'égalité des sexes* (Paris: Centre national de documentation pédagogique).

MARX, K., and ENGELS, F., (1962), *Manifesto of the Communist Party in Selected Works* (Moscow: Foreign Languages Publishing House, Moscow), i.

MARX-FERREE, M. (1991), 'The Gender Division of Labour in Two-Earner Marriages', *Journal of Family Issues*, 12/2: 158–80.

MASTEKAASA, A. (1992). 'Fravær blant småbarnsforeldre: Betydningen av egen sykdom og sykdom hos barna', *Søkelys på arbeidsmarkedet*, 9: 153–7.

MATHIEU, NICOLE-CLAUDE (1992), *L'Anatomie politique: Catégorisations et idéologies du sexe* (Paris: Éditions Côté-Femmes).

MAURICE, M., SELLIER, F., and SILVESTRE, J. J. (1986), *The Social Foundations of Industrial Power* (Cambridge Mass.: MIT Press).

MAYNARD, M. (1995), 'Beyond the "Big Three": The Development of Feminist Theory into the 1990s', *Women's History Review*, 4/3: 259–81.

MEAD, MARGARET (1966), *L'un et l'autre sexe* (Paris: Éditions Denoël/ Gonthier).

MENKEL-MEADOW, C. (1989), 'Exploring a Research Agenda of the Feminization of the Legal Profession: Theories of Gender and Social Change', *Law and Social Enquiry*, 14/2: 289–319

MILLAR, J. (1996), 'Mothers, Workers, Wives: Policy Approaches to Supporting Lone Mothers', in Silva E. Bortolaia (ed.), *Good Enough Mothering? Feminist Perspectives on Lone Motherhood* (London: Routledge).

—— (1997), 'Family Obligations and Social Policy: The Case of Child Support, *Policy Studies*, 17/3:181–93.

—— and WARMAN, A. (1996), *Family Obligations in Europe* (London: Family Policy Studies Centre).

MINISTÈRE DU TRAVAIL ET DES AFFAIRES SOCIALES (1996), 'Les Medicins par specialité au 1er Janvier 1995', *SESI*, 249.

MORAN, M., and WOOD, B. (1993), *States, Regulation, and the Medical Profession* (Buckingham: Open University Press).

MORRIS, L. (1990), *The Workings of the Household* (Cambridge: Polity).

MÓSESDÓTTIR, LILJA (1995), 'The State and the Egalitarian, Ecclesiastical and Liberal Regimes of Gender Relations', *British Journal of Sociology*, 46/4 (Dec.), 623–42.

MOSS P. (1990), *Childcare in the European Community* (Brussels: Commission of the European Communities).

—— (1991), 'Day Care for Young Children in the United Kingdom', in M. Melhuish and P. Moss (eds.), *Day Care for Young Children* (London, Tavistock/Routledge).

—— (1996), 'Parental Employment in the European Union 1985–1993', *Labour Market Trends*, 104/12 (Dec.).

MOZNY, I. (1993), 'The Czech Family in Transition from Social to Economic Capital' (Central European University, Prague).

NÄTTI, JOUKO (1995), 'Working Time Policy and Work Sharing in Finland', paper presented at the International Workshop on 'Work-Sharing in Order to Protect and Expand Employment', Brussels.

NIKANDER, TIMO (1992), *The Woman's Life Course and the Family Formation* (Helsinki: Statistics Finland).

NOU (1995), *Et apparat for likestilling.* NOU 1995:15 (Oslo: Statens forvaltningstjeneste).

—— (1996), *Offentlige overføringer til barnefamilier.* NOU 1996:13 (Oslo: Statens forvaltningstjeneste).

OECD (1990): Organization for Economic Cooperation and Development, *Employment Outlook* (Paris: OECD).

—— (1991), *Employment Outlook: July 1991* (Paris: OECD).

—— (1992), *Employment Outlook: July 1992* (Paris: OECD).

—— (1994) *Women and Structural Change* (Paris: OECD).

—— (1995), *Employment Outlook: July 1995* (Paris: OECD).

—— (1996), *Employment Outlook: July 1996* (Paris: OECD).

—— (1997), *Observer*, 206 (June–July).

O'REILLY, JACQUELINE (1995), 'Teilzeitarbeit in Ost- und Westdeutschland: Ansätze zu einem geschlechterspezifischen gesellschaftlichen Modell', unpublished paper, Berlin: Wissenschaftszentrum Berlin.

—— (1996), 'Theoretical Considerations in Cross-National Employment Research', *Sociological Research Online*, 1/1:http:\\www.soc.surrey. ac.uk.

—— and FAGAN, C. (1998) (eds.), *Part-Time Prospects* (London: Routledge).

ORLOFF, A. (1993), 'Gender and the Social Rights of Citizenship: The Comparative Analysis of Gender Relations and Welfare States', *American Sociological Review*, 58: 303–28.

—— (1996a), *Gender and the Welfare State* (Madrid: Centro de Estudios Avanzados en Ciencias Sociales, Instituto Juan Mrach de Estudis e Investigaciones).

ORLOFF, A. (1996*b*), 'Gender in the Welfare State', *Annual Review of Sociology*, 22: 51–78.

—— (1997), 'Commentary on Jane Lewis', *Social Politics*, 4/2: 188–202.

OSBORNE, T. (1993), 'On Liberalism, Neo-Liberalism and the "Liberal Profession of Medicine" ', *Economy and* Society, 22/3: 345–55.

OSTNER, ILONA (1993), 'Slow Motion: Women, Work and the Family in Germany', in Lewis (1993).

—— (1995), 'Arm ohne Ehemann? Sozialpolitische Regulierung von Lebenschancen für Frauen im internationalen Vergleich', *Aus Politik und Zeitgeschichte, Beilage zur Wochenzeitung Das Parlament*, B 36–37: 3–12.

PARSONS, T. (1939), 'The Professions and Social Structure', *Social Forces*, 17, reprinted in *Essays in Sociological Theory* (New York: Free Press, 1954).

PASCALL, G. (1997), *Social Policy: A New Feminist Analysis* (London: Routledge).

PATEMAN, C. (1988), *The Sexual Contract* (Cambridge: Polity).

—— (1989), 'The Patriarchal Welfare State', in C. Pateman (ed.), *The Disorder of Women* (Cambridge: Polity).

PERKIN, H. (1989), *The Rise of Professional Society* (London: Routledge).

PERSSON, I. (1990), 'The Third Dimension', in I. Persson (ed.), *Generating Equality in the Welfare State* (Oslo: Scandinavian University Press).

PEYRE, EVELYNE, WIELS, JOËLLE, and FONTON, MICHÈLE (1991), 'Sexe biologique et sexe social', in M.-C. Hurtig, M. Kail, and H. Rouch (eds.), *Sexe et genre: De la hiérarchie entre les sexes* (Paris: Éditions du CNRS).

PFAU-EFFINGER, BIRGIT (1990), *Erwerbsverlauf und Risiko. Arbeitsmarktrisiken im Generationenvergleich* (Weinheim/Basel: Deutscher Studien-Verlag).

—— (1993), 'Modernisation, Culture and Part-Time Employment: The Example of Finland and West Germany', *Work Employment and Society*, 3/7: 383–410.

—— (1994), 'The Gender Contract and Part-Time Paid Work by Women: A Comparative Perspective', in S. S. Duncan (ed.), *Spatial Divisions of Patriarchy in Western Europe*, Special Issue of *Environment and Planning A*, 26/2: 1355–76.

—— (1996*a*) 'Analyse internationaler Differenzen in der Erwerbsbeteiligung von Frauen—theoretischer Rahmen und empirische Ergebnisse', *Kölner Zeitschrift für Soziologie und Sozialpsychologie*, 48/3: 462–92.

—— (1996*b*), 'Theorizing Cross-National Differences in the Labour Force Participation of Women', paper presented at the 'Seminar on Gender Relations, Employment and Occupational Segregation: A Cross-National Study', University of Leicester.

—— (1998*a*) 'Gender Cultures and the Gender Arrangement—a Theoretical Framework for Cross-National Comparisons on Gender', in Simon S. Duncan (ed.), *Gender Inequalities in Europe: Cultures, States and Regions*,

Special Issue of *Innovation. European Journal of Social Sciences*, 11/2: 147–66.

—— (1998*b*), 'Culture or Structure as Explanations for Differences in Part-Time Work in Germany, Finland and the Netherlands?', in Colette Fagan and Jacqueline O'Reilly (eds.), *Part-Time Perspectives* (London: Routledge).

—— (1999) *Kultur oder Institutionen? Kultur wohlfahrtsstaat und Frauenarbeit im europäischen Vergleich* (Opladen: Leske & Budrich).

—— and GEISSLER, BIRGIT (1992), 'Institutioneller und soziokultureller Kontext der Entscheidung verheirateter Frauen für Teilzeitarbeit—Ein Beitrag zur Soziologie des Erwerbsverhaltens', *Mitteilungen aus der Arbeitsmarkt- und Berufsforschung*, 25/3: 358–70.

PHILLIPS, A., and MOSS, P. (1988), *Who Cares for Europe's Children?* (Brussels: EC).

PIERSON, P. (1994), *Dismantling the Welfare State? Reagan, Thatcher and the Politics of Retrenchment* (Cambridge: Cambridge University Press).

PILLINGER, J (1992), *Feminising the Market: Women's Pay and Employment in the European Community* (Basingstoke: Macmillan).

PINNARÒ, G., and PUGLIESE, E. (1985), 'Informalization and Social Resistance: The Case of Naples', in N. Redclift and E. Mingione (eds.), *Beyond Employment: Household, Gender and Subsistence* (Oxford: Blackwell).

PLANTENGA, JANNEKE (1992*a*), 'Women and Work in the Netherlands: Some Notes about Female Labour Force Participation and the Nature of the Welfare State', in G. Buttler, H.-J. Hoffmann-Nowotny, and G. Schmitt-Rink (eds.), *Acta Demographica* (Heidelberg: Physika), 47–56.

—— (1992*b*), 'Differences and Similarities: The Position of Women on the Dutch Labour Market from a European Perspective', *Bevolking en Gezin*, 1: 101–20.

—— and VAN VELZEN, S. (1994), 'Changing Patterns of Work and Working-Time for Men and Women: Towards the Integration or the Segmentation of the Labour Market: External Report Commissioned by and Presented to the European Commission' (Utrecht: Economic Institute/CIAV).

PLUMMER, K. (1983), *Documents of Life: An Introduction to the Problems and Literature of a Humanist Method* (London: Allen & Unwin).

POLLERT, A. (1996), 'Gender and Class Revisited', *Sociology*, 30/4: 639–59.

POOLE, M. E., and LANGAN-FOX, J. (1997), *Australian Women and Careers: Psychological and Contextual Influences over the Life Course* (Cambridge: Cambridge University Press).

POTT-BUTER, HETTIE (1993), *Facts and Fairy Tales about Female Labor: Family and Fertility: A Seven-Country Comparison 1850–1950* (Amsterdam: Amsterdam University Press).

PRINGLE, R. (1988), *Secretaries Talk: Sexuality, Power and Work* (London: Verso).

QUACK, SIGRID (1993), *Dynamik der Teilzeitarbeit. Implikationen für die soziale Sicherung von Frauen* (Berlin: Sigma).

—— and MAIER, FRIEDERIKE (1994), 'From State Socialism to Market Economy—Women's Employment in East Germany, *Environment and Planning A*, 26/8: 117–1328.

RAINBIRD, H. (1993), 'Vocational Education and Training', in M. Gold (ed.), *The Social Dimension: Employment Policy in the European Community* (Basingstoke: Macmillan).

RERRICH, M. (1996), 'Modernizing the Patriarchal Family in West Germany', *European Journal of Women's Studies*, 3/1: 27–37.

RESKIN, B. F., and ROOS, P. A. (1990), *Job Queues, Gender Queues* (Philadelphia, Pa.: Temple University Press).

RICHARDS, T. J., and RICHARDS, L. (1994), 'Using Computers in Qualitative Research' in N. K. Denzin and Y. S. Lincoln (eds.), *Handbook of Qualitative Research* (London: Sage).

RISKA, E. (1989), 'The Professional Status of Physicians in the Nordic Countries', *Millbank Quarterly*, 133–47.

—— (1993), 'Introduction', in E. Riska and K. Wegar, *Gender Work and Medicine* (London: Sage).

—— and WEGAR, K. (1993), *Gender Work and Medicine* (London: Sage).

RØNSEN, M. (1993), 'Hva betyr barnehager for kvinners fruktbarhet og yrkesdeltakelse?', *Samfunnsspeilet*, 7: 8–11.

RUBERY, J. (1988) (ed.), *Women and Recession* (London: Routledge & Kegan Paul).

—— and FAGAN, C. (1995), 'Gender Segregation in Societal Context', *Work, Employment and Society*, 9/2: 213: 40.

—— SMITH, M., and FAGAN, C. (1997), 'Explaining Working-Time Patterns by Gender: Societal and Sectoral Effects', presented at the 15th International Labour Process Conference, University of Edinburgh.

—— —— —— and GRIMSHAW, D. (1998), *Women and European Employment* (London: Routledge).

RUELLAND, N. (1995), 'Revenu des médecins libéraux: 10 ans d'évolution', *Solidarité Santé*, 1: 51–64.

RUSTIN, M. (1994), 'Incomplete Modernity: Ulrich Beck's "Risk Society" ', *Radical Philosophy*, 67: 3–12.

SAINSBURY, D. (1994) (ed.), *Gendering Welfare States* (London: Sage).

—— (1996), *Gender, Equality and Welfare States* (Cambridge: Cambridge University Press).

SARACENO, C. (1992), 'Women's Paid and Unpaid Work in Times of Economic Crisis', in L. Benería and S. Feldman, *Unequal Burden: Economic Crises, Persistent Poverty, and Women's Work* (Boulder, Colo.: Westview Press).

Sassoon, A. (1997), 'Commentary on Jane Lewis', *Social Politics*, 4/2: 178–81.

Savage, M. (1992), 'Women's Expertise, Men's Authority: Gendered Organization and the Contemporary Middle Classes', in M. Savage and A. Witz (eds.), *Gender and Bureaucracy* (Oxford: Blackwell).

Schei, B., Botten, G., and Sundby, J. (1993) (eds.) *Kvinnemedisin: 100 år med kvinnelige leger* (Oslo: Ad Notam Gyldendal).

Scheiwe, K. (1994), 'Labour Market, Welfare State and Family Institutions: The Links to Mothers' Poverty Risks: A Comparison between Belgium, Germany and the United Kingdom', *European Journal of Social Policy*, 4/3: 201–24.

Schmid, Günter (1991), *Women and Employment Restructuring: Women in the Public Sector* (Paris: OECD).

—— (1992), 'Flexible Koordination: Instrumentarium erfolgreicher Beschäftigungspolitik aus internationaler Perspektive', *Mitteilungen aus der Arbeitsmarkt- und Berufsforschung*, 25: 323–50.

Schömann, K., Rogowski, R., and Kruppe, T. (1994), 'Fixed Term Contracts in the European Union', *European Observatory Policies*, 24 (Brussels: European Commission).

Schupp, Jürgen (1991), 'Teilzeitarbeit als Möglichkeit der beruflichen (Re-)Integration', in K.-U. Mayer, J. Allmendinger, and J. Huinink (eds.), *Vom Regen in die Traufe: Frauen zwischen Beruf und Familie* (Frankfurt: Campus).

Scott, H. (1974), *Does Socialism Liberate Women?* (Boston: Beacon Press).

Segal, L. (1987), *Is the Future Female?* (London: Virago).

Sejersted, F. (1995), *Demokratisk kapitalisme* (Oslo: Universitetsforlaget).

Simmel, George (1986), *La Sociologie de l'expérience du monde modern* (Paris: Méridiens-Kleincksieck).

Simonen, Leila (1990), 'Contradictions of the Welfare State: Women and Caring', *Acta Universitatis Tamperensis*, ser. A, 295 (Tampere: University of Tampere).

Social Trends (1998) (London: HSMO).

Snyder, P. (1992), *The European Women's Almanac* (London: Scarlet Press).

Sørhaug, T. (1996), *Om ledelse* (Oslo: Universitetsforlaget).

Sporton, D. (1993), 'Fertility: The Lowest Level in the World', in D. Noin and R. Woods (eds.), *The Changing Population of Europe* (Oxford: Blackwell).

St.prp. nr. 1 (1994–5). (Oslo: Barne- og familiedepartmentet).

Statistics Norway (1995), *Working Environment 1993* (Oslo: Statistics Norway)

—— (1996), *Child Care Institutions and Educational Programmes for 6 Years Olds* (Oslo: Statistics Norway).

Statistics Norway (1998), *Labour Market Statistics 1996–1997* (Oslo: Statistics Norway).

STRAUSS, ANSELM (1978), *Negotiations, Varieties, Contexts, Processes and Social Order* (San Francisco: Berkely).

TAIT, A., and PLATT, M. J. (1995), 'Women Consultants, their Background and Training: Some Myths Explored', *Medical Education*, 29: 372–6.

TARALDSET, A. (1998), *Statistics on Medical Specialties* (Oslo: Norwegian Medical Association).

TEAGUE, P. (1989), *The European Community: The Social Dimension: Labour Market Policies for 1992* (London: Kogan Page).

THERBORN, G. (1995), *European Modernity and Beyond: The Trajectory of European Societies 1945–2000* (London: Sage).

THOMAS, J. J. R. (1985), 'Rationalisation and the Status of Gender Divisions', *Sociology*, 19/3: 409–20.

TORP, H. (1990), 'Fleksibel arbeidskraft', in H. Torp and K. Skollerud (eds.), *Organisasjon, arbeidsmiljø og mobilitet* (Oslo: Institute for Social Research).

TRIFILETTI, R. (1995), ' The Gendered "Rationalization" of Italian Family Policies in the Nineties', paper presented to the second ESA Conference, Budapest.

UNGERSON, C. (1995), 'Gender, Cash and Informal Care: European Perspectives and Dilemmas', *Journal of Social Policy*, 24/1: 31–52.

VAN DEN PUTTE, BAS, and PELZER, ANS (1993), 'Wensen, motieven en belemmeringen ten aanzien van de arbeidsduur', *Sociaal Maandblad Arbeid*, 47: 487–95.

VILAIN, A. (1995), 'La Feminisation du corps medical', *Solidarité Santé*, 1: 23–34.

VOGLER, C., and PAHL, J. (1993), 'Social and Economic Change and the Organisation of Money within Marriage', *Work, Employment and Society*, 7/1: 71–95.

WALBY, S. (1986), *Patriarchy at Work* (Cambridge: Polity).

—— (1990), *Theorizing Patriarchy* (Oxford: Blackwell).

—— (1994), 'Methodological and Theoretical Issues in the Comparative Analysis of Gender Relations in Western Europe', *Environment and Planning A*, 26: 1339–54.

—— (1997), *Gender Transformations* (London: Routledge).

WALLACE, C. (1994), 'Education and Training', in J. Clasen and R. Freeman (eds.), *Social Policy in Germany* (London: Harvester Wheatsheaf).

WARDE, A., and HETHERINGTON, P. (1993), 'A Changing Domestic Division of Labour? Issues of Measurement and Interpretation', *Work, Employment and Society*, 7/1: 23–45.

WARMAN, A., and MILLAR, J. (1996), 'Researching Family Obligations: Some Reflections on Methodology', in L. Hantrais and M. Letablier (eds.), *Reflections on International Comparisons of Families, the Family–Employment Relationship and Family Policies in Europe* (Loughborough: Centre for European Studies, University of Loughborough).

WATSON, G. (1992), 'Hours of Work in Great Britain and Europe: Evidence from the UK and European Labour Force Surveys', *Employment Gazette*, 11: 539–58.

WEBER, Max (1971), *Économie et société* (Paris: Plon; first published 1922).

WIESENTHAL, HELMUT (1987), *Strategie und Illusion—Rationalitätsgrenzen kollektiver Akteure am Beispiel der Arbeitszeitpolitik 1980–1985* (Frankfurt: Campus).

WILSON, E. (1977), *Women and the Welfare State* (London: Tavistock).

WITZ, A. (1992), *Professions and Patriarchy* (London: Routledge).

WRIGHT, E. O. (1997), *Class Counts* (Cambridge: Cambridge University Press).

YEANDLE, S. (1996), 'Change in the Gender Composition of the Workforce: Recent Analyses and their Significance for Social Theory', Sheffield Hallam University CRESR Gender and Women's Studies Series GW7, ISBN 0863396461.

—— (1999), 'Gender Contracts, Welfare Systems and "Non-Standard Working": Diversity and Change in Denmark, France, Germany, Italy and the UK', in A. Felstead and N. Jewson (eds.), *Global Trends in Flexible Labour* (Basingstoke: Macmillan).

—— GORE, T., and HERRINGTON, A. (1998), *Employment, Family and Community Activities: A New Balance for Women and Men* (report for the European Foundation for the Improvement of Living and Working Conditions, Dublin).

YOUNG, M., and WILMOTT, P. (1973) *The Symmetrical Family* (London: Routledge & Kegan Paul).

ZEIHER, H., and ZEIHER, H. J. (1991), 'Wie Kinderalltage zustandekommen', in I. Berg (ed.), *Kinderwelten* (Suhrkamp: Frankfurt/Main).

INDEX